A WORLD ATLAS OF MILITARY HISTORY

Volume One - to 1500

A WORLD ATLAS

by ARTHUR BANKS

*with an Introduction
by Lord Chalfont*

OF MILITARY HISTORY

VOLUME ONE
TO 1500

HIPPOCRENE
BOOKS, INC.
New York City

CONTENTS

viii

PREFACE

For twenty years I have been fighting to impress upon publishers, authors and cartographical draughtsmen the need and value of clear maps in text-books. I became an historical cartographer largely because so many of the maps I saw in books and atlases were difficult to understand. Maps are visual aids: they do not supersede text-books. What are required are simple, clear drawings that one can assimilate with ease.

The greatest drawback to historical maps is that historians are not usually good draughtsmen and cartographers are not usually well-read in history. Furthermore, there is an important difference between a *cartographer* (who can devise and plan a map) and a *cartographical draughtsman* who can only draw the final result from a cartographer's draft. And whereas authors obviously want as many maps as possible in their books, publishers try to keep these to a minimum for economic reasons.

This atlas is an attempt to produce a book of clear and simple maps printed in black and grey with a 'story' line attached. One cannot satisfy everyone's requirements within 154 pages and I can only hope that it proves useful and informative to the reader. In this opening volume I have included 'general' maps in addition to 'war' maps since one cannot readily grasp military campaigns in early times unless one has a background map to assist one.

ARTHUR BANKS
Oxshott
June, 1972

ACKNOWLEDGEMENTS

During the preparation of this volume I consulted some six hundred reference works, examined innumerable maps and general atlases and had the good fortune to be advised on various items by friends, colleagues and associates.

I should like to thank Dr R. A. Banks (my brother) for his expert suggestions on the Vikings and Alfred the Great maps in particular, and for his inspection of the various story panels.

Mr I. Baxter of the India Records Office supplied details on the maps dealing with India and Asia, and Mr Lim and Mr Freeberne of the School of African and Oriental Studies meticulously checked my spellings in the Chinese, Indian and Asian maps and proffered detailed advice on Far Eastern geography and history in general.

Mr A. Henderson checked my ancient and classical sections with diligence and vigour, and suggested much information to assist my work throughout. Mr R. B. Welsh, my friend since childhood, nobly read extensive notes I supplied, and researched much material for me, notably on Egypt, India, China and Asia. General Sir James Marshall-Cornwall supplied details on guns, rocketry and gunpowder items.

I must also thank Mr I. Rudd, Miss J. Gibbs and Mr J. Watkins for their assistance with the cartographical draughtsmanship on certain maps.

The Chief Librarian and Staff of the Study and Information Department of the Surrey County Library Headquarters and the Branch Library at Leatherhead, Surrey went to great lengths to assist me in my research. To them also I proffer my thanks.

Before the maps were printed Mr Alan Palmer and his wife Veronica gave them a detailed scrutiny for which I am indebted.

INTRODUCTION

BY LORD CHALFONT

I am particularly pleased to have been invited to write the introduction to this and to the later volumes in this series. The project is one of immense interest and value.

Arthur Banks' technique, which seems to me altogether admirable, is especially suited to the extremely challenging task of explaining in clear and easily understood terms campaigns, strategies and developments in military history which are often regarded as complicated and difficult to understand.

War is one of the most profoundly important manifestations of the human condition. From the first tentative experiments in the organisation of society disputes have been resolved, insults avenged and goods and territory seized or defended by violence, by force of arms, by war. It has been condemned as an obscenity; justified by theological scholars as the last resort against intolerable tyranny; and even, from time to time, glorified as the status symbol of the sovereign nation state. To the civilized mind it is astonishing that men are capable of inflicting upon each other the appalling cruelty and suffering of war; but so far no-one has been able to devise any other way of settling international quarrels or achieving political aims against determined opposition. There have been attempts to bring about disarmament by international agreement; to achieve peaceful settlement of disputes by arbitration; and to impose order on chaos by the establishment of such ambitious institutions as the League of Nations and its successor, the United Nations. None of them has succeeded. Organised violence remains the ultimate sanction in international affairs; it is still considered legitimate for a government in the pursuit of its foreign policy to indulge in the killing or maiming of thousands of human beings, and the destruction of their homes, their crops and their possessions. And it is arguable that the situation will remain unchanged so long as the nation state remains the basic unit of the structure of world society.

The phenomenon of war permeates every aspect of human behaviour. Its vocabulary fills our everyday language with vivid metaphors—the war on want, the battle for survival, the population explosion. It has inspired unforgettable music, immortal painting and some of our greatest literature. It has produced men of greatness and compassion; and others of indescribable evil. Napoleon called it "a simple art, consisting entirely of execution". For Erasmus it was the one human activity which "it is encumbent on every man, by every lawful means, to avoid, to deprecate, to oppose". But perhaps the most perceptive, if possibly the most cynical reflection was that of Thomas Hardy—"My argument is that War makes rattling good history; but Peace is poor reading."

The history of war, then, is at least as old as the recorded history of man. Most military historians divide it into periods roughly corresponding with the principal developments in the technology of war. The primitive, or ancient period of warfare is generally regarded as beginning in about 5,000 BC, when the Sumerians, who lived in the fertile lands between the Tigris and the Euphrates, became the targets of attack by the desert and mountain tribes. One of the earliest Sumerian sculptures shows soldiers carrying spears and shields; and on the ivory handle of a flint-bladed knife, found at Gebel el-Arak in Egypt and dated about 3,000 BC, there is a carving depicting soldiers fighting on a beach. Historic, or medieval warfare dates roughly from AD 500 to 1500, and modern warfare from then on.

Until about 3,000 BC it is probable that war was mainly a highly formalised method of avenging insults between one tribe and another—it was only rarely a matter of economic gain or political conquest. It was the transition from man's hunting and collecting period to that of primitive agriculture which almost certainly brought with it the military organisation designed to further political and economic aims. The ability of some tribes to till fertile lands and to establish reserves of food—the beginnings of organised society—aroused the envy of others, who sought by violence to acquire what they had been unable to provide for themselves. As the nomadic life gave way to the development of permanent communities and villages, the phenomenon later to be described as the "territorial imperative" began to emerge in a recognizable form, and success in war began to confer a hierarchical title to pleasant living space and productive lands. The development of primitive military technology was at first a matter almost entirely of the manufacture of new weapons—swords, shields, spears and bows and arrows. The first significant innovation was the introduction of the horse and the impact of cavalry on military tactics, a development which enabled the Hyksos, a warlike Indo-European people, probably nomads, to conquer Egypt in 1750 BC and to occupy the country for a century and a half.

Much of our knowledge of early military history is indeed identified with Ancient Egypt and its Asiatic Empire, although China and India too provide essential evidence of the various stages in the development of warfare. The Egyptians created one of the greatest and most enduring civilisations in history. It lasted 3000 years and passed through three great eras—the Old and Middle Kingdoms, from 2700 to 1500 BC, when the Egyptians consolidated and improved their occupation of the valley of the River Nile; and the New Kingdom, or Empire, when they occupied lands outside the boundaries of present day Egypt. This period, between 1560 and 1085 BC, represents the summit of Egyptian military power. It opened with the expulsion of the Hyksos ('the desert charioteers') by the Pharaoh Amosis (or Ahmose) I, who also reorganised northern Nubia (originally occupied by Sesostris II about 1850 BC). The successor of Ahmose, Thutmosis (or Thutmose) I, carried on the expansion of Egypt both to the south, beyond the fourth and fifth cataracts of the Nile, and north-eastwards through Palestine and Syria to the banks of the Euphrates. This was, in effect, the cradle of military history.

For almost five hundred years the Egyptians maintained a regular army to secure its great new Empire. Although the basic arm was infantry, much use was made now of the horse-drawn chariot, a weapon adapted from the Hyksos; and the pikes and spears of the Old and Middle Kingdoms were augmented by bows, swords, battle-axes and daggers. At this time also there began to appear the first signs of cohesive military organisation. A quartermaster corps was formed to take care of logistical supplies, and as the Empire developed the traditional skirmishing and head-on pitched battles gave way to more sophisticated tactical methods. The technique of the battle square emerged and the two-man chariots were used as a primitive cavalry, either in massed charges or individually in support of infantry operations.

After 1085 BC the Egyptian Empire began to decline as the power of the military caste grew and the generals began to set themselves up, together with the priests, as the feudal overlords of independent regions. Eventually Egypt collapsed under the invasion of the Assyrians, a cruel and warlike people under whose dominion there were further developments in organisation and tactics. Larger chariots, each drawn by two horses and driven by three men, made their appearance. The foot soldiers were organised into heavy and light infantry, and a corps of engineers was established. Some of the first signs of total war began to emerge, with the massacre of prisoners, mass deportations and the plundering and pillaging of enemy towns and villages. The Assyrians in their turn were expelled with the aid of Greek mercenaries, but in 525 BC Egypt was once again invaded and occupied, this time by the Persians under King Cambyses. The Persians made comparatively little impact on the science of war and the only interesting military innovations of this period were the introduction of the elephant and the development of flexible tactical doctrines which allowed for operations both by large massed formations and by small detachments of troops. Meanwhile the size of armies had grown substantially. Whereas in the early Sumerian period the typical city state had perhaps 1000 foot soldiers, some estimates put the strength of Darius's Persian Army at the Battle of Arbela, against Alexander the Great, in 331 BC, at a million foot soldiers and 40,000 horsemen. The most conservative estimate suggests that the strength was certainly not less than 300,000. In 332 BC the conquest of Egypt by Alexander brought to an end the long supremacy of the Egyptian Empire. The centre of power had moved decisively to Greece.

The Greek civilisation, later to become the Greco-Roman, had already, in the fifth century BC, entered a period of almost continuous warfare which was to last nearly four hundred years. Before the Greco-Persian wars, military operations in the Greek peninsula had been primitive affairs; the early Minoan civilization on the island of Crete had been conquered by the Achaeans in 1600 BC and for the next eight hundred years the Greek mainland and islands were subjected to a series of invasions from the north—the Dorians, Ionians and eventually the Aeolians. There then arose the city states of Classic Greece, dominated by Athens and Sparta. It was the liberal, civilised Athens which rose first to pre-eminence, principally through its leading part in the wars with Persia. At the beginning of the fifth century Darius sent his army to invade Greece and was defeated in 490 by the Athenians at Marathon. Ten years later the Persians returned in greater numbers under Xerxes, but were again defeated. This time the Persians came within striking distance of Athens, and attempts to halt them in a naval battle off Artemisium and a land battle at Thermopylae were unsuccessful, in spite of a heroic Greek stand at Thermopylae under a Spartan—Leonidas. The way to Athens was now open, but an Athenian-Spartan coalition inflicted a heavy defeat on the Persians at Plataea in 479 BC. Thirty years later, in 449 BC, the Persians finally admitted defeat and abandoned the Aegean to the Greeks.

As has so often been the case throughout history, the disappearance of the external threat meant the beginning of internal struggles in Greece. The Peloponnesian War of 431-404 BC led to the defeat of Athens by Sparta and the establishment of over half a century of Spartan hegemony. This was followed by a brief period of Theban predominance, during which there emerged a tactical development of some significance—the device employed by Epaminondas of Thebes in his battle with the Spartans at Leuctra in 371 BC. The Spartan commander, King Cleumbrotus, formed his Army of 1,000 cavalrymen and 10,000 *hoplites* in traditional phalanx formation, with his élite troops, as usual, on the right flank. Instead of doing the same, Epaminondas concentrated his numerically inferior force in great strength on his *left* flank, in a striking phalanx, four times as deep as the enemy immediately to their front. They smashed into the Spartan ranks like a battering ram—the first recorded example of a commander exerting irresistible force at a chosen point of attack.

A little later in the fourth century BC Macedonia began to emerge as a significant military power, and in 338 BC Philip II of Macedonia defeated the Greeks, who had succeeded in forming a coalition of their warring city states in an attempt to meet this new threat at Chaeronea. It was a battle in which his son, Alexander, played a decisive part when he massacred the 'Sacred Band' (a battalion of élite Theban troops) on the right flank of the Greek United Armies, and then wheeled behind the Greek lines in a classic cavalry manoeuvre.

With the makeshift coalition of Greek city states crushed, Alexander, who had succeeded Philip in 336 BC, proclaimed Greek unity and required each of the City States to provide troops for his Asian campaigns. There followed, over a period of twelve years, one of the greatest military campaigns in history, as Alexander the Great set out to punish the Persians for their earlier invasions of Greece and to create an Empire extending over most of the known world. He defeated the Persians in three great battles at Granicus (334 BC), Issus (333 BC) and Arbela (331 BC), and swept on to the frontiers of India where, on the River Hydaspes (now the Jhelum River) a tributary of the Indus, he fought one of his most brilliant battles against the Indians in 326 BC. This was, however, the last of his great victories. Three years later he died, at the age of 32, in Babylon, and his Empire gradually disintegrated.

Technically the art and science of war had advanced considerably during this period. The main weapon of the Greek city states was the thrusting spear carried by the *hoplites* or heavy infantrymen, who were formed in compact masses of up to 5,000—the phalanx—which formed the centre of the basic battle formation, with cavalry and light infantry on the flanks and the *psiloi*—special skirmishing forces—out in front. The Athenian armies also had well organised auxiliary services, including a medical corps of a rudimentary kind. Their tactics were fairly simple, often involving no more than a head-on confrontation between phalanxes.

When Alexander the Great succeeded his father, however, his impact on the military art was dramatic. Tactically he refined the rudimentary but original ideas of Epaminondas of Thebes, developing a system in which the individual phalanx did not advance 'in line'—that is to say in a straight battle front—but roughly in the shape of a V pointing at the enemy. This created a dent in the opposing line and enabled the *hoplites* to pin down the opposing infantry, allowing the cavalry to sweep in on the flanks. The cavalry thus became the decisive arm in battle instead of being used principally as a protection for the infantry. At the same time new engines of war began to make their appearance, the siege tower, the catapult or *ballista*, and the *testudo*, a battering ram under a protective covering of shields. The artillery began to emerge as an organised arm. But the principal factor in the military developments of the era was Alexander the Great himself—one of the greatest generals in history. He showed an extraordinary and precocious skill in combining and manoeuvring forces of all arms; his mastery of tactics was complete and he was able to adapt his method to any form of warfare with which he was confronted, from guerilla warfare to the investing of fortified villages. He was a strategist of remarkable skill and imagination; yet he did not hesitate to lead his own cavalry on the battlefield. Although his basic instincts were aggressive, he never moved on to a new phase in a campaign without first consolidating his gains. In the course of the great twelve year campaign which took him to the borders of India, he never outran his lines of communication or his administrative support. He brought a new dimension to the military art.

Alexander's vision of an Empire encompassing the known world was, however, achieved not by the Greeks, but by the Romans, who had become the masters of Italy in 275 BC after four centuries of war—principally against the Etruscans in the North and the Greek colonists in the south. There followed the period of the Punic Wars, in which Rome and Carthage fought for the control of the Mediterranean. When the First Punic War began in 264 BC, Carthage dominated the north coast of Africa, the south coast of Spain and most of the Mediterranean islands, including part of Sicily. After destroying the Carthaginian fleet at Mylae in Sicily in 260, the Romans landed in Africa but were defeated at Tunis in 255 by Xanthippus. The Second Punic War, which lasted from 218-201 BC, began when Hannibal, crossing the Pyrenees from Spain, defeated the Romans at the River Trebia, Lake Trasimene and Cannae; but after the defeat of Hannibal's brother, Hasdrubal, at the Metaurus River in 207 BC, the Romans sent Scipio to Africa. Hannibal, having returned to Carthage in 203, was defeated by Scipio at the Battle of Zama and Carthage was reduced to the status of a trading port. The defeat of Carthage was finally completed in the Third Punic War (149-146 BC) and by 100 BC the Roman Empire had been extended to cover Spain, Cisalpine Gaul, Illyria, Macedonia, Greece, Tripolitania, and Proconsular Africa.

The principal contribution of the Romans to military organisation and tactics was the legion. It consisted of 4,000 to 6,000 men in three ranks, the first of *hastati*, the second of *principes* and the third of *triarii*. Each rank was divided into 10 *maniples*, each of 120 to 160 men, organised into two *centuries* of 60-80. In the third rank of *triarii* this was varied—each maniple consisting of only one century. Each legion had horsemen in support on the flanks, and *velites* for skirmishing in front. The main advantage over the phalanx was tactical flexibility. With each maniple operating on a 20 yard front, with a similar distance between maniples, it was possible to adapt quickly to uneven terrain or to change formation and pass units rapidly through each other's positions as the tactical situation required. This flexibility was reflected in the equipment of the legion, the *hastati* in the front rank carrying shields, swords and javelins; the *principes* and *triarii* carrying pikes instead of javelins; and the *velites* carrying light javelins or *iacula*. The Romans also developed siege engines, mobile bridging equipment, catapults designed to fire huge arrows and bolts, and the technique of the fortified camp. Administrative arrangements became relatively elaborate and signalling and communications systems were comparatively highly organised.

It was upon this military basis that the great campaigns of Julius Caesar, Pompey, Augustus and Mark Antony were fought. From 61 to 51 BC Caesar's Gallic Wars extended the Roman Empire through Spain and Gaul as far as Britain. He then returned to Rome and a period of civil war followed, in which he defeated his rival Pompey. Caesar's successor Octavian (later the Emperor Augustus) defeated *his* main rival Mark Antony and then began a series of campaigns in Germany and Central Europe from 15 BC to 10 AD.

The reign of Augustus was the beginning of the end of the military power of Rome. He reduced the professional army to just over 300,000 men and disarmed the free civilians. For the next four hundred years the Roman Army underwent fundamental changes. The size of the legion was progressively reduced and large numbers of barbarians were enlisted to protect the Empire from external attack. When, in the third century, the Gothic frontier invasion began, the Army was reorganised into the Palatine Army—a campaign force of shock troops, and *limitani* or border troops. Meanwhile two factors had combined to consolidate the superior status of the cavalry; the need for a high degree of mobility in an Army used mainly for dealing with border raids, and the generally low calibre of the infantry which required them to be massed together for the purpose of improving their morale, thus allowing horsemen to predominate as the offensive arm. There were corresponding changes in arms, and by the 4th century the bow and the sling were beginning to rival the sword and the javelin. At the same time a vast complex of defensive works (the *limes*) had been built up by Rome in Europe, Africa and the Middle East.

There were persistent attacks on this, notably by the Goths and Visigoths in the 2nd, 3rd and 4th centuries; by the Vandals over the same period; and finally by the Huns under Attila, in the 5th century. At the same time the Angles, Picts and Jutes had invaded Britain and the Herulians had established a kingdom in Italy, only to be defeated by the Ostrogoths under Theodoric. Under these repeated assaults the Roman Empire, for all practical purposes, disintegrated. It was split up into barbarian kingdoms ruled by *foederati*, the leaders of Roman auxiliary troops raised from the barbarian peoples.

In 481, as the Roman Empire withered away, Europe came under the Merovingian dynasty; the Frankish King, Clovis, extended his rule through most of Gaul and he and his successors expanded their Empire gradually until in 771 Charlemagne inherited the Frankish Kingdom from his father Pepin III, and rapidly pushed south and east into Italy, Bavaria and Carinthia, south-west into Spain and north-east to the River Elbe. In 800 Charlemagne was crowned Emperor by the Pope in Rome, but in 843 the Treaty of Verdun divided the Empire into three kingdoms. The Carolingian Army was surprisingly small—6,000 to 10,000 men, of whom more than half were mounted troops. Heavy chariots carried supplies in convoys. It was a cumbersome, unimpressive Army, but Charlemagne commanded it in person and his intelligence and boundless energy enabled him to make the best of his limited resources.

When the Carolingian Empire came to its end the feudal system began its period of domination in European history and warfare moved into its historic or medieval phase of development. For more than two hundred years the Vikings from Scandinavia ranged over most of England, Ireland and Northern France. They were a fierce, well-disciplined fighting force, who landed in their shallow-draft long ships, seized horses and weapons from their enemies and used them in marauding cavalry tactics. Their most effective series of campaigns were those against Britain throughout the 9th century.

Meanwhile there began that great period of history, lasting from the end of the Carolingian Empire to the Italian Renaissance in the 15th century, which saw the birth of modern Europe. In the military sense it was not at first a period of dramatic change. The basic fighting unit was the knight, or armoured horseman. The manufacture of armour was raised almost to the level of an art; and there were impressive developments in the techniques of fortification and siege warfare; but tactics remained basically simple. A typical battle would begin with the cavalry formed up within a wall of infantry, which at a given signal would open, allowing the cavalry to charge upon the enemy. The infantry were generally either pikemen or bowmen, armed with either the crossbow or the longbow—the latter enthusiastically adopted by the English armies fighting against the Welsh and the Scots in the 13th century. It was a weapon which was later to have a decisive effect at the Battle of Crécy on August 26th, 1346, the first great English victory over the French in the Hundred Years' War.

Meanwhile William the Conqueror had invaded Britain in 1066 and transformed the structure of English society; and from 1096 to 1192 the Crusades had taken armies from Western Europe on three great expeditions to the Middle East. A number of military lessons emerged from the Crusades—including the importance of sea-power and the value of being able to manoeuvre rapidly with mixed forces of infantry and cavalry. But possibly the most important lesson affected the construction of fortifications and defence systems. The Middle Ages was the great era of fortification, although it was not until the end of the twelfth century that true castles and fortified cities began to replace the feudal residence with its rudimentary protective wall. With the development of strongly fortified areas, siege machinery began to play an increasingly important role. Explosives were still unknown, but it was possible to hurl huge projectiles, at first with giant catapults mounted on towers and later with the *trebuchet*, a counter-weighted sling. The arts of sapping and mining were refined and an early example of 'artificial moonlight' appeared when the trees surrounding medieval fortresses were soaked in oil and set alight to illuminate the surrounding countryside and so discourage night attacks.

While these developments in military science and technology were taking place in Europe, there had been a remarkable century of conquest by the Arabs from 632-732. Within this period they had conquered territory from the Syrian border in the east, across Egypt and North Africa, and north through Spain to the Pyrenees. This extraordinary interlude, however, had little impact on the development of warfare. The campaigns were fought by tribes using camel-borne cavalry and infantry armed with bows and arrows. The Bedouin techniques of surprise attack and rapid movement were fully exploited. Battles usually began with a volley from the archers followed by a cavalry charge with sabre and lance. Even against the comparatively unsophisticated feudal militia their success was predictably short-lived.

The Middle Ages, in spite of the apparent pre-occupation with invasion and counter-invasion, was in fact a period characterised by certain obvious limitations on the scope and scale of warfare. As the Roman Empire gave way to Christendom, the moral authority of the Church increased, and with it the inhibitions against organised violence. Even the great battles of medieval history were trivial affairs by modern standards (at Poitiers and Agincourt, for example, fewer than 30,000 men were engaged) and even long bitter campaigns could be conducted without great hardship to the general population or serious disruption of society. It was not until the 14th and 15th centuries that this situation began to change, leading to the vastly different all pervading experience of modern war. The crucial period of transition was the Hundred Years' War from 1337 to 1453. While it raged in France, the Anglo-Scottish conflict which had begun in 1297 ended when the Scots were defeated at Homildon Hill in 1402; and Owain Glyndwr's brief but brave attempt to achieve independence for Wales finally failed in 1412. Meanwhile, in Europe, Switzerland had emerged as a substantial military power, with a special reputation for effective infantry, highly disciplined and meticulously trained. Military organisation during this period was totally transformed and for the first time there appeared the 'regular Army'—a paid Army owing allegiance to the Crown and not to a feudal lord. Tactically the infantry became once again the Queen of Battles, ending a thousand years of cavalry predominance; gunpowder artillery appeared to change irrevocably the nature of war.

The great battles of the Hundred Years' War were at Crécy (1346), Poitiers (1356) and Agincourt (1415)—all decisive victories for the English. In 1429, however, the French resurgence began with Joan of Arc, and by 1453 the English had been driven from France, their only territorial gain after over a century of war being the port of Calais. This was the end of the Hundred Years' War and, by common consent of most historians, the end of the Middle Ages. The Wars of the Roses, between York and Lancaster, ravaged England for another thirty years, but in general Medieval Europe began to give way to the modern Europe of the nation state—a crucial development in political, economic and military history.

It is, however, not only in Europe, North Africa and the Middle East that military history has its origins—China was at one time the most militarily advanced country in the ancient world. The dates of the early Chinese dynasties and the development of their armies are the subject not of history but of legend. It is likely that in the first two dynasties, the Hsia and the Shang (or Yin), the warrior class became predominant. Certainly the third dynasty, the Chou, who defeated the Shang and moved into Anyang, the Shang capital, in about 1028 BC, were basically a military hierarchy. In about 770 BC they established their capital at Loyang, and there followed a period of internal struggle in China. The country split into a series of loose confederations and until 221 BC there was almost continuous civil war, with enormous walls being built after 450 BC to protect the border states from attacks by the Asiatic Huns. In 221 BC one of the fiercest of the warring leaders—Cheng, who at the age of 22 had come to power in the state of Ch'in—succeeded in reuniting China and, as Shih Huang Ti (First Emperor), founded the fourth (Ch'in) dynasty. Under his rule the sections of wall built under the Chou dynasty were linked together to form the Great Wall of China, and the country was divided into 36 regions. In spite of his efforts, however, China again split into kingdoms at the beginning of the third century BC and it was not until 206 BC that the country was reunited again under Wu Ti, who founded the Han Dynasty, which was to last for four centuries (Western Han 206 BC-24 AD and Eastern Han 25-221 AD). Although he was a soldier, Wu Ti established a civil administration; under his rule, however, there was almost continuous fighting against the

Huns, and the military hierarchy achieved great power and prestige. The Chinese cavalry was improved by a systematic horse-breeding policy and iron weapons were widely used. The Huns were not only driven out of the regions of northern China which they had occupied while China was still in a state of internal disorder; they were also driven west from the borders of China in a series of military campaigns between 128 and 36 BC.

In 221 AD, however, the Han dynasty fell, and yet another period of unrest followed. The period of the Three Kingdoms (San Huo) saw renewed attacks by barbarians from the north and under the Western Tsin Dynasty (265-317) the Huns invaded North China and established a Hun Dynasty. There followed a period of division and conflict, with North and South China under separate dynasties for nearly two centuries. It was not until the end of the Sixth century that the Sui dynasty was founded by Yang Chien (also called Wen Ti) who made a determined attempt to reunite China. He had the Great Wall of China extended and repaired and the country began to enjoy a period of comparative tranquility, under which Chinese civilisation began to flower. The barbarians on the frontiers, however, remained a serious threat, and under the T'ang Dynasty (618-907) the Emperor Li Yuan (also called T'ae Tsu) defeated the Turks with an Army which came to be feared and respected all over Asia. It was towards the end of the T'ang dynasty that gunpowder made its first recorded appearance.

In the tenth century there was yet another internal struggle in China, which culminated in the seizure of power in 960 by a general, Chao K'uang-yin (also called Sung T'ai Tsu) who founded the Sung Dynasty. Chao was a great military leader, but like his predecessor Wu Ti, he insisted on the army being subordinated to the civil authority. The Army, however, continued to develop and it soon reached a strength of one million men—mostly volunteers. Arms and equipment, however, were still rudimentary, the cross-bow being still the basic weapon of the Chinese soldier. Gunpowder was now being used for making bombs launched by catapult and China was centuries ahead of Europe in its siege techniques.

Chao K'uang-yin's successors in the Sung dynasty, however, lacked his military talents and in about 1260 after a period of progressive degeneration in the army, the great Mongol invasion of China began.

The Mongol Army was almost exclusively an Army of horsemen, drawn from a barbarian, patriarchal community living on the Eurasian Steppes. Their military organisation and tactics were simple and effective, and military skills were highly regarded in the Mongol tribes. The cavalrymen were mounted on small, tough horses; they wore leather breast-plates, carried leather shields and were armed with bows and arrows, javelins and lances. They were expert archers and ruthless, savage soldiers. Their tactics were based on the exploitation of surprise and mobility, using small numbers of infantry only to pin down an enemy and set the scene for their cavalry attacks. These were terrifying affairs, carried out at first in total silence, messages being sent by flags; in the final charge they terrorised the enemy with battle cries. This implacable, highly disciplined, military hierarchy produced two of the greatest but most terrifying warriors in History—Genghis Khan and Tamerlane. It was Genghis Khan who, in a sustained military campaign between 1219 and 1225 penetrated into Turkestan, Iran and Afghanistan; and reached the banks of the Indus, Azerbaijan, the Caucasus and South Russia. Under his command no method of waging war was too frightful—civilians, men, women and children, were used as a living screen for his attacks; cities were ruthlessly sacked and mutilation, rape and desecration were systematically used as instruments of terror.

When he died in 1227, Genghis Khan's successors were marginally less barbaric and notably less bellicose, and it was not until the middle of the 14th century that the Mongol military tradition was revived under Tamerlane (Timur i leng or Timur the lame), who between 1380 and 1395 overran Khurasan and Eastern Persia, Iraq, Azerbaijan, Armenia, Mesopotamia and Georgia. During his campaigns he proved to be an apt disciple of Genghis Khan, destroying cities, murdering whole populations and building towns out of the skulls of beheaded prisoners. Like Genghis Khan, he organised his soldiers meticulously; his tactics were imaginative and well-planned, and his disciple draconian and rigid.

The Mongol invasion of China reached its peak in 1279, with the establishment of the Yuan dynasty, and ended nearly a century later with the establishment of the Ming dynasty. In the East, as in the West, the scene was set for a new era in military history.

A WORLD ATLAS OF
MILITARY HISTORY

Volume One - to 1500

FOUR EARLY VERSIONS OF THE WORLD

❶ As visualised by Hecataeus c. 500 B.C.

Hecataeus of Miletus was a much-travelled Greek historian and geographer who thought the world was round. His works have perished

❷ As visualised by Herodotus c. 450 B.C.

Herodotus, born in Halicarnassus in 484 B.C., was a much-travelled Greek historian who wrote a detailed account of the ancient world.

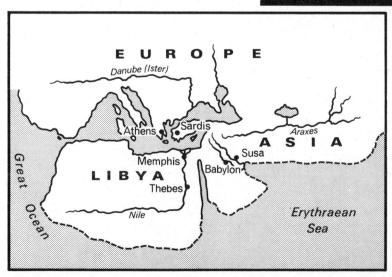

❸ As visualised by Eratosthenes c.200 B.C.

Eratosthenes,born at Cyrene in 276 B.C., was a scholar of geography, history, astronomy, philosophy, and geometry, and chief librarian at Alexandria. Most of his works have perished.

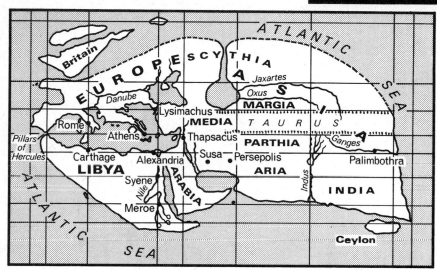

❹ As visualised by Ptolemy c. A.D. 150

Ptolemy (Ptolemaeus, Claudius) was a geographer, astronomer, and mathematician.

IDENTIFIABLE TRENDS IN EARLY MILITARY HISTORY

NOTE: EARLY HISTORY IS MUCH-DISPUTED BY SCHOLARS

❶ The Fertile Riverine Areas

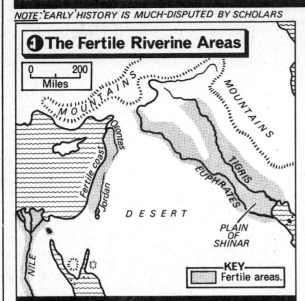

KEY
Fertile areas.

Early wars (in the sense of organized struggles) appear to have occurred in the area now known loosely as the Middle East and came about due to geography. In about 5000 B.C., people known as Sumerians occupied the area called the Plain of Shinar, and this fertile region became the envy of surrounding desert and mountain tribes.

❷ Early Wars and Invasions

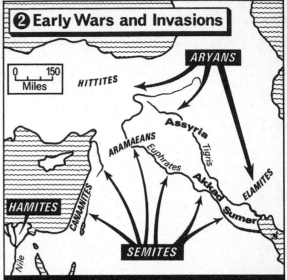

There were three main tribal groupings: Hamites, Semites, and Aryans (or Indo-Europeans). About 3000 B.C., Semitic tribes invaded Akkad-Sumer, and Aryans attacked Assyria. A long struggle ensued, and at one time (c.2320 B.C.), the tribes appear to have occupied the complete area between the rivers Tigris and Euphrates (under Sargon of Akkad).

❸ The Middle East c.2300-1500 B.C.

KEY
❶ Hittites.
❷ Mitannians.
❸ Assyrians.
❹ Kassites.
❺ Elamites.
❻ Canaanites.
❼ Thebans.

By c.2300 B.C., the main groups had split up into smaller tribes. Fierce struggles continued for the 'land of the two rivers', now known as Babylonia. Raids on the Nile delta were made by desert horsemen (Hyksos) who set up a base at Avaris. They were opposed by the Thebans. An Aryan group from the Black Sea (Hittites) expanded southwards.

❹ The Middle East c.1500-1000 B.C.

KEY
Egyptian Empire c.1450B.C.
❶ Hittites.
❷ Mitannians.
❸ Assyrians.
❹ Hebrews.
❺ Philistines.
❻ Elamites.
❼ Libyans.
❽ Achaeans.

The Egyptian peoples eventually expelled the Hyksos, and despite attacks from similar border groups, established a great empire. The Phoenicians, a sea-faring people, settled at Tyre and Sidon. The Achaean peoples of Aryan stock advanced southwards from Greece, occupied Minoan Crete, and then expanded eastward into the Middle East.

⑤ India before c.600 B.C.

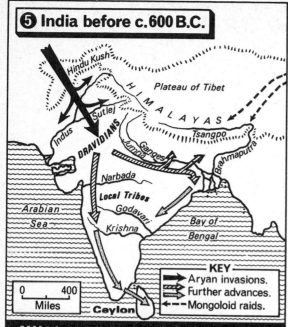

KEY
→ Aryan invasions.
⇨ Further advances.
⤍ Mongoloid raids.

c.2000 B.C., migrations from Asia into India occurred in a pattern similar to the Middle East. Aryan tribal groups advanced over the Hindu Kush to the riverine areas of the Indus and Ganges, and later moved south, even to Ceylon. Infrequent Mongoloid invasions from the north-east were hindered by the Himalayas and Tibetan plateaux.

⑥ China before c.600 B.C.

c.1766 B.C., the Shang dynastic empire was created in the region of Anyang, its capital. After c.1130 the semi-barbaric Chou from the Wei area moved eastwards, defeated the Shang, and later formed a great empire from the Yangtze to present-day Manchuria. From 800-600 B.C. there were constant feuds between autonomous war-lords.

⑦ Italy before c.600 B.C.

INDO-EUROPEANS

Founded c.700 B.C., possibly as a border post.

c.900 B.C., the Etruscans arrive by sea from the east and settle here.

KEY
→ Early penetrations.
⇨ Etruscan invasions.
⇦ Greek colonization.

c.2000 B.C., Indo-European tribes migrated across the Alps and pressed southwards bringing the Bronze Age to Italy and Sicily. c.900 B.C., Etruscans (of different racial origin), arrived by sea and infiltrated north-west Italy. From 750-600 B.C., there were frequent wars between the two groups. Meanwhile, Greeks were colonizing Sicily and southern Italy.

⑧ Greece before c.600 B.C.

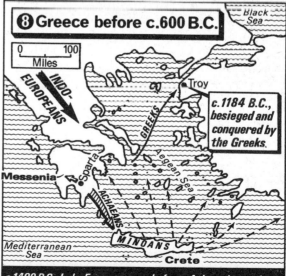

INDO-EUROPEANS

c.1184 B.C., besieged and conquered by the Greeks.

c.1400 B.C., Indo-European people from Achaea in southern Greece (which had been invaded by the Dorians) conquered the highly civilized Minoans of Crete, whose culture had spread over most of the Aegean. From c.1000 B.C., Sparta became militarily dominant and won two wars against the Messenians (c.700-680 B.C., and c.640-620 B.C.).

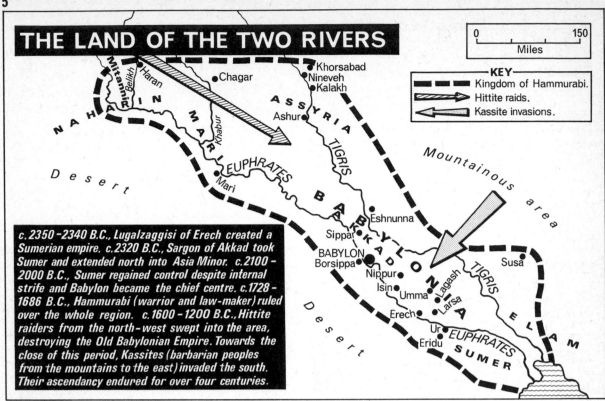

THE LAND OF THE TWO RIVERS

0   150
Miles

KEY
- — — — Kingdom of Hammurabi.
- ⇨ Hittite raids.
- ⟸ Kassite invasions.

Haran   Chagar   Khorsabad   Nineveh   Kalakh

MITANNI   NAHARIN   MARI

Belikh   Khabur   ASSYRIA   Ashur

Desert

EUPHRATES   Mari   TIGRIS   BABYLONIA

Mountainous area

Eshnunna   Sippar   BABYLON   Borsippa   Nippur   Isin   Umma   Erech   Lagash   Larsa   Ur   Eridu

AKKAD   Susa   TIGRIS   ELAM

Desert   EUPHRATES   SUMER

c. 2350 – 2340 B.C., Lugalzaggisi of Erech created a Sumerian empire. c. 2320 B.C., Sargon of Akkad took Sumer and extended north into Asia Minor. c. 2100 – 2000 B.C., Sumer regained control despite internal strife and Babylon became the chief centre. c. 1728 – 1686 B.C., Hammurabi (warrior and law-maker) ruled over the whole region. c. 1600 – 1200 B.C., Hittite raiders from the north-west swept into the area, destroying the Old Babylonian Empire. Towards the close of this period, Kassites (barbarian peoples from the mountains to the east) invaded the south. Their ascendancy endured for over four centuries.

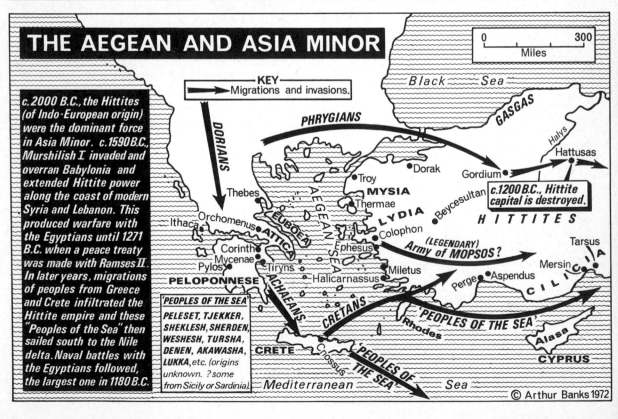

THE AEGEAN AND ASIA MINOR

0   300
Miles

KEY
→ Migrations and invasions.

Black Sea

GASGAS

c. 2000 B.C., the Hittites (of Indo-European origin) were the dominant force in Asia Minor. c. 1590 B.C., Murshilish I invaded and overran Babylonia and extended Hittite power along the coast of modern Syria and Lebanon. This produced warfare with the Egyptians until 1271 B.C. when a peace treaty was made with Ramses II. In later years, migrations of peoples from Greece and Crete infiltrated the Hittite empire and these "Peoples of the Sea" then sailed south to the Nile delta. Naval battles with the Egyptians followed, the largest one in 1180 B.C.

DORIANS   PHRYGIANS   Halys   Hattusas

Troy   Dorak   Gordium

Thebes   MYSIA   Thermae   LYDIA   Beycesultan

c. 1200 B.C., Hittite capital is destroyed.

HITTITES

Ithaca   Orchomenus   EUBOEA   ATTICA   AEGEAN SEA   Colophon   Ephesus

(LEGENDARY) Army of MOPSOS?

Tarsus   Mersin   CILICIA

Corinth   Mycenae   Pylos   Tiryns   ACHAEANS   Miletus   Halicarnassus

PELOPONNESE   CRETANS   Perge   Aspendus

'PEOPLES OF THE SEA'

Rhodes   Alasa   CYPRUS

'PEOPLES OF THE SEA'
PELESET, TJEKKER, SHEKLESH, SHERDEN, WESHESH, TURSHA, DENEN, AKAWASHA, LUKKA, etc. (origins unknown. ? some from Sicily or Sardinia).

CRETE   Cnossus   'PEOPLES OF THE SEA'

Mediterranean Sea

© Arthur Banks 1972

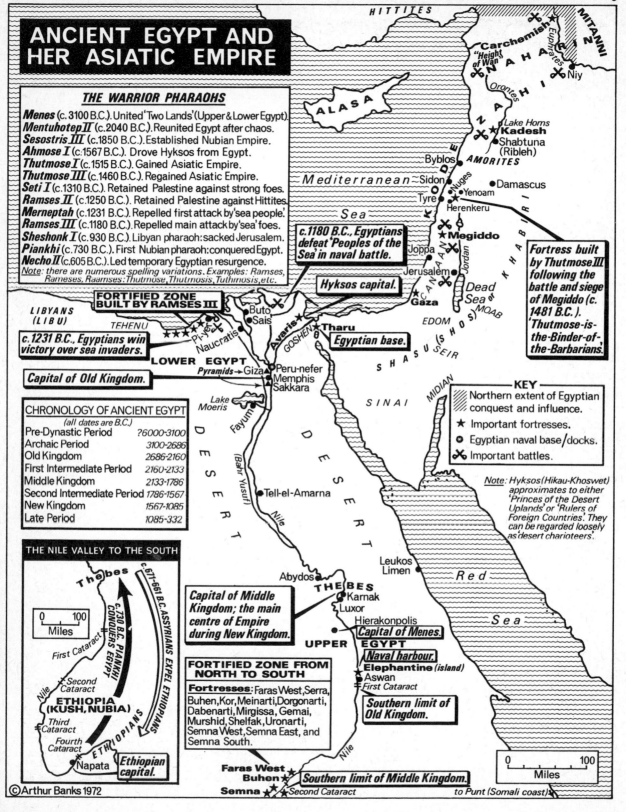

6

ANCIENT EGYPT AND HER ASIATIC EMPIRE

THE WARRIOR PHARAOHS

Menes (c.3100 B.C.). United 'Two Lands' (Upper & Lower Egypt).
Mentuhotep II (c.2040 B.C.). Reunited Egypt after chaos.
Sesostris III (c.1850 B.C.). Established Nubian Empire.
Ahmose I (c.1567 B.C.). Drove Hyksos from Egypt.
Thutmose I (c.1515 B.C.). Gained Asiatic Empire.
Thutmose III (c.1460 B.C.). Regained Asiatic Empire.
Seti I (c.1310 B.C.). Retained Palestine against strong foes.
Ramses II (c.1250 B.C.). Retained Palestine against Hittites.
Merneptah (c.1231 B.C.). Repelled first attack by 'sea people'.
Ramses III (c.1180 B.C.). Repelled main attack by 'sea' foes.
Sheshonk I (c.930 B.C.). Libyan pharaoh: sacked Jerusalem.
Piankhi (c.730 B.C.). First Nubian pharaoh: conquered Egypt.
Necho II (c.605 B.C.). Led temporary Egyptian resurgence.
Note: there are numerous spelling variations. Examples: Ramses, Rameses, Raamses: Thutmose, Thutmosis, Tuthmosis, etc.

CHRONOLOGY OF ANCIENT EGYPT
(all dates are B.C.)

Pre-Dynastic Period	?6000-3100
Archaic Period	3100-2686
Old Kingdom	2686-2160
First Intermediate Period	2160-2133
Middle Kingdom	2133-1786
Second Intermediate Period	1786-1567
New Kingdom	1567-1085
Late Period	1085-332

THE NILE VALLEY TO THE SOUTH

0 — 100 Miles

c.671-661 B.C. ASSYRIANS EXPEL ETHIOPIANS
c.730 B.C. PIANKHI CONQUERS EGYPT
Thebes
First Cataract
Second Cataract
ETHIOPIA (KUSH, NUBIA)
Third Cataract
Fourth Cataract
ETHIOPIANS
Napata — **Ethiopian capital.**
Nile

FORTIFIED ZONE BUILT BY RAMSES III
c.1231 B.C., Egyptians win victory over sea invaders.
Capital of Old Kingdom.

LIBYANS (LIBU)
TEHENU
Pi-Yer
Naucratis
LOWER EGYPT
Pyramids → Giza
Peru-nefer
Memphis
Sakkara
Lake Moeris
Fayum
(Bahr Yusuf)
DESERT
Nile
Tell-el-Amarna
Abydos

Buto
Sais
Avaris — **Hyksos capital.**
GOSHEN
Tharu — **Egyptian base.**
SINAI
MIDIAN

c.1180 B.C., Egyptians defeat 'Peoples of the Sea' in naval battle.

Mediterranean Sea
ALASA
HITTITES
Carchemish — Euphrates — MITANNI
"Height of Wan"
NAHARIN
Niy
Orontes
Lake Homs
Kadesh
Shabtuna (Ribleh)
AMORITES
Byblos
Sidon
Tyre
Nuges
Yenoam
Herenkeru
Damascus
KHABIRI
CANAAN
Megiddo
Joppa
Jordan
Jerusalem
Gaza
Dead Sea
EDOM
MOAB
SEIR
SHASU (SHOS)

Fortress built by Thutmose III following the battle and siege of Megiddo (c.1481 B.C.). 'Thutmose-is-the-Binder-of-the-Barbarians'.

KEY
- //// Northern extent of Egyptian conquest and influence.
- ★ Important fortresses.
- ⊕ Egyptian naval base/docks.
- ✕ Important battles.

Note: Hyksos (Hikau-Khoswet) approximates to either 'Princes of the Desert Uplands' or 'Rulers of Foreign Countries'. They can be regarded loosely as 'desert charioteers'.

Capital of Middle Kingdom; the main centre of Empire during New Kingdom.

Leukos Limen
Red Sea
THEBES
Karnak
Luxor
Hierakonpolis — **Capital of Menes.**
UPPER EGYPT
Naval harbour.
Elephantine (island)
Aswan
First Cataract
Southern limit of Old Kingdom.

FORTIFIED ZONE FROM NORTH TO SOUTH
Fortresses: Faras West, Serra, Buhen, Kor, Meinarti, Dorgonarti, Dabenarti, Mirgissa, Gemai, Murshid, Shelfak, Uronarti, Semna West, Semna East, and Semna South.

Faras West
Buhen
Semna
Second Cataract
Southern limit of Middle Kingdom.
to Punt (Somali coast)

0 — 100 Miles

© Arthur Banks 1972

THE BATTLE AND SIEGE OF MEGIDDO 1481 B.C.

The Battle (?15 May)

Note: the king of Kadesh slips away to north.

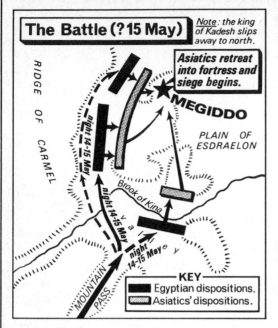

Asiatics retreat into fortress and siege begins.

RIDGE OF CARMEL

night 14-15 May

MEGIDDO

PLAIN OF ESDRAELON

Brook of Kina

night 14-15 May

v a l l e y

night 14-15 May

MOUNTAIN PASS.

KEY
▰ Egyptian dispositions.
▱ Asiatics' dispositions.

Egyptian Pre-Battle Strategy

0 — 3 Miles

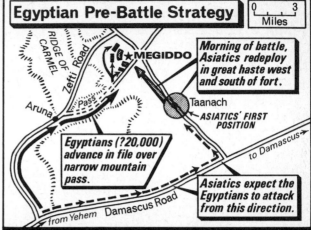

RIDGE OF CARMEL

Zefti Road

MEGIDDO

Aruna Pass

Taanach

Morning of battle, Asiatics redeploy in great haste west and south of fort.

ASIATICS' FIRST POSITION

to Damascus

Egyptians (?20,000) advance in file over narrow mountain pass.

Asiatics expect the Egyptians to attack from this direction.

from Yehem   Damascus Road

In May 1481 B.C., the king of Kadesh led a revolt of the Egyptian Empire's Asiatic city kings against the pharoah, Thutmose III. The Egyptian army marched to Megiddo, defeated the insurgents in battle, and besieged the fortress. After a campaign to secure the northern regions, Thutmose III returned to Thebes in October.

THE BATTLE OF KADESH 1288 B.C.

The Egyptian Advance

Hittite army concentrates north of Kadesh. As Ramses II and the Amon division advance, Hittites manœuvre to intercept Re.

Lake Homs

Orontes

KADESH

KEY
Ⓔ Egyptian encampment at night (?29 May).
▪ Egyptian divisions at dawn (?30 May).
Ⓗ Hittites first position at dawn (?30 May).

noon ?30 May

Ramses II leads advance

Orontes

ford

Shabtuna

Ramses II
Amon Division
Aranami
Re Division

Ptah Division

Sutekh Division

The Egyptian army was arranged in four divisions: Amon, Re, Ptah, and Sutekh. Ramses II took personal command over Amon and led in front during advance.

0 — 3 Miles

Ⓔ As Egyptians move out, Ptah and Sutekh lag behind.

The Hittite Ambush

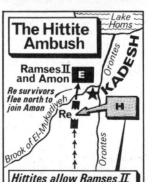

Lake Homs

Ramses II and Amon

Ⓔ

KADESH

Orontes

Re survivors flee north to join Amon

Re

Ⓗ

Brook of El-Mukadiyeh

Orontes

Hittites allow Ramses II and Amon to pass before emerging to attack Re. The Egyptian advance is cut in two as Ptah is far behind.

The Egyptian 'Victory'

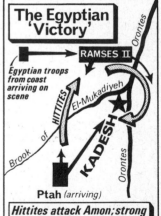

Orontes

RAMSES II

Egyptian troops from coast arriving on scene

HITTITES

El-Mukadiyeh

Brook of

KADESH

Orontes

Ptah (arriving)

Hittites attack Amon; strong Egyptian defence aided by unexpected arrival of 'recruit' troops. Hittites driven back into Kadesh as Ptah arrives.

By 1288 B.C., the Hittites under Metella had swept southwards and made Kadesh their base. Ramses II led his army to engage them and a battle ensued at Kadesh. Each army numbered about 20,000 and despite gaining an early tactical success, Metella was beaten. This battle is notable for the extensive use of chariots in warfare.

8

ANCIENT PALESTINE AND THE ISRAELITES

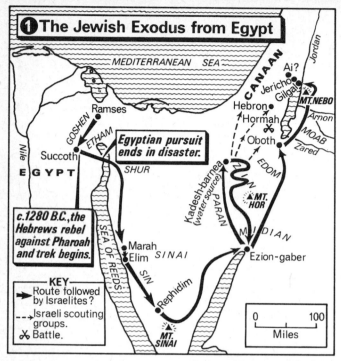

① The Jewish Exodus from Egypt

MEDITERRANEAN SEA

CANAAN

Ai? Jericho Gilgal MT.NEBO

Hebron Hormah Oboth MOAB Arnon Zared EDOM

Ramses GOSHEN ETHAM

Nile Succoth SHUR

Egyptian pursuit ends in disaster.

EGYPT

c.1280 B.C., the Hebrews rebel against Pharoah and trek begins.

Kadesh-barnea (water source) PARAN MT. HOR

Marah Elim SINAI SIN Rephidim MIDIAN Ezion-gaber

SEA OF REEDS

MT. SINAI

KEY
→ Route followed by Israelites?
- - - Israeli scouting groups.
✗ Battle.

0 ——— 100 Miles

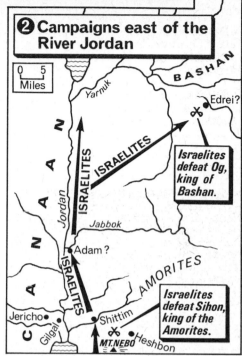

② Campaigns east of the River Jordan

0 ——— 5 Miles

BASHAN Yarnuk Edrei?

CANAAN ISRAELITES

Israelites defeat Og, king of Bashan.

Jordan Jabbok Adam?

ISRAELITES AMORITES

Jericho Gilgal Shittim Heshbon MT.NEBO

Israelites defeat Sihon, king of the Amorites.

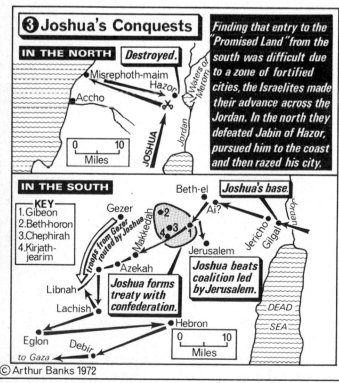

③ Joshua's Conquests

IN THE NORTH *Destroyed.*

Misrephoth-maim Hazor Waters of Merom

Accho JOSHUA Jordan

0 — 10 Miles

Finding that entry to the "Promised Land" from the south was difficult due to a zone of fortified cities, the Israelites made their advance across the Jordan. In the north they defeated Jabin of Hazor, pursued him to the coast and then razed his city.

IN THE SOUTH

KEY
1. Gibeon
2. Beth-horon
3. Chephirah
4. Kirjath-jearim

Beth-el *Joshua's base.* Ai?

Gezer Makkedah Jericho Gilgal

troops from Gezer routed by Joshua

Azekah Jerusalem *Joshua beats coalition led by Jerusalem.*

Joshua forms treaty with confederation.

Libnah Lachish Hebron

Eglon Debir to Gaza

DEAD SEA

0 — 10 Miles

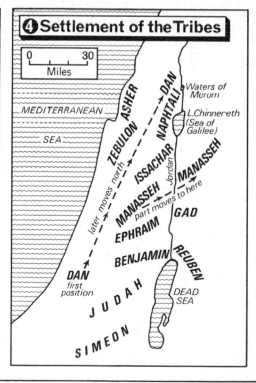

④ Settlement of the Tribes

0 ——— 30 Miles

MEDITERRANEAN SEA

ASHER ZEBULON NAPHTALI DAN Waters of Merom L.Chinnereth (Sea of Galilee)

later moves north ISSACHAR MANASSEH MANASSEH part moves to here

EPHRAIM GAD

DAN first position BENJAMIN REUBEN

JUDAH DEAD SEA

SIMEON

© Arthur Banks 1972

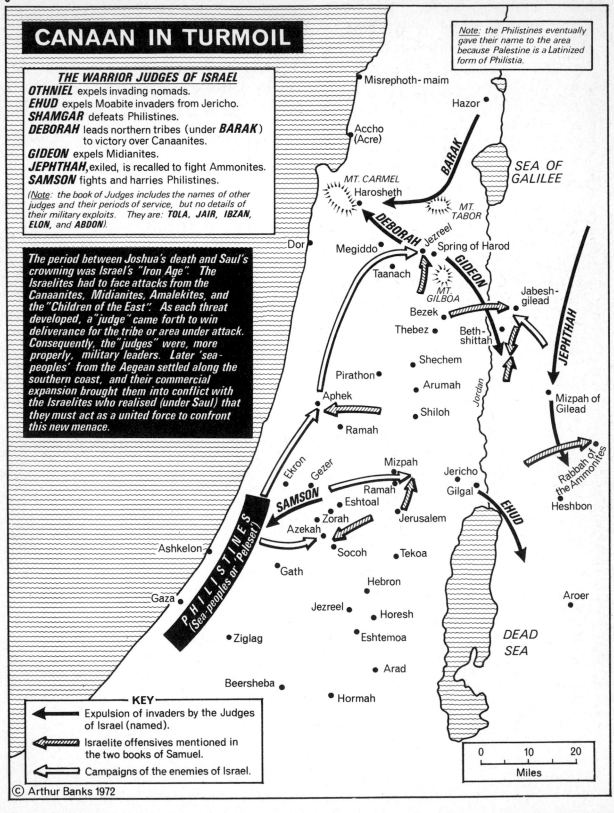

CANAAN IN TURMOIL

THE WARRIOR JUDGES OF ISRAEL

OTHNIEL expels invading nomads.
EHUD expels Moabite invaders from Jericho.
SHAMGAR defeats Philistines.
DEBORAH leads northern tribes (under **BARAK**) to victory over Canaanites.
GIDEON expels Midianites.
JEPHTHAH, exiled, is recalled to fight Ammonites.
SAMSON fights and harries Philistines.

(*Note*: the book of Judges includes the names of other judges and their periods of service, but no details of their military exploits. They are: **TOLA**, **JAIR**, **IBZAN**, **ELON**, and **ABDON**).

The period between Joshua's death and Saul's crowning was Israel's "Iron Age". The Israelites had to face attacks from the Canaanites, Midianites, Amalekites, and the "Children of the East". As each threat developed, a "judge" came forth to win deliverance for the tribe or area under attack. Consequently, the "judges" were, more properly, military leaders. Later 'sea-peoples' from the Aegean settled along the southern coast, and their commercial expansion brought them into conflict with the Israelites who realised (under Saul) that they must act as a united force to confront this new menace.

Note: the Philistines eventually gave their name to the area because Palestine is a Latinized form of Philistia.

Misrephoth-maim

Hazor

Accho (Acre)

SEA OF GALILEE

BARAK

MT. CARMEL
Harosheth

MT. TABOR

DEBORAH

Dor

Megiddo

Jezreel

Spring of Harod

GIDEON

Taanach

MT. GILBOA

Jabesh-gilead

Bezek

Thebez

Beth-shittah

JEPHTHAH

Shechem

Arumah

Pirathon

Shiloh

Jordan

Aphek

Mizpah of Gilead

Ramah

Rabbah of the Ammonites

Ekron

Gezer

Mizpah

Jericho

Heshbon

SAMSON

Ramah

Gilgal

EHUD

Eshtoal

Jerusalem

Zorah

Azekah

Socoh

Tekoa

Ashkelon

Gath

Hebron

Aroer

Gaza

Jezreel

Horesh

DEAD SEA

P H I L I S T I N E S
(Sea-peoples or 'Peleset')

Ziglag

Eshtemoa

Arad

Beersheba

Hormah

KEY

- Expulsion of invaders by the Judges of Israel (named).
- Israelite offensives mentioned in the two books of Samuel.
- Campaigns of the enemies of Israel.

0   10   20
Miles

© Arthur Banks 1972

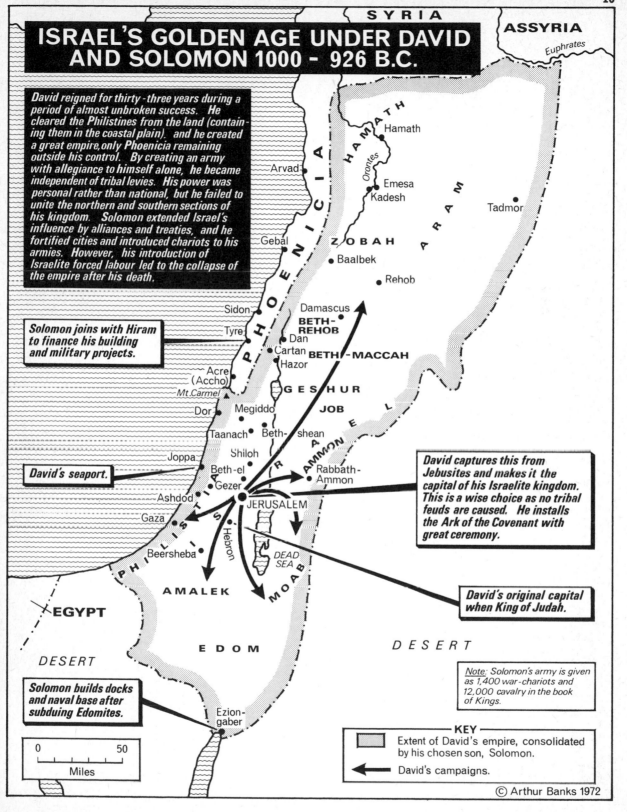

ISRAEL'S GOLDEN AGE UNDER DAVID AND SOLOMON 1000 - 926 B.C.

David reigned for thirty-three years during a period of almost unbroken success. He cleared the Philistines from the land (containing them in the coastal plain), and he created a great empire, only Phoenicia remaining outside his control. By creating an army with allegiance to himself alone, he became independent of tribal levies. His power was personal rather than national, but he failed to unite the northern and southern sections of his kingdom. Solomon extended Israel's influence by alliances and treaties, and he fortified cities and introduced chariots to his armies. However, his introduction of Israelite forced labour led to the collapse of the empire after his death.

Solomon joins with Hiram to finance his building and military projects.

David's seaport.

David captures this from Jebusites and makes it the capital of his Israelite kingdom. This is a wise choice as no tribal feuds are caused. He installs the Ark of the Covenant with great ceremony.

David's original capital when King of Judah.

Solomon builds docks and naval base after subduing Edomites.

Note: Solomon's army is given as 1,400 war-chariots and 12,000 cavalry in the book of Kings.

SYRIA

ASSYRIA

Euphrates

Hamath

Arvad

Orontes

Emesa
Kadesh

Tadmor

ARAM

ZOBAH

Baalbek

Rehob

Gebal

Sidon

Damascus

BETH-REHOB

Tyre

Dan
Cartan

BETH-MACCAH

Hazor

Acre (Accho)

Mt.Carmel

GESHUR

JOB

Dor

Megiddo

Beth-shean

Taanach

Shiloh

Joppa

Beth-el

AMMON

Rabbath-Ammon

Gezer

Ashdod

JERUSALEM

Gaza

Hebron

Beersheba

DEAD SEA

AMALEK

MOAB

EGYPT

EDOM

DESERT

DESERT

Ezion-gaber

PHOENICIA

PHILISTIA

ISRAEL

0   50
Miles

KEY
Extent of David's empire, consolidated by his chosen son, Solomon.
David's campaigns.

© Arthur Banks 1972

BASIC CHINESE CHRONOLOGY

Dynasties:

HSIA (legend only)	before c.1766 B.C.
SHANG (YIN)	1766 - 1122 B.C.
CHOU	1122 - 221 B.C.
CH'IN	221 - 206 B.C.
HAN { WESTERN HAN	206 B.C. - A.D. 24
HAN { LATER HAN (EASTERN)	25 - 221
THE THREE { SHU-HAN	221 - 263
KINGDOMS { WEI	220 - 265
{ WU	222 - 279
TSIN { WESTERN TSIN	265 - 317
TSIN { EASTERN TSIN	317 - 419

North

TOBA (WEI)	386 - 534
WESTERN WEI	535 - 556
EASTERN WEI	534 - 550
NORTHERN CH'I	550 - 577
NORTHERN CHOU	557 - 581
SUI	581 - 618
T'ANG	618 - 907
WU-TAI (FIVE SHORT DYNASTIES)	907 - 960
SUNG	960 - 1279
LIAO (KITAN TARTARS)	916 - 1119
CHIN (GOLDEN TARTARS)	1115 - 1234
YUAN (MONGOLS)	1260 - 1368
MING	1368 - 1644
CH'ING (MANCHU)	1644 - 1911

South

SUNG (LIU SUNG)	420 - 479
CH'I	479 - 502
LIANG	502 - 557
CH'EN	557 - 589

Chronology of the Bamboo Books and the orthodox dates vary until the year 827 B.C. After this, they coincide. The Chou period (1122 - 221 B.C.) can be broken down into 3 divisions: the Early Chou (1122-722 B.C), the Ch'un Ch'iu (722 - 481 B.C.), and the Warring States period (481 - 221 B.C.). This map shows China during the Ch'un Ch'iu period.

ANCIENT CHINA

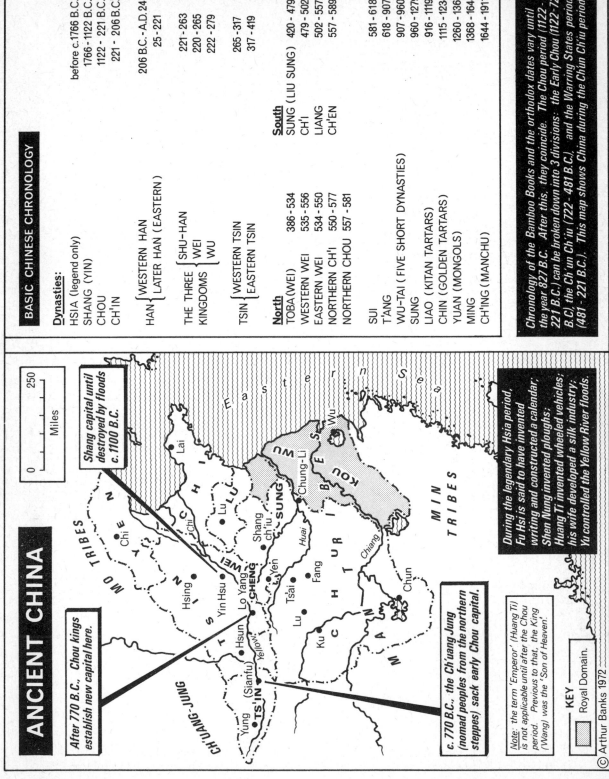

0 — 250 Miles

Shang capital until destroyed by floods c.1100 B.C.

After 770 B.C., Chou kings establish new capital here.

c. 770 B.C., the Ch'uang Jung (nomad peoples from the northern steppes) sack early Chou capital.

During the legendary Hsia period, Fu Hsi is said to have invented writing and constructed a calendar. Shen Nung invented ploughs. Huang Ti invented wheeled vehicles: his wife developed a silk industry: Yu controlled the Yellow River floods.

Note: the term 'Emperor' (Huang Ti) is not applicable until after the Chou period. Previous to that, the King (Wang) was the 'Son of Heaven'.

KEY

Royal Domain.

© Arthur Banks 1972

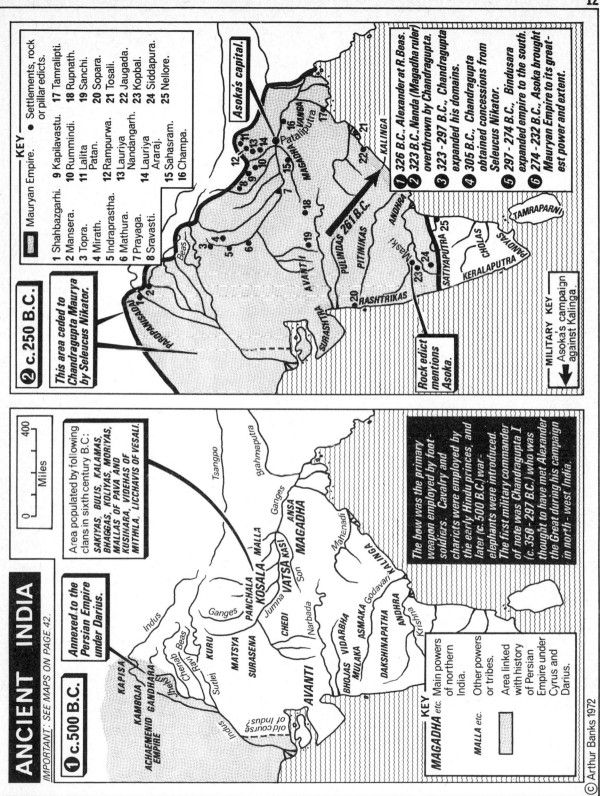

ANCIENT GREECE

13

Note: place-names are in traditional Latinized form. Thus, island names end in -os and mainland names in -us.

P A E O N I A

THRACIA

Strymon

Axius

Nestus

ILLYRIA

PELAGONIA

CRESTONIA

EDONES

Abdera

Epidamnus

L. Lychnidus

ALMOPIA

ANTHEMUS

Amphipolis

Eion

Eordaicus

Cellae

Pella

Therma

Apsus

Pelium

ORESTIS

Aegae

Apollonia

CHALCIDICE

ACTE

Thasos

Apsus

MACEDONIA

Methone

Pydna

Acanthus

Olynthus

Dium

MT. ATHOS

Aous

BOTTIAEA

Haliacmon

Petra

Potidaea

Singus

Oricus

ELIMEA

Philace

PIERIA

MT. OLYMPUS

Torone

SITHONIA

Heracleum

Mende

PALLENE

Cassiope

Scione

Buthrotum

E

Chalcis

Aeginium

MT. OSSA

Corcyra

P

Dodona

Tricca

THESSALY

I

Peneus

Polyaegos

Corcyra

R

Crannon

Pherae

Pagasae

Sciathos

Icos

Paxos

U

ATHAMANIA

Ithome

Thebes

Peparethos

S

Pharsalus

Scyros

AMBRACIA

PHTHIOTIS

Pteleum

Artemisium

Nicopolis

Argos

(ACHAEA)

Oreus

Amphilochicum

Achelous

MALIS

Cerinthus

Leucas

ACARNANIA

E

Cyme

Leucas

AETOLIA

Thermum

Heraclea

LOCRIS

C. Chersonesus

Ithaca

Naupactus

Thermopylae

Elatea

PHOCIS

Chalcis

Eretria

W. LOCRIS

Delphi

Cirrha

BOEOTIA

Cephallenia

Bulis

Thebes

Delium

C.

Plataea

Caphereus

Patrae

Aegium

GULF OF CORINTH

Marathon

Dyme

ACHAEA

Sicyon

Eleusis

ATHENS

Cyllene

Tritaea

Corinth

Megara

ATTICA

Helena

Elis

Clitor

Phlius

Mycenae

Salamis

Andros

ELIS

Olympia

ARCADIA

ARGOLIS

Piraeus

Ceos

Zacynthos

Mantinea

Argos

Tiryns

Aegina

Cythnos

Phigalia

Tegea

Troezen

Seriphos

Syros

Alpheus

CYNURIA

Hydrea

Eurotas

Prasiae

Siphnos

MESSENIA

Pharae

SPARTA

Pylus

LACONIA

Zarax

Methone

Epidaurus

Melos

C. Acritas

Limera

Pholegandros

C. Taenarum

C. Malea

Cythera

c.700 B.C., under Lycurgus, Sparta became an entirely military society. Its army dominated the whole area of the Peloponnese, being noted for its iron discipline, unit manœuvrability, and higher organization.

c.560 - 500 B.C., the city state of Athens rose to challenge the supremacy of Sparta. Occupied by Spartans, Athens expelled them in 507 B.C.

ANCIENT CRETE

0   40
Miles

Cydonia

Rhithymna

Lappa

MT. IDA

Cnossus

Mallia

Gortyna

Phaestus

Myrtos

Hierapytna

0   50
Miles

© Arthur Banks 1972

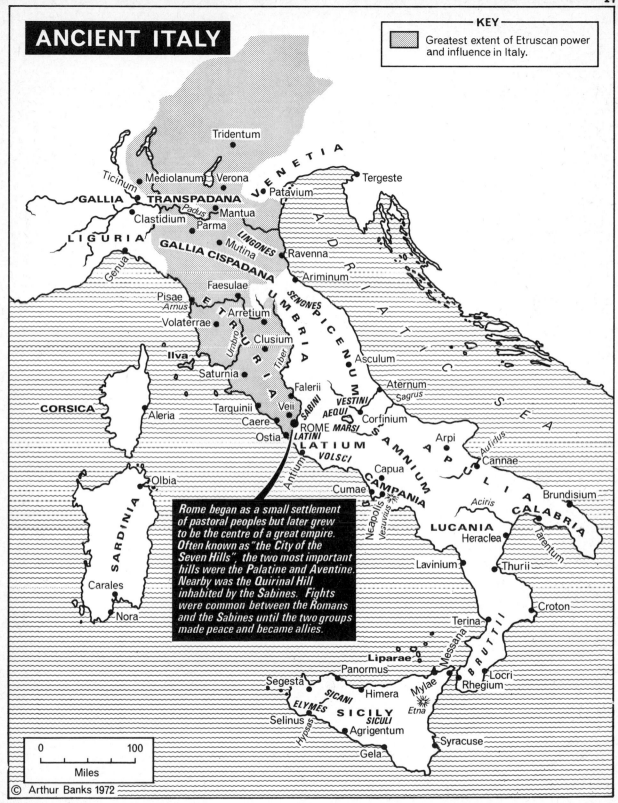

ANCIENT ITALY

KEY

Greatest extent of Etruscan power and influence in Italy.

Tridentum

VENETIA

Ticinum Mediolanum Verona

Patavium Tergeste

GALLIA TRANSPADANA

Padus Mantua

Clastidium Parma

LIGURIA

Mutina LINGONES

GALLIA CISPADANA

Ravenna

Genua

Faesulae

Ariminum

Pisae Arnus

ETRURIA

Arretium

SENONES

UMBRIA

PICENUM

Volaterrae

Umbro Clusium

Tiber

Asculum

Ilva

Saturnia

Falerii

Aternum
Sagrus

CORSICA

Tarquinii Veii SABINI VESTINI AEQUI

Aleria

Caere MARSI Corfinium

ROME

Ostia LATINI SAMNIUM

LATIUM

Arpi

VOLSCI

Antium Cannae Aufidus

Capua APULIA

Olbia Cumae CAMPANIA Brundisium

Neapolis Aciris CALABRIA

SARDINIA Vesuvius LUCANIA Tarentum

Heraclea

Lavinium Thurii

Rome began as a small settlement of pastoral peoples but later grew to be the centre of a great empire. Often known as "the City of the Seven Hills", the two most important hills were the Palatine and Aventine. Nearby was the Quirinal Hill inhabited by the Sabines. Fights were common between the Romans and the Sabines until the two groups made peace and became allies.

Carales Croton

Nora Terina BRUTTII

Messana

Liparae Locri

Panormus Mylae Rhegium

Segesta SICANI Himera Etna

ELYMES SICILY SICULI

Selinus Agrigentum

Hypsas Syracuse

Gela

ADRIATIC SEA

0   100

Miles

© Arthur Banks 1972

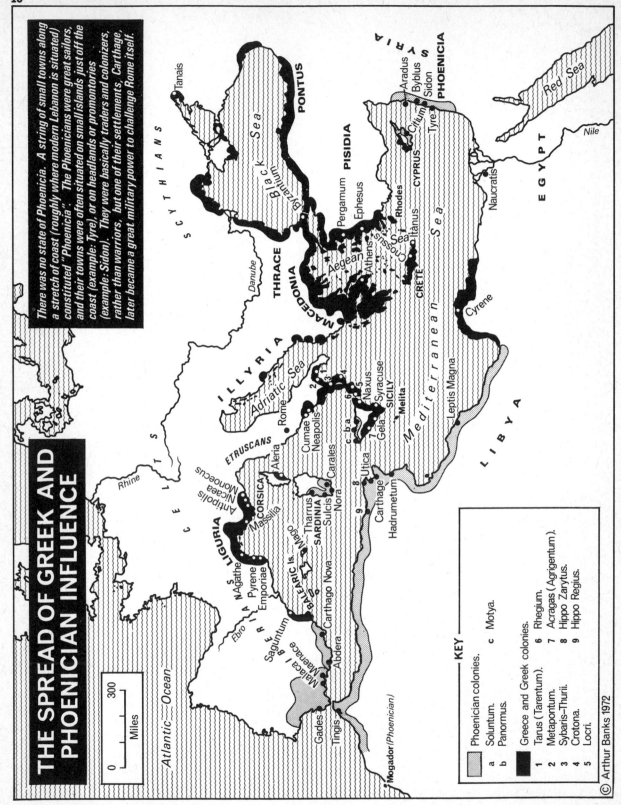

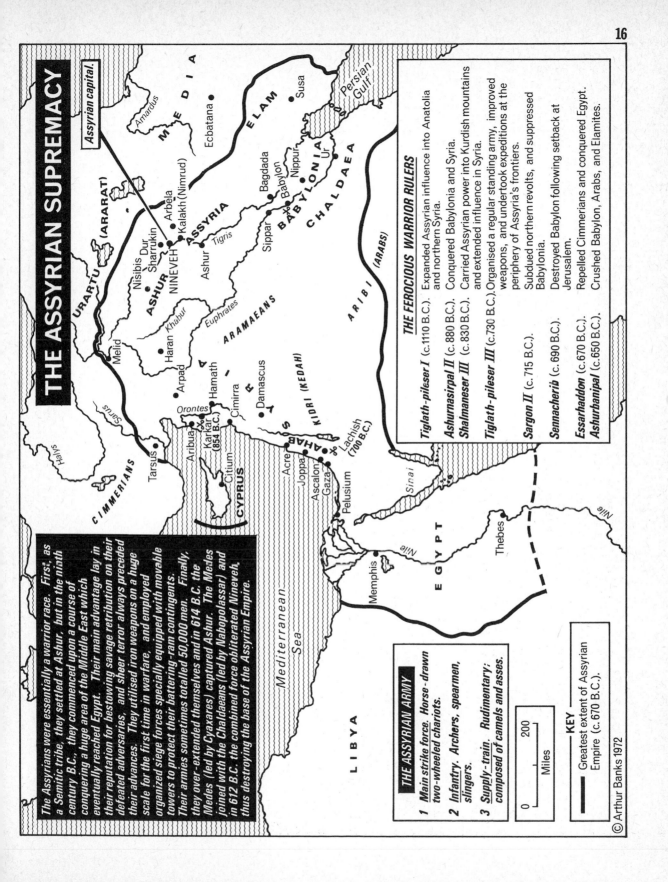

THE ASSYRIAN SUPREMACY

Assyrian capital.

The Assyrians were essentially a warrior race. First, as a Semitic tribe, they settled at Ashur, but in the ninth century B.C., they commenced upon a course of conquering a huge area of the Middle East which eventually reached Egypt. Their main advantage lay in their reputation for bestowing savage retribution on their defeated adversaries, and sheer terror always preceded their advances. They utilised iron weapons on a huge scale for the first time in warfare, and employed organized siege forces specially equipped with movable towers to protect their battering-ram contingents. Their armies sometimes totalled 50,000 men. Finally, they over-extended themselves and in 614 B.C. the Medes (led by Cyaxares) captured Ashur. The Medes joined with the Chaldaeans (led by Nabopolassar) and in 612 B.C. the combined force obliterated Nineveh, thus destroying the base of the Assyrian Empire.

THE FEROCIOUS WARRIOR RULERS

Tiglath-pileser I (c.1110 B.C.). Expanded Assyrian influence into Anatolia and northern Syria.

Ashurnasirpal II (c.880 B.C.). Conquered Babylonia and Syria.

Shalmaneser III (c.830 B.C.). Carried Assyrian power into Kurdish mountains and extended influence in Syria.

Tiglath-pileser III (c.730 B.C.). Organised a regular standing army, improved weapons, and undertook expeditions at the periphery of Assyria's frontiers.

Sargon II (c.715 B.C.). Subdued northern revolts, and suppressed Babylonia.

Sennacherib (c.690 B.C.). Destroyed Babylon following setback at Jerusalem.

Essarhaddon (c.670 B.C.). Repelled Cimmerians and conquered Egypt.

Ashurbanipal (c.650 B.C.). Crushed Babylon, Arabs, and Elamites.

THE ASSYRIAN ARMY

1 *Main strike force.* Horse-drawn two-wheeled chariots.

2 *Infantry.* Archers, spearmen, slingers.

3 *Supply-train.* Rudimentary; composed of camels and asses.

KEY

— Greatest extent of Assyrian Empire (c. 670 B.C.).

0   200
Miles

© Arthur Banks 1972

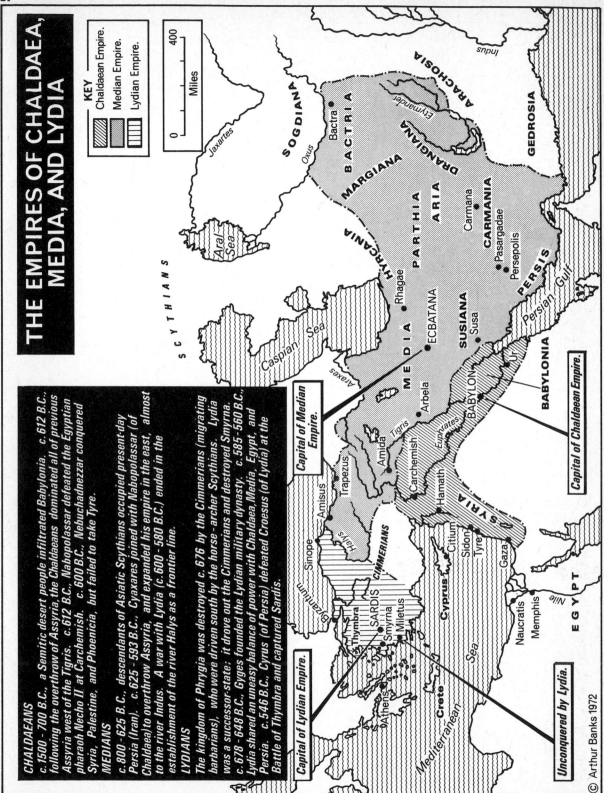

THE EMPIRES OF CHALDAEA, MEDIA, AND LYDIA

KEY
- Chaldaean Empire.
- Median Empire.
- Lydian Empire.

0 ——— 400 Miles

CHALDAEANS

c. 1500 - 700 B.C.. a Semitic desert people infiltrated Babylonia. c. 612 B.C.. following the overthrow of Assyria, the Chaldaeans dominated all of previous Assyria west of the Tigris. c. 612 B.C.. Nabopolassar defeated the Egyptian pharaoh Necho II at Carchemish. c. 600 B.C.. Nebuchadnezzar conquered Syria, Palestine, and Phoenicia, but failed to take Tyre.

MEDIANS

c. 800 - 625 B.C.. descendants of Asiatic Scythians occupied present-day Persia (Iran). c. 625 - 593 B.C.. Cyaxares joined with Nabopolassar (of Chaldaea) to overthrow Assyria, and expanded his empire in the east, almost to the river Indus. A war with Lydia (c. 600 - 580 B.C.) ended in the establishment of the river Halys as a frontier line.

LYDIANS

The kingdom of Phrygia was destroyed c. 676 by the Cimmerians (migrating barbarians). who were driven south by the horse- archer Scythians. Lydia was a successor-state: it drove out the Cimmerians and destroyed Smyrna. c. 678 - 648 B.C.. Gyges founded the Lydian military dynasty. c. 565 - 560 B.C.. Lydia shared an uneasy balance of power with Chaldaea, Media, Egypt, and Persia. c. 546 B.C.. Cyrus (of Persia) defeated Croesus (of Lydia) at the Battle of Thymbra and captured Sardis.

Capital of Median Empire.

Capital of Chaldaean Empire.

Capital of Lydian Empire.

Unconquered by Lydia.

SCYTHIANS

SOGDIANA

Jaxartes

Aral Sea

Oxus

Indus

ARACHOSIA

BACTRIA

Bactra

MARGIANA

DRANGIANA

Etymander

ARIA

GEDROSIA

HYRCANIA

PARTHIA

Rhagae

CARMANIA

Carmana

Pasargadae

Persepolis

PERSIS

Caspian Sea

MEDIA

ECBATANA

SUSIANA

Susa

Persian Gulf

Araxes

Arbela

BABYLON

BABYLONIA

Ur

Amida

Tigris

Euphrates

Carchemish

Hamath

SYRIA

Trapezus

Amisus

Sinope

Halys

CIMMERIANS

Byzantium

SARDIS

Thymbra

Smyrna

Miletus

Athens

Crete

Mediterranean Sea

Cyprus

Citium

Sidon

Tyre

Gaza

Naucratis

Memphis

Nile

EGYPT

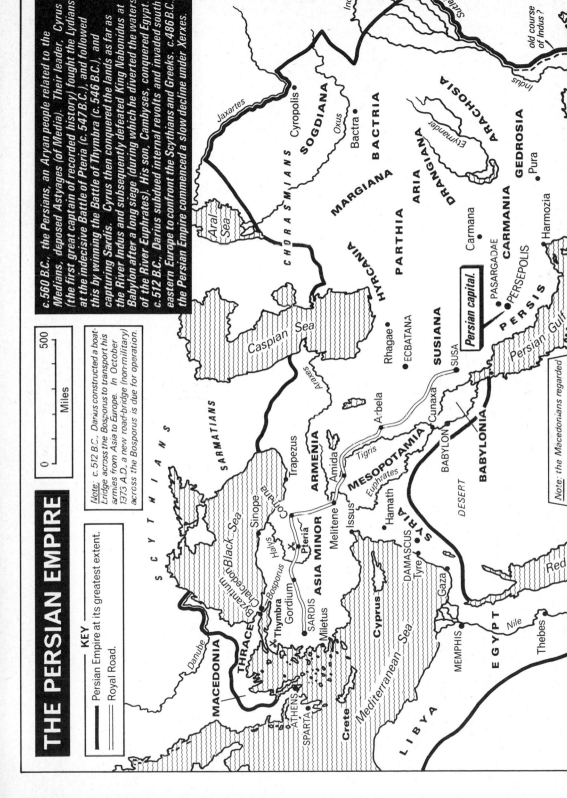

THE PERSIAN EMPIRE

KEY

━━━ Persian Empire at its greatest extent.

▨▨▨ Royal Road.

500

0

Miles

Note: c. 512 B.C., Darius constructed a boat-bridge across the Bosporus to transport his armies from Asia to Europe. In October 1973 A.D. a new road-bridge (non-military) across the Bosporus is due for operation.

c. 560 B.C., the Persians, an Aryan people related to the Medians, deposed Astyages (of Media). Their leader, Cyrus (the first great captain of recorded history) fought the Lydians at the indecisive Battle of Pteria (c. 547 B.C.) and followed this by winning the Battle of Thymbra (c. 546 B.C.), and capturing Sardis. Cyrus then conquered the lands as far as the River Indus and subsequently defeated King Nabonidus at Babylon after a long siege (during which he diverted the waters of the River Euphrates). His son, Cambyses, conquered Egypt. c. 512 B.C. Darius subdued internal revolts and invaded south eastern Europe to confront the Scythians and Greeks. c. 486 B.C., the Persian Empire commenced a slow decline under Xerxes.

Persian capital.

Note: the Macedonians regarded Persepolis (capital of Persis) as the Empire's capital. Greek historians mention Susa, Babylon, and Ecbatana.

© Arthur Banks 1972

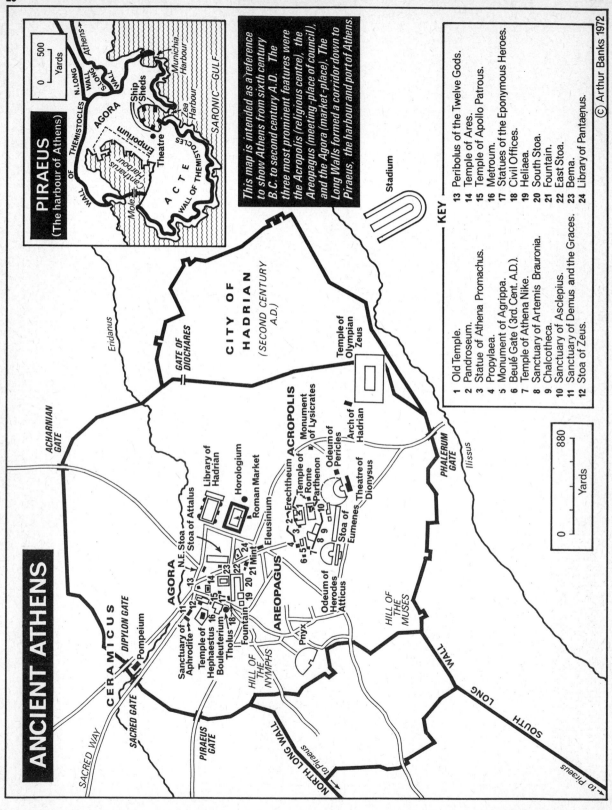

ANCIENT ATHENS

PIRAEUS
(The harbour of Athens)

WALL OF THEMISTOCLES
N.LONG WALL
S.LONG WALL
To Athens →
AGORA
Ship Sheds
Theatre
EMPORIUM
Cantharus Harbour
Mole
WALL OF THEMISTOCLES
ACTE
Zea Harbour
Munichia Harbour
SARONIC GULF

0 500 Yards

This map is intended as a reference to show Athens from sixth century B.C. to second century A.D. The three most prominent features were the Acropolis (religious centre), the Areopagus (meeting-place of council), and the Agora (market-place). The Long Walls formed a corridor down to Piraeus, the harbour and port of Athens.

© Arthur Banks 1972

CERAMICUS
SACRED WAY
Pompeium
DIPYLON GATE
SACRED GATE
ACHARNIAN GATE
Eridanus
AGORA
N.E. Stoa of Attalus
Library of Hadrian
Horologium
Roman Market
GATE OF DIOCHARES
CITY OF HADRIAN
(SECOND CENTURY A.D.)
Sanctuary of Aphrodite
Temple of Hephaestus
Bouleuterium
Tholus
Fountain
Mint
Eleusinium
ACROPOLIS
Erechtheum
Temple of Rome
Parthenon
Temple of Athena Nike
Monument of Lysicrates
Odeum of Pericles
Theatre of Dionysus
Arch of Hadrian
Temple of Olympian Zeus
Stadium
AREOPAGUS
Stoa of Eumenes
Odeum of Herodes Atticus
Pnyx
HILL OF THE NYMPHS
HILL OF THE MUSES
PHALERUM GATE
Ilissus
PIRAEUS GATE
NORTH LONG WALL
to Piraeus →
SOUTH LONG WALL
to Piraeus →

0 880 Yards

KEY

1 Old Temple.
2 Pandroseum.
3 Statue of Athena Promachus.
4 Propylaea.
5 Monument of Agrippa.
6 Beulé Gate (3rd. Cent. A.D.).
7 Temple of Athena Nike.
8 Sanctuary of Artemis Brauronia.
9 Chalcotheca.
10 Sanctuary of Asclepius.
11 Sanctuary of Demus and the Graces.
12 Stoa of Zeus.
13 Peribolus of the Twelve Gods.
14 Temple of Ares.
15 Temple of Apollo Patrous.
16 Metroum.
17 Statues of the Eponymous Heroes.
18 Civil Offices.
19 Heliaea.
20 South Stoa.
21 Fountain.
22 East Stoa.
23 Bema.
24 Library of Pantaenus.

20

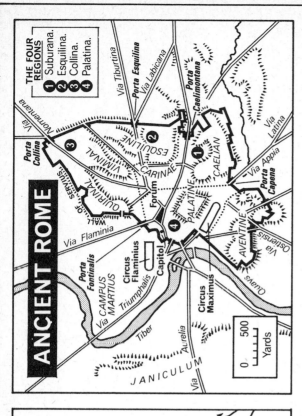

ANCIENT ROME

THE FOUR REGIONS
1 Suburana.
2 Esquilina.
3 Collina.
4 Palatina.

Via Nomentana
Porta Collina
Via Flaminia
Via Tiburtina
Porta Esquilina
Via Labicana
Porta Caelimontana
Via Latina
Via Appia
Porta Capena
Via Ostiensis
VIMINAL
QUIRINAL
ESQUILINE
CARINAE
CAELIAN
PALATINE
AVENTINE
WALL OF SERVIUS
Forum
Capitol
Porta Fontinalis
Circus Flaminius
Via Triumphalis
CAMPUS MARTIUS
Circus Maximus
Quays
Tiber
Aurelia
JANICULUM
Via

0   500
Yards

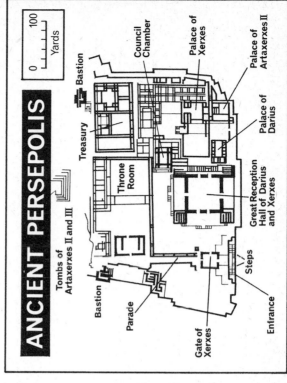

ANCIENT PERSEPOLIS

0   100
Yards

Bastion
Treasury
Council Chamber
Palace of Xerxes
Palace of Artaxerxes II
Palace of Darius
Throne Room
Great Reception Hall of Darius and Xerxes
Tombs of Artaxerxes II and III
Bastion
Parade
Gate of Xerxes
Steps
Entrance

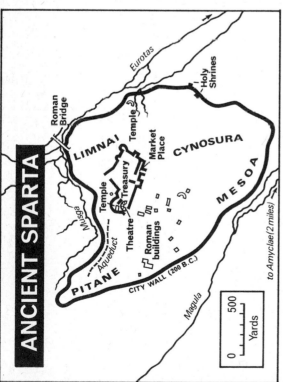

ANCIENT SPARTA

Eurotas
Roman Bridge
Holy Shrines
LIMNAI
Temple
Temple
Market Place
CYNOSURA
Musga
Temple
Treasury
Theatre
Roman buildings
MESOA
Aqueduct
PITANE
CITY WALL (200 B.C.)
Magula
to Amyclae (2 miles)

0   500
Yards

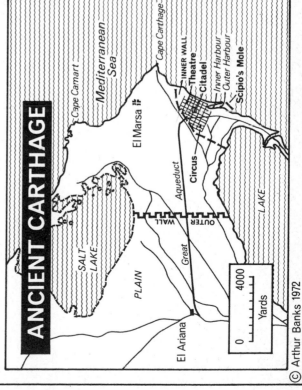

ANCIENT CARTHAGE

Cape Camart
Mediterranean Sea
Cape Carthage
El Marsa
INNER WALL
Theatre
Citadel
Inner Harbour
Outer Harbour
Scipio's Mole
Circus
Aqueduct
OUTER WALL
LAKE
SALT LAKE
PLAIN
Great
El Ariana

0   4000
Yards

© Arthur Banks 1972

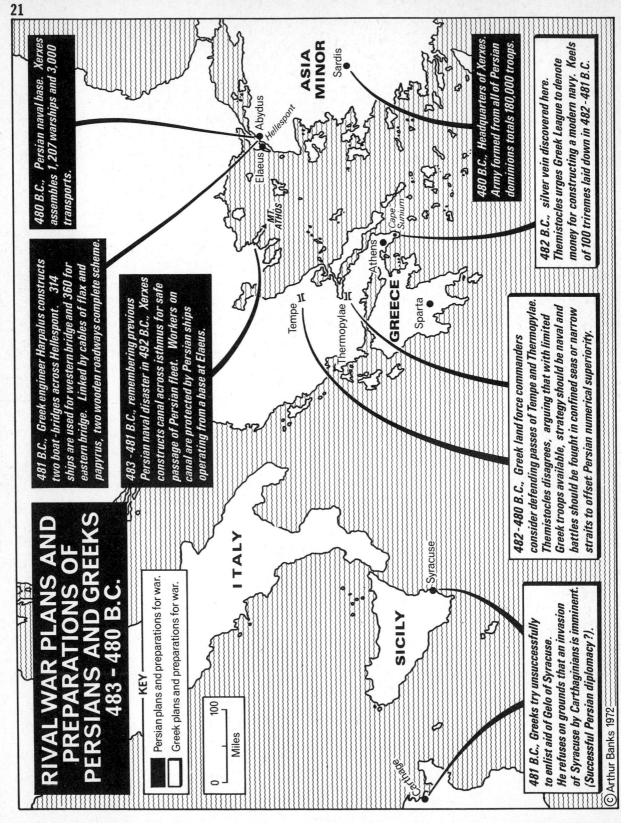

RIVAL WAR PLANS AND PREPARATIONS OF PERSIANS AND GREEKS 483 - 480 B.C.

KEY

Persian plans and preparations for war.

Greek plans and preparations for war.

0 — 100 Miles

© Arthur Banks 1972

480 B.C., Persian naval base. Xerxes assembles 1,207 warships and 3,000 transports.

481 B.C., Greek engineer Harpalus constructs two boat - bridges across Hellespont. 314 ships are used for western bridge and 360 for eastern bridge. Linked by cables of flax and papyrus, two wooden roadways complete scheme.

483 - 481 B.C., remembering previous Persian naval disaster in 492 B.C., Xerxes constructs canal across isthmus for safe passage of Persian fleet. Workers on canal are protected by Persian ships operating from a base at Elaeus.

480 B.C., Headquarters of Xerxes. Army formed from all of Persian dominions totals 180,000 troops.

482 B.C., silver vein discovered here. Themistocles urges Greek League to denote money for constructing a modern navy. Keels of 100 triremes laid down in 482 - 481 B.C.

482 - 480 B.C., Greek land force commanders consider defending passes of Tempe and Thermopylae. Themistocles disagrees, arguing that with limited Greek troops available, strategy should be naval and battles should be fought in confined seas or narrow straits to offset Persian numerical superiority.

481 B.C., Greeks try unsuccessfully to enlist aid of Gelo of Syracuse. He refuses on grounds that an invasion of Syracuse by Carthaginians is imminent. (Successful Persian diplomacy?).

ASIA MINOR

Sardis

Abydus

Hellespont

Elaeus

MT. ATHOS

Cape Sunium

Athens

GREECE

Tempe

Thermopylae

Sparta

ITALY

SICILY

Syracuse

Carthage

PERSIAN MILITARY AND NAVAL EXPEDITIONS AGAINST GREECE

The Persians launched three assaults against the Greeks: all of them ended in failure. In 492 B.C. a gale wrecked the Persian fleet; in 490 B.C. they were defeated at Marathon; in 480 B.C., the largest invasion of the three ended in the defeats at Salamis and Plataea, and in 479, at Cape Mycale.

KEY

Persian army invasion 492 B.C.
Persian naval invasion 492 B.C.
Persian naval invasion 490 B.C.
Persian army invasion 480 B.C.
Persian naval invasion 480 B.C.
Important battle.
Persian naval disaster due to gale.
The Persian Empire.
Persian vassal-state from 492 B.C.
Allied with Persia in 480 B.C.

© Arthur Banks 1972

THE GREEK VICTORY AT MARATHON 490 B.C.

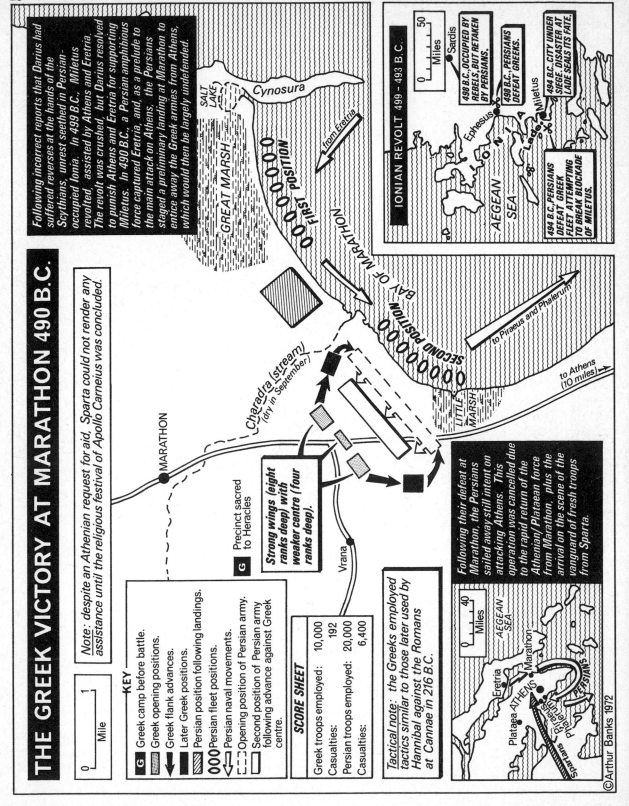

Following incorrect reports that Darius had suffered reverses at the hands of the Scythians, unrest seethed in Persian-occupied Ionia. In 499 B.C., Miletus assisted by Athens and Eretria. The revolt was crushed, but Darius resolved to punish Athens and Eretria for supporting Miletus. In 490 B.C., a Persian amphibious force captured Eretria, and, as a prelude to the main attack on Athens, the Persians staged a preliminary landing at Marathon to entice away the Greek armies from Athens, which would then be largely undefended.

Note: despite an Athenian request for aid, Sparta could not render any assistance until the religious festival of Apollo Carneius was concluded.

KEY

- **G** Greek camp before battle.
- Greek opening positions.
- Greek flank advances.
- Later Greek positions.
- Persian position following landings.
- **OOO** Persian fleet positions.
- Persian naval movements.
- Opening position of Persian army.
- Second position of Persian army following advance against Greek centre.

G Precinct sacred to Heracles

Strong wings (eight ranks deep) with weaker centre (four ranks deep).

SCORE SHEET

Greek troops employed:	10,000
Casualties:	192
Persian troops employed:	20,000
Casualties:	6,400

Tactical note: the Greeks employed tactics similar to those later used by Hannibal against the Romans at Cannae in 216 B.C.

Following their defeat at Marathon, the Persians sailed away still intent on attacking Athens. This operation was cancelled due to the rapid return of the Athenian/Plataean force from Marathon, plus the arrival on the scene of the vanguard of fresh troops from Sparta.

SALT LAKE

Cynosura

GREAT MARSH

from Eretria

FIRST POSITION

BAY OF MARATHON

SECOND POSITION

LITTLE MARSH

to Piraeus and Phalerum

to Athens (10 miles)

MARATHON

Charadra (stream) (dry in September)

Vrana

0   1   Mile

IONIAN REVOLT 499 - 493 B.C.

0   50   Miles

Sardis

498 B.C. OCCUPIED BY REBELS, BUT RETAKEN BY PERSIANS.

498 B.C. PERSIANS DEFEAT GREEKS.

494 B.C. CITY UNDER SIEGE. DISASTER AT LADE SEALS ITS FATE.

Ephesus

Miletus

Lade

I O N I A

AEGEAN SEA

494 B.C. PERSIANS DEFEAT GREEK FLEET ATTEMPTING TO BREAK BLOCKADE OF MILETUS.

0   40   Miles

AEGEAN SEA

Eretria

Plataea

ATHENS

Marathon

PERSIANS

Spartans

© Arthur Banks 1972

GREEK EFFORTS TO STEM PERSIAN ADVANCE

In 480 B.C., Xerxes' expedition against Greece was within striking distance of Athens and the Isthmus of Corinth, and the Athenian-dominated Greek Congress decided to stage two simultaneous actions to the north to stem the Persian advance. The first, a naval battle fought off Artemisium, proved indecisive despite the occurrence of two storms which wrecked over 500 Persian warships. The second, a land battle at the narrow Pass of Thermopylae, ended in disaster despite an heroic stand by 7,000 Greek troops led by the Spartan, Leonidas. 20,000 Persians and 4,000 Greeks perished in the fight, the outcome of which was determined when 10,000 Persians outflanked the main Greek position by traversing a mountain track to attack Leonidas from the rear. The way to Athens was now unguarded and its citizens were hurriedly evacuated.

KEY

- ⚔ Battles of Artemisium and Thermopylae.
- **L** Main Greek force under Leonidas (6,000 men).
- **P** Greek (Phocian) detachment (1,000 men) guarding mountain track.
- 〰 Ancient wall sheltering Greeks.
- ⊗ Final stand of Greeks on mound.
- ⬆ Main Persian advance.
- ⬆ Persian outflanking movement.

① At Artemisium

Persians lose many warships in storms prior to battle.

EUBOEA

Euboic Channel

Artemisium

Pass of Thermopylae

Plataea

ATHENS

Salamis

Corinth

0 — 20 Miles

② At Thermopylae

Citadel of Trachis

Melas

PERSIAN CAMP

Asopus

WEST GATE

Anthela

Main Persian Advance

GULF OF MALIS

ANCIENT COASTLINE

MIDDLE GATE

EAST GATE

Alpeni

Supply base of Leonidas.

Main Greek force withdraws leaving Leonidas and 2,000 to make last stand.

L

⊗

Hydarnes attacks and forces Phocians to fall back to higher ground.

P

Dracospilia

ANOPAEA (mountain track)

MOUNTAINS

CALLIDROMUS

HYDARNES and the 10,000 'IMMORTALS'

0 — 1 — 2 Miles

© Arthur Banks 1972

THE GREEK NAVAL VICTORY AT SALAMIS 480 B.C.

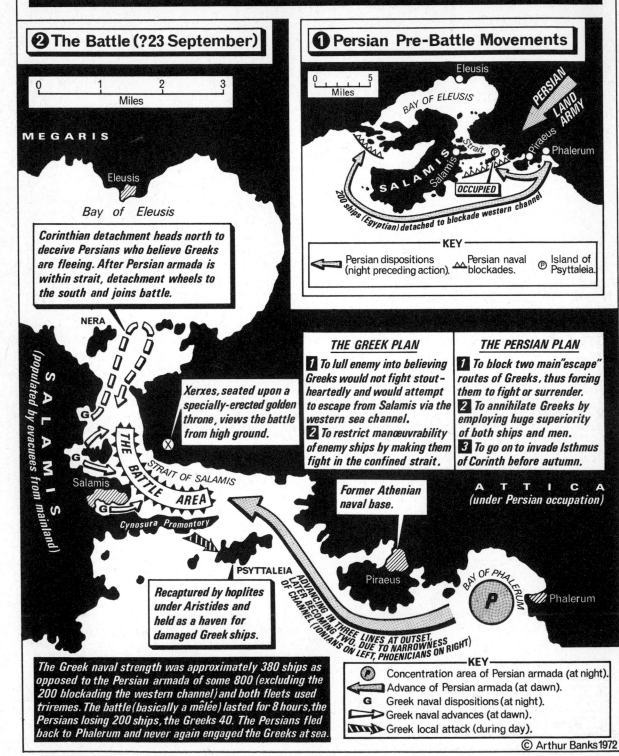

② The Battle (?23 September)

0   1   2   3
Miles

MEGARIS

Eleusis

Bay of Eleusis

Corinthian detachment heads north to deceive Persians who believe Greeks are fleeing. After Persian armada is within strait, detachment wheels to the south and joins battle.

NERA

S A L A M I S
(populated by evacuees from mainland)

G

G

Xerxes, seated upon a specially-erected golden throne, views the battle from high ground.

THE BATTLE AREA

STRAIT OF SALAMIS

G

Salamis

Cynosura Promontory

PSYTTALEIA

Recaptured by hoplites under Aristides and held as a haven for damaged Greek ships.

Former Athenian naval base.

Piraeus

A T T I C A
(under Persian occupation)

ADVANCING IN THREE LINES AT OUTSET, LATER BECOMING TWO, DUE TO NARROWNESS OF CHANNEL (IONIANS ON LEFT, PHOENICIANS ON RIGHT)

BAY OF PHALERUM
P

Phalerum

① Persian Pre-Battle Movements

0   5
Miles

Eleusis

BAY OF ELEUSIS

PERSIAN LAND ARMY

S A L A M I S

Strait

Piraeus

Phalerum

Salamis

OCCUPIED

200 ships (Egyptian) detached to blockade western channel

── KEY ──

⬅ Persian dispositions (night preceding action). ▲▲ Persian naval blockades. Ⓟ Island of Psyttaleia.

THE GREEK PLAN

1 To lull enemy into believing Greeks would not fight stout-heartedly and would attempt to escape from Salamis via the western sea channel.
2 To restrict manœuvrability of enemy ships by making them fight in the confined strait.

THE PERSIAN PLAN

1 To block two main "escape" routes of Greeks, thus forcing them to fight or surrender.
2 To annihilate Greeks by employing huge superiority of both ships and men.
3 To go on to invade Isthmus of Corinth before autumn.

The Greek naval strength was approximately 380 ships as opposed to the Persian armada of some 800 (excluding the 200 blockading the western channel) and both fleets used triremes. The battle (basically a mêlée) lasted for 8 hours, the Persians losing 200 ships, the Greeks 40. The Persians fled back to Phalerum and never again engaged the Greeks at sea.

── KEY ──

Ⓟ Concentration area of Persian armada (at night).
⬅ Advance of Persian armada (at dawn).
G Greek naval dispositions (at night).
⬜➡ Greek naval advances (at dawn).
▨➤ Greek local attack (during day).

© Arthur Banks 1972

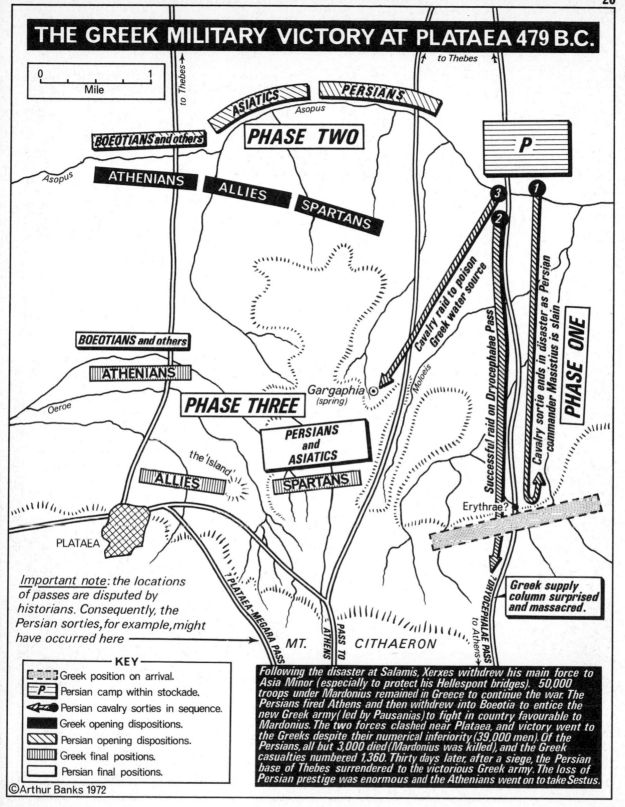

THE GREEK MILITARY VICTORY AT PLATAEA 479 B.C.

0 _____ 1
Mile

to Thebes

to Thebes

ASIATICS
PERSIANS
Asopus

PHASE TWO

BOEOTIANS and others

Asopus

ATHENIANS
ALLIES
SPARTANS

P

3
2
1

Cavalry raid to poison Greek water source

Successful raid on Dryocephalae Pass

Cavalry sortie ends in disaster as Persian commander Masistius is slain

PHASE ONE

BOEOTIANS and others

ATHENIANS

Oeroe

PHASE THREE

Gargaphia
(spring)

Moloeis

PERSIANS
and
ASIATICS

SPARTANS

the 'Island'

ALLIES

Erythrae?

Greek supply column surprised and massacred.

PLATAEA

Important note: the locations of passes are disputed by historians. Consequently, the Persian sorties, for example, might have occurred here ➤

?PLATAEA-MEGARA PASS

?DRYOCEPHALAE PASS

to Athens

PASS TO ATHENS

MT. CITHAERON

KEY
- ⬚⬚⬚ Greek position on arrival.
- P Persian camp within stockade.
- ◅— Persian cavalry sorties in sequence.
- ▬ Greek opening dispositions.
- ▨ Persian opening dispositions.
- ⦀ Greek final positions.
- ▭ Persian final positions.

©Arthur Banks 1972

Following the disaster at Salamis, Xerxes withdrew his main force to Asia Minor (especially to protect his Hellespont bridges). 50,000 troops under Mardonius remained in Greece to continue the war. The Persians fired Athens and then withdrew into Boeotia to entice the new Greek army (led by Pausanias) to fight in country favourable to Mardonius. The two forces clashed near Plataea, and victory went to the Greeks despite their numerical inferiority (39,000 men). Of the Persians, all but 3,000 died (Mardonius was killed), and the Greek casualties numbered 1,360. Thirty days later, after a siege, the Persian base of Thebes surrendered to the victorious Greek army. The loss of Persian prestige was enormous and the Athenians went on to take Sestus.

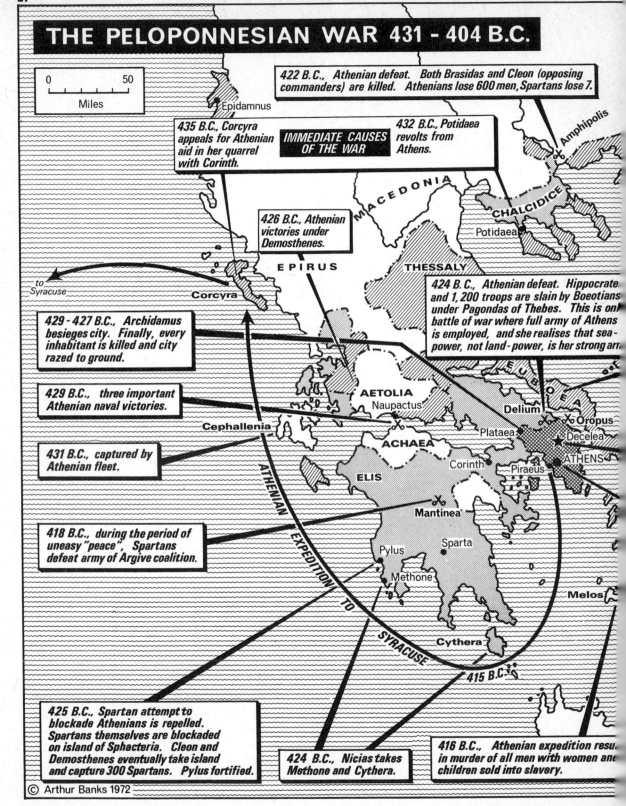

THE PELOPONNESIAN WAR 431 - 404 B.C.

0 50
Miles

Epidamnus

422 B.C., Athenian defeat. Both Brasidas and Cleon (opposing commanders) are killed. Athenians lose 600 men, Spartans lose 7.

435 B.C., Corcyra appeals for Athenian aid in her quarrel with Corinth.

IMMEDIATE CAUSES OF THE WAR

432 B.C., Potidaea revolts from Athens.

Amphipolis

MACEDONIA

CHALCIDICE

Potidaea

426 B.C., Athenian victories under Demosthenes.

EPIRUS

THESSALY

424 B.C., Athenian defeat. Hippocrate and 1,200 troops are slain by Boeotians under Pagondas of Thebes. This is onl battle of war where full army of Athens is employed, and she realises that sea-power, not land-power, is her strong arm

to Syracuse

Corcyra

429 - 427 B.C., Archidamus besieges city. Finally, every inhabitant is killed and city razed to ground.

429 B.C., three important Athenian naval victories.

Cephallenia

431 B.C., captured by Athenian fleet.

AETOLIA

Naupactus

Delium

Oropus

Decelea

Plataea

ACHAEA

Corinth

ATHENS

Piraeus

ELIS

ATHENIAN EXPEDITION TO SYRACUSE

418 B.C., during the period of uneasy "peace", Spartans defeat army of Argive coalition.

Mantinea

Pylus

Sparta

Methone

Melos

Cythera

415 B.C.

425 B.C., Spartan attempt to blockade Athenians is repelled. Spartans themselves are blockaded on island of Sphacteria. Cleon and Demosthenes eventually take island and capture 300 Spartans. Pylus fortified.

424 B.C., Nicias takes Methone and Cythera.

416 B.C., Athenian expedition resu in murder of all men with women an children sold into slavery.

© Arthur Banks 1972

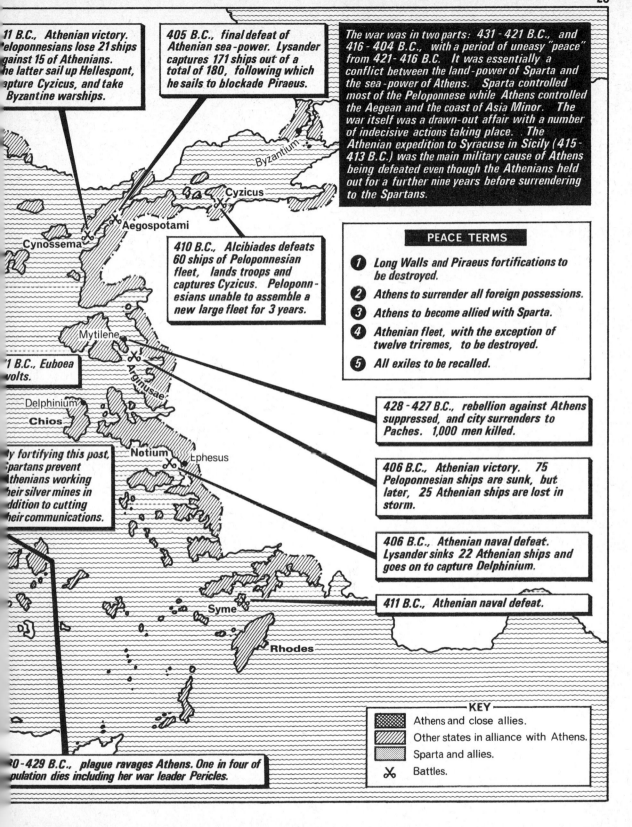

411 B.C., Athenian victory. Peloponnesians lose 21 ships against 15 of Athenians. The latter sail up Hellespont, capture Cyzicus, and take Byzantine warships.

405 B.C., final defeat of Athenian sea-power. Lysander captures 171 ships out of a total of 180, following which he sails to blockade Piraeus.

The war was in two parts: 431 - 421 B.C., and 416 - 404 B.C., with a period of uneasy "peace" from 421 - 416 B.C. It was essentially a conflict between the land-power of Sparta and the sea-power of Athens. Sparta controlled most of the Peloponnese while Athens controlled the Aegean and the coast of Asia Minor. The war itself was a drawn-out affair with a number of indecisive actions taking place. The Athenian expedition to Syracuse in Sicily (415 - 413 B.C.) was the main military cause of Athens being defeated even though the Athenians held out for a further nine years before surrendering to the Spartans.

Byzantium

Cyzicus

Aegospotami

Cynossema

410 B.C., Alcibiades defeats 60 ships of Peloponnesian fleet, lands troops and captures Cyzicus. Peloponnesians unable to assemble a new large fleet for 3 years.

PEACE TERMS

1. Long Walls and Piraeus fortifications to be destroyed.
2. Athens to surrender all foreign possessions.
3. Athens to become allied with Sparta.
4. Athenian fleet, with the exception of twelve triremes, to be destroyed.
5. All exiles to be recalled.

Mytilene

Arginusae

1 B.C., Euboea revolts.

Delphinium

Chios

428 - 427 B.C., rebellion against Athens suppressed, and city surrenders to Paches. 1,000 men killed.

Notium

Ephesus

ly fortifying this post, Spartans prevent Athenians working heir silver mines in addition to cutting heir communications.

406 B.C., Athenian victory. 75 Peloponnesian ships are sunk, but later, 25 Athenian ships are lost in storm.

406 B.C., Athenian naval defeat. Lysander sinks 22 Athenian ships and goes on to capture Delphinium.

Syme

411 B.C., Athenian naval defeat.

Rhodes

KEY

- Athens and close allies.
- Other states in alliance with Athens.
- Sparta and allies.
- ✗ Battles.

30 - 429 B.C., plague ravages Athens. One in four of population dies including her war leader Pericles.

THE DISASTROUS SICILIAN EXPEDITION 415-413 B.C.

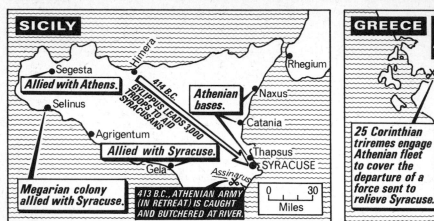

SICILY

- Himera
- Segesta — **Allied with Athens.**
- Rhegium
- Naxus
- Selinus
- **414 B.C. GYLIPPUS LEADS 3000 TROOPS TO AID SYRACUSANS**
- **Athenian bases.**
- Catania
- Agrigentum
- **Allied with Syracuse.**
- Thapsus
- SYRACUSE
- Gela
- Assinarus
- **Megarian colony allied with Syracuse.**
- **413 B.C., ATHENIAN ARMY (IN RETREAT) IS CAUGHT AND BUTCHERED AT RIVER.**

0 — 30 Miles

GREECE

By fortifying Decelea, Sparta severed communications to Athens, forcing her to fight a war on two fronts.

- Naupactus
- Decelea
- Corinth
- Athens
- Sparta

25 Corinthian triremes engage Athenian fleet to cover the departure of a force sent to relieve Syracuse.

0 — 50 Miles

SYRACUSE

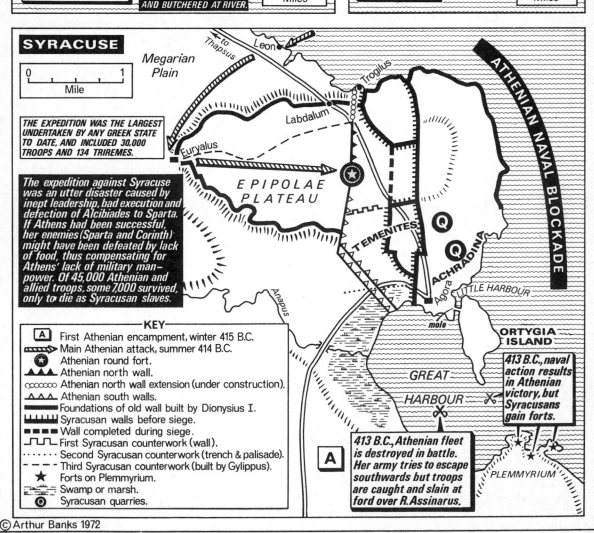

0 — 1 Mile

Megarian Plain

THE EXPEDITION WAS THE LARGEST UNDERTAKEN BY ANY GREEK STATE TO DATE, AND INCLUDED 30,000 TROOPS AND 134 TRIREMES.

The expedition against Syracuse was an utter disaster caused by inept leadership, bad execution and defection of Alcibiades to Sparta. If Athens had been successful, her enemies (Sparta and Corinth) might have been defeated by lack of food, thus compensating for Athens' lack of military man-power. Of 45,000 Athenian and allied troops, some 7,000 survived, only to die as Syracusan slaves.

- to Thapsus
- Leon
- Trogilus
- ATHENIAN NAVAL BLOCKADE
- Labdalum
- Euryalus
- E P I P O L A E P L A T E A U
- TEMENITES
- Q
- Q
- ACHRADINA
- Agora
- LITTLE HARBOUR
- Anapus
- mole
- ORTYGIA ISLAND
- GREAT HARBOUR
- PLEMMYRIUM

413 B.C., naval action results in Athenian victory, but Syracusans gain forts.

A *413 B.C., Athenian fleet is destroyed in battle. Her army tries to escape southwards but troops are caught and slain at ford over R. Assinarus.*

KEY

- **A** — First Athenian encampment, winter 415 B.C.
- Main Athenian attack, summer 414 B.C.
- Athenian round fort.
- Athenian north wall.
- Athenian north wall extension (under construction).
- Athenian south walls.
- Foundations of old wall built by Dionysius I.
- Syracusan walls before siege.
- Wall completed during siege.
- First Syracusan counterwork (wall).
- Second Syracusan counterwork (trench & palisade).
- Third Syracusan counterwork (built by Gylippus).
- ★ Forts on Plemmyrium.
- Swamp or marsh.
- **Q** Syracusan quarries.

© Arthur Banks 1972

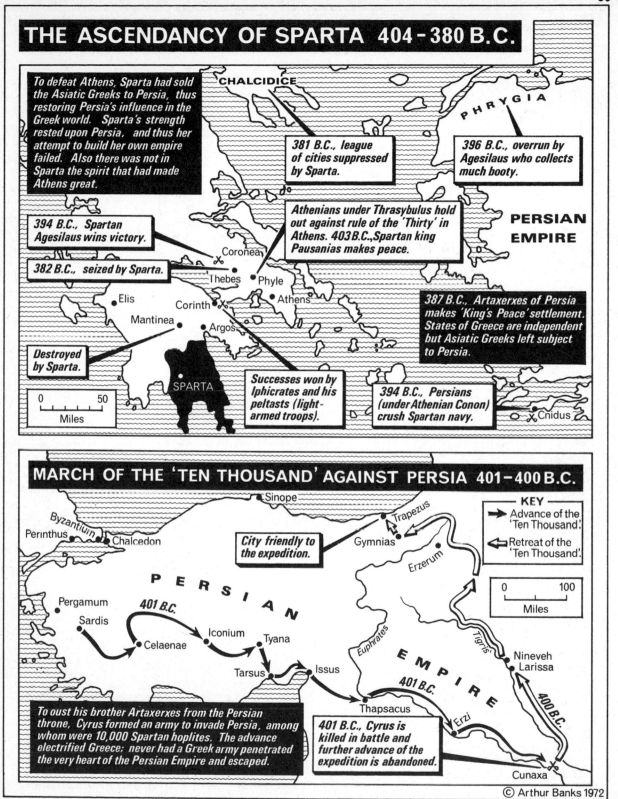

THE ASCENDANCY OF SPARTA 404-380 B.C.

CHALCIDICE

PHRYGIA

PERSIAN EMPIRE

To defeat Athens, Sparta had sold the Asiatic Greeks to Persia, thus restoring Persia's influence in the Greek world. Sparta's strength rested upon Persia, and thus her attempt to build her own empire failed. Also there was not in Sparta the spirit that had made Athens great.

381 B.C., league of cities suppressed by Sparta.

396 B.C., overrun by Agesilaus who collects much booty.

394 B.C., Spartan Agesilaus wins victory.

Athenians under Thrasybulus hold out against rule of the 'Thirty' in Athens. 403 B.C., Spartan king Pausanias makes peace.

382 B.C., seized by Sparta.

Coronea

Thebes   Phyle

Elis

Corinth   Athens

Mantinea   Argos

387 B.C., Artaxerxes of Persia makes 'King's Peace' settlement. States of Greece are independent but Asiatic Greeks left subject to Persia.

Destroyed by Sparta.

SPARTA

Successes won by Iphicrates and his peltasts (light-armed troops).

394 B.C., Persians (under Athenian Conon) crush Spartan navy.

Cnidus

0   50
Miles

MARCH OF THE 'TEN THOUSAND' AGAINST PERSIA 401-400 B.C.

Sinope

Byzantium   Trapezus
Perinthus   Chalcedon   Gymnias   KEY
→ Advance of the 'Ten Thousand'.
← Retreat of the 'Ten Thousand'.

City friendly to the expedition.

Erzerum

P E R S I A N

0   100
Miles

Pergamum

Sardis

401 B.C.

Celaenae   Iconium   Tyana

Tarsus   Issus

Euphrates   E M P I R E   Tigris

Nineveh
Larissa

401 B.C.

Thapsacus   Erzi   400 B.C.

To oust his brother Artaxerxes from the Persian throne, Cyrus formed an army to invade Persia, among whom were 10,000 Spartan hoplites. The advance electrified Greece; never had a Greek army penetrated the very heart of the Persian Empire and escaped.

401 B.C., Cyrus is killed in battle and further advance of the expedition is abandoned.

Cunaxa

© Arthur Banks 1972

THE ASCENDANCY OF THEBES 379–362 B.C.

Thebes rose for a short time to be the ruling state in Greece due to two main factors.
1 The war-weariness of Sparta and Athens.
2 Thebes possessed two leaders of great stature, Epaminondas and Pelopidas. The former fortified Thebes and created a cadre of 300 élite warriors – the Sacred Band.

364 B.C., Thebans fight a drawn battle against the Athenian ally, Alexander of Pherae, but lose Pelopidas.

375 B.C., Sacred Band of Thebes defeat two units of Spartans (600 men) plus killing both generals.

371 B.C., Epaminondas forms military ties with Jason of Pherae, who commands force of 8,000 cavalry, 20,000 hoplites, and peltasts.

376 B.C., Chabrias (of Athens–allied with Thebes at this time) defeats 60 Spartan warships in naval battle.

369 B.C., founded by Epaminondas. Became capital of new state hostile to Sparta.

362 B.C., Thebans out-manoeuvre opposing army of Arcadians, Spartans, Athenians. Each army consists of 25,000 troops. Utilising the tactics successful at Leuctra, Thebans gain victory, but Epaminondas is killed during battle.

THE BATTLE OF LEUCTRA 371 B.C.

Strong left wing.
SPARTANS
THEBANS

THEBAN VICTORY. SPARTANS NUMBERED 1,000 CAVALRY AND 10,000 HOPLITES (1,000 MEN SLAIN). THEBANS NUMBERED 600 IN CAVALRY AND 6,000 HOPLITES. FIRST INSTANCE OF DEEP COLUMN ATTACK AND REFUSED FLANK.

KEY

- Thebes and allies.
- Athens and allies.
- Sparta and allies.
- Chalcidian League.
- Neutral states.
- ✗ Important battles.
- Theban attacks against the Spartans, with dates.
- Theban naval expedition to Byzantium (100 ships).

0 50 Miles

© Arthur Banks 1972

THRACE · PHRYGIA · MYSIA · LYDIA · IONIA · CARIA · Rhodes · Bosporus · Byzantium · Cyzicus · Samos · Icaria · Naxos · Thera · Melos · Chios · Lesbos · Andros · Lemnos · Imbros · Samothrace · Thasos · CHALCIDICE · Pydna · Cynoscephalae · Pherae · THESSALY · Cnoscephalae · Tegyra · Orchomenus · THEBES · Leuctra · EUBOEA · ATHENS · AETOLIA · ACHAEA · Mantinea · SPARTA · Messene · Olympia · Cythera · EPIRUS · Corcyra · 384 B.C. · 370 B.C. · 362 B.C.

THE BATTLE OF MANTINEA JUNE 362 B.C.

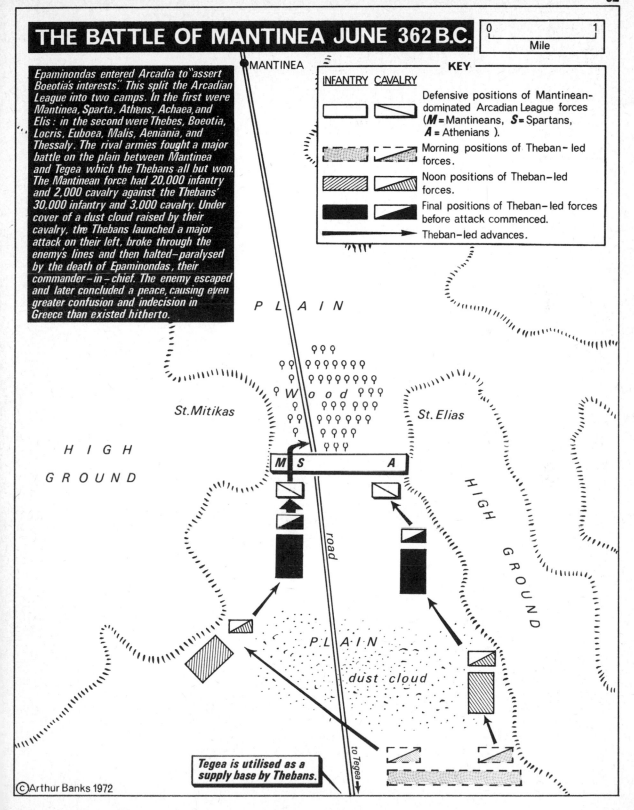

0   1
Mile

MANTINEA

Epaminondas entered Arcadia to "assert Boeotia's interests." This split the Arcadian League into two camps. In the first were Mantinea, Sparta, Athens, Achaea, and Elis: in the second were Thebes, Boeotia, Locris, Euboea, Malis, Aeniania, and Thessaly. The rival armies fought a major battle on the plain between Mantinea and Tegea which the Thebans all but won. The Mantinean force had 20,000 infantry and 2,000 cavalry against the Thebans' 30,000 infantry and 3,000 cavalry. Under cover of a dust cloud raised by their cavalry, the Thebans launched a major attack on their left, broke through the enemy's lines and then halted—paralysed by the death of Epaminondas, their commander-in-chief. The enemy escaped and later concluded a peace, causing even greater confusion and indecision in Greece than existed hitherto.

KEY

INFANTRY   CAVALRY

Defensive positions of Mantinean-dominated Arcadian League forces (**M** = Mantineans, **S** = Spartans, **A** = Athenians).

Morning positions of Theban-led forces.

Noon positions of Theban-led forces.

Final positions of Theban-led forces before attack commenced.

Theban-led advances.

P L A I N

W o o d

St. Mitikas

St. Elias

H I G H

G R O U N D

M S   A

H I G H   G R O U N D

road

P L A I N

dust cloud

to Tegea

Tegea is utilised as a supply base by Thebans.

© Arthur Banks 1972

MACEDONIA'S GROWTH AS A MILITARY POWER 359 – 336 B.C.

0 ___ 50
Miles

357 B.C., Philip besieges town and secures gold mines, thus making Macedonia the richest state in Greece.

Renamed as Philippi by Philip.

340 - 339 B.C., Philip besieges seaports without success. Only serious military setbacks in his career.

Macedonian capital.

PAEONIA

THRACE

Strymon

Nestos

Hebros

Axios

Aegae
PELLA
Amphipolis
Methone
Pydna
Olynthus
Potidaea
Stagirus
Crenides
Maronea
Perinthus
Byzantium
Bosporus

Abydus

THESSALY

Pherae

Ambracia

352 B.C., Philip gains victory of the 'Crocus Field'. Phocian general Onomarchus is killed.

PERSIAN EMPIRE

Oreus

Pass of Thermopylae
Delphi
Naupactus
Elatea
Chaeronea
Thebes
Corinth
Athens

Sardis

338 B.C., Philip becomes master of Greece by defeating Athens, Thebes and allies. Alexander plays important part in battle.

346 B.C., during Pythian Games, Isocrates calls on Philip to unite Greece and fight Persia.

338 B.C., Philip creates Hellenic League. Parmenion is later sent to Asia to carry out a reconnaissance in force (336 B.C.).

Sparta

Miletus

Halicarnassus

PHILIP'S AIMS

❶ To establish his base of operations (wars to the west, north, and east of Macedonia).

❷ To gain control of Thessaly (wars to the south of Macedonia).

❸ To establish his dominion over Thrace and gain command of the Bosporus.

❹ To impose Macedonian authority over the whole of Greece south of Thermopylae.

KEY
▨ Macedonia in 359 B.C.
▢ The Persian Empire.
✂ Important battles.

Philip organized the Macedonian army into the finest fighting force the world had yet seen.

Note: In 359 B.C., Amyntas (infant son of Perdiccas) was elected king by the people of Macedonia, with Philip nominated as regent. Following the defeat of Illyria in 358 B.C., Philip was made King Philip II of Macedon.

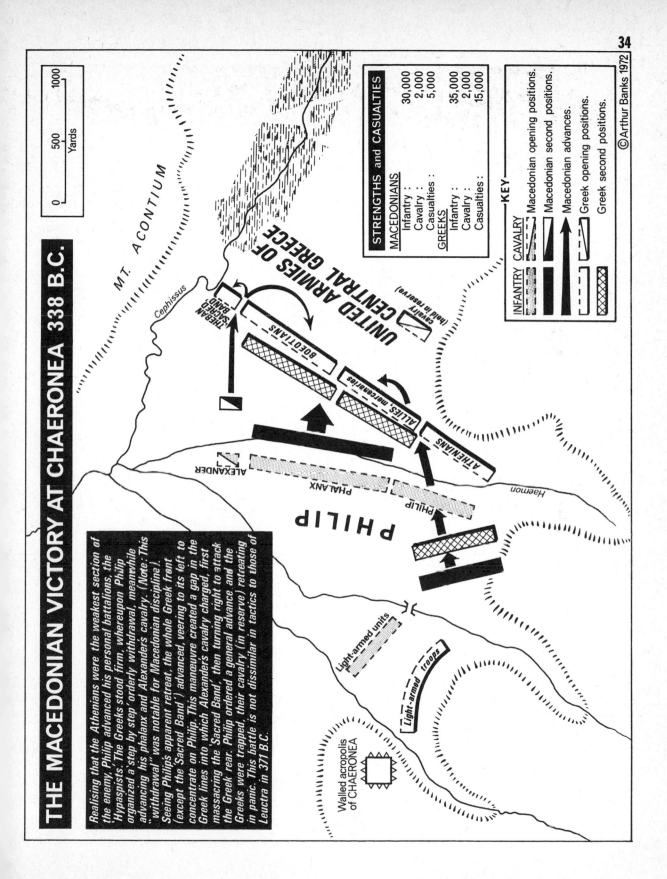

THE MACEDONIAN VICTORY AT CHAERONEA 338 B.C.

34

Realising that the Athenians were the weakest section of the enemy, Philip advanced his personal battalions, the 'Hypaspists'. The Greeks stood firm, whereupon Philip organized a 'step by step' orderly withdrawal, meanwhile advancing his phalanx and Alexander's cavalry. (Note: This "withdrawal" was notable for Macedonian discipline). Seeing Philip's apparent retreat, the whole Greek front (except the Sacred Band') advanced, veering to its left to concentrate on Philip. This manoeuvre created a gap in the Greek lines into which Alexander's cavalry charged, first massacring the 'Sacred Band', then turning right to attack the Greek rear. Philip ordered a general advance, and the Greeks were trapped, their cavalry (in reserve) retreating in panic. This battle is not dissimilar in tactics to those of Leuctra in 371 B.C.

MT. ACONTIUM

Cephissus

UNITED CENTRAL GREECE

PHILIP

PHALANX

ALEXANDER

ATHENIANS

ALLIES, mercenaries

BOEOTIANS

THEBAN 'SACRED BAND'

CAVALRY held in reserve

Haemon

Light-armed units

Light-armed troops

Walled acropolis of CHAERONEA

STRENGTHS and CASUALTIES

MACEDONIANS	
Infantry :	30,000
Cavalry :	2,000
Casualties :	5,000
GREEKS	
Infantry :	35,000
Cavalry :	2,000
Casualties :	15,000

KEY

INFANTRY CAVALRY
Macedonian opening positions.
Macedonian second positions.
Macedonian advances.
Greek opening positions.
Greek second positions.

© Arthur Banks 1972

Yards 0 500 1000

THE CAMPAIGNS OF ALEXANDER THE GREAT
336-323 B.C.

ALEXANDER'S OBJECTIVES

1. To secure his home base.
2. To establish a stable overseas base.
3. To gain command of the seas.
4. To defeat the Persians on land.

ALEXANDER'S ARMY OF INVASION
(Total: 40,000)

INFANTRY
12,000 Macedonians.
7,000 Greek League hoplites.
6,000 Agrianian javelin-men, Thracians, Cretan archers.
5,000 mercenary hoplites.

CAVALRY
2,000 Companions.
2,000 Thessalians.
1,000 Thracians, Paeonians, Greek allied horse, lancers.

MISCELLANEOUS
5,000 artillerists, sappers surveyors, siege-engineer: transport-drivers, servant camp-followers, etc.

The aim of the invasion wa ideological: to avenge wrong done to Hellas by Xerxes.

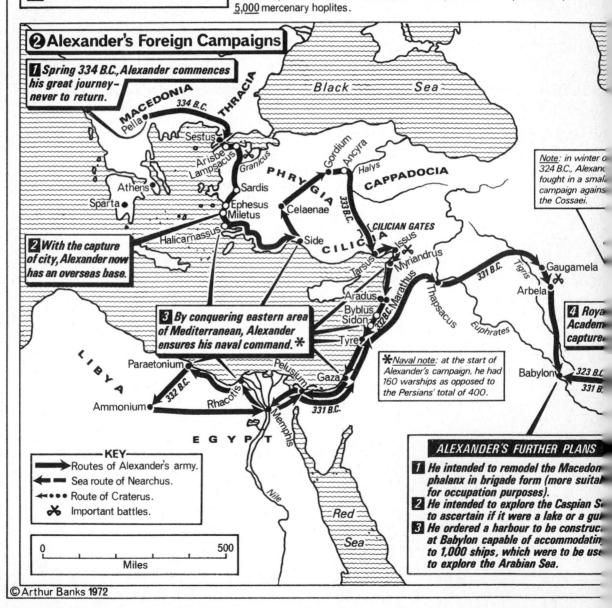

② Alexander's Foreign Campaigns

1. Spring 334 B.C., Alexander commences his great journey - never to return.

2. With the capture of city, Alexander now has an overseas base.

3. By conquering eastern area of Mediterranean, Alexander ensures his naval command. *

4. Roya Academ capture:

Note: in winter o 324 B.C., Alexand fought in a smal campaign agains the Cossaei.

*Naval note: at the start of Alexander's campaign, he had 160 warships as opposed to the Persians' total of 400.

ALEXANDER'S FURTHER PLANS

1. He intended to remodel the Macedon phalanx in brigade form (more suital for occupation purposes).
2. He intended to explore the Caspian S to ascertain if it were a lake or a gul
3. He ordered a harbour to be construc at Babylon capable of accommodatin to 1,000 ships, which were to be use to explore the Arabian Sea.

KEY
- Routes of Alexander's army.
- Sea route of Nearchus.
- Route of Craterus.
- Important battles.

0 — 500
Miles

© Arthur Banks 1972

➊ Securing the Home Base

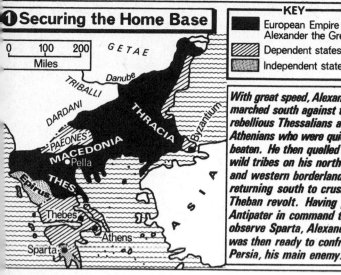

— KEY —

◼ European Empire of Alexander the Great.

▨ Dependent states.

▦ Independent states.

Scale: 0 — 100 — 200 Miles

With great speed, Alexander marched south against the rebellious Thessalians and Athenians who were quickly beaten. He then quelled the wild tribes on his northern and western borderlands, returning south to crush a Theban revolt. Having put Antipater in command to observe Sparta, Alexander was then ready to confront Persia, his main enemy.

Alexander lived from 356 B.C. to 323 B.C. Son of Philip II of Macedonia (who was murdered in 336 B.C.), he became king at the early age of 19, and in the following twelve years created by conquest a large empire extending from Greece eastwards across Asia to the borders of India. After first establishing his authority in Greece in the early years of his reign between 336 B.C. and 334 B.C., he recruited and led an army against the Persian Empire, whose armies he defeated in a long series of battles and sieges. Following a number of small wars in the east, he returned to Babylon to consolidate his empire. There he died of malaria at the age of 33.

As well as being a great military captain, Alexander was a statesman, diplomat and explorer. He founded at least seventeen "Alexandrias" during his career.

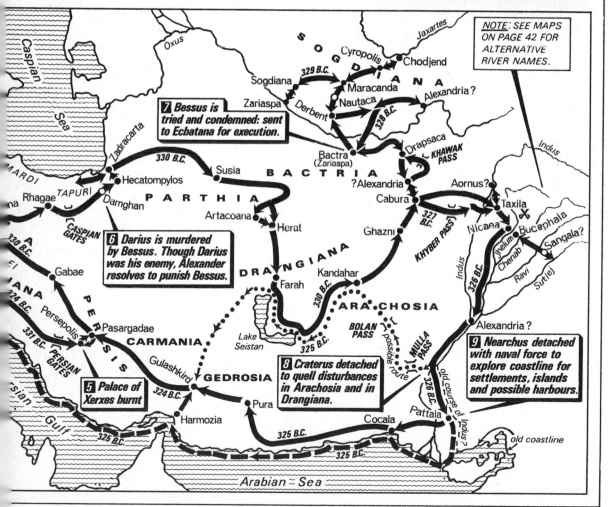

NOTE: SEE MAPS ON PAGE 42 FOR ALTERNATIVE RIVER NAMES.

7 Bessus is tried and condemned: sent to Ecbatana for execution.

6 Darius is murdered by Bessus. Though Darius was his enemy, Alexander resolves to punish Bessus.

5 Palace of Xerxes burnt

8 Craterus detached to quell disturbances in Arachosia and in Drangiana.

9 Nearchus detached with naval force to explore coastline for settlements, islands and possible harbours.

ALEXANDER'S GREAT BATTLES AND SIEGES

*Army strength
and losses are
estimates only*

- ■ Macedonian infantry.
- ◩ Macedonian cavalry.
- → Main Macedonian attacks, numbered in sequence
- ▭ Persian infantry.
- ◪ Persian cavalry.

❶ Battle of the Granicus 334 B.C.

MACEDONIANS
Total strength: 40,000
Casualties: 250

CALAS
PHILIP
AGATHON
CRATERUS
MELEAGER
PHILIP
AMYNTAS
COENUS
PERDICCAS
NICANOR
AMYNTAS
PHILOTAS
CLEARCHUS
ATTALUS
ALEXANDER
Parmenion
River Granicus
to Sea of Marmara
RHEOMITHRES
ARSITES
SPITHRIDATES
ARSAMENES
Greek mercenaries
OMARES
MEMNON
MEMNON OF RHODES
Lake

0 — 1000 Yards

Persian movements in this battle
have been omitted for clarity.
They were mainly defensive, for
the Macedonians made the first
attack. In early warfare it was
essential to kill or capture the
opposing commanders since panic
among their soldiers invariably
followed. Thus the Persians were
intent on eliminating Alexander
but he survived. On the other
hand, the Persians lost a number
of their own unit commanders, a
factor of some significance in
the battles to come. In view of
the importance of the leaders,
units are shown with the names
of their respective commanders

PERSIANS
Total strength: 15,000
Casualties: 2,000
Captured: 2,000

❷ Siege of Halicarnassus 334 B.C.

0 — 500 Yards

to Myndus
from Myndus
WALL
HALICARNASSUS
WALL
HARBOUR
road to Myndus (12 miles)
GULF OF COS
MOAT (45 feet wide 22 feet deep)
ARCONNESUS ISLAND
GULF OF COS
road to Mylasa
(25 mls.)
M

Persians reinforce and supply citadels by sea.

—KEY—
▨ Citadels of Halicarnassus
1 Acropolis.
2 Fortress of Salmacis.
3 King's Castle.
Gates of Halicarnassus.
A Myndus Gate.
B Triple Gate.
C Mylasa Gate.
M Macedonian encampment
⇨ Sortie by the garrison.
◀ Macedonian reconnaissance of the walls.
•••◀ Alexander's abortive march to subdue Myndus.
➤ Main Macedonian attack.
⇦ Garrison's abortive counter attack.
▬▬ Garrison's attempt to fill the breached wall.
Garrison's retreat into the citadels. Despite the Macedonian land blockade citadels resisted for a year.

©Arthur Banks 1972

❸ Battle of Issus 333 B.C.

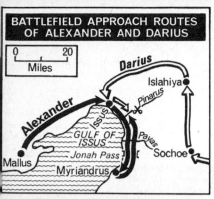

BATTLEFIELD APPROACH ROUTES OF ALEXANDER AND DARIUS

0 — 20 Miles

Islahiya
Darius
Alexander
Pinarus
Issus
GULF OF ISSUS
Jonah Pass
Payas
Sochoe
Mallus
Myriandrus

*Alexander marched from Issus en route for Myriandrus, just missing Darius who reached Issus twenty-four hours later. On his arrival at Myriandrus, Alexander was surprised to learn that Darius was advancing **behind** him. Realising that his line of retreat had been cut, Alexander resolved to surprise Darius in return by reversing his line of advance and resting his men, then launching a rapid attack on the weary Persians.*

PERSIANS
Total strength: 100,000
Killed: 50,000
Escaped: 8,000

MACEDONIANS
Total strength: 40,000
Killed: 450
Wounded: 4,500

0 — 1000 Yards

KEY

Macedonian infantry.
Macedonian cavalry.
Macedonian thrusts.
Persian infantry.
Persian cavalry.
Persian archers.
Persian advances.

MACEDONIANS
A Allied Greek cavalry.
B Thessalian cavalry.
C Thracian javelin-men.
D Cretan archers.
E Phalanx (Amyntas).
F Phalanx (Ptolemy).
G Phalanx (Meleager).
H Phalanx (Craterus).
I Phalanx (Perdiccas).
J Phalanx (Coenus).
K Hypaspists.
L Companion cavalry.
M Macedonian archers.
N Agrianians.
O Greek mercenaries.
P Lancers.
Q Paeonian light horsemen.
R Agrianians.
S Light horse squadron.

PERSIANS
A Cavalry (Nabarzanes).
B Asiatic levies.
C Cardaces.
D Greek mercenaries.
E Bodyguard (Darius).
F Archers.
G Light troop detachment.

❹ Siege of Tyre 332 B.C.

0 — 500 Yards

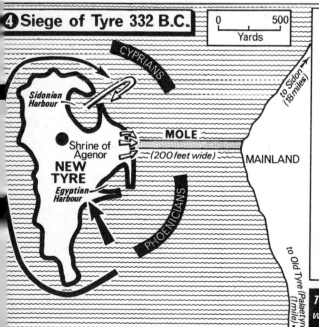

CYPRIANS
Sidonian Harbour
Shrine of Agenor
NEW TYRE
Egyptian Harbour
MOLE (200 feet wide)
MAINLAND
PHOENICIANS
to Sidon (18 miles)
to Old Tyre (Palaetyros) (1 mile)

1 *Alexander's first task is to construct a mole from the mainland to New Tyre. The work is hindered by Tyrian attacks, including a fire-ship's sortie.*

2 *Alexander decides to blockade the two Tyrian harbours with two fleets.*

3 *Tyrian navy sorties out from Sidonian Harbour, but despite initial success, it is thwarted by Alexander sailing round west coast of island to reinforce his Cyprian contingent.*

4 *Alexander finally breaches city wall south of Egyptian Harbour and advances into city. Simultaneously his naval contingents storm the two harbours.*

5 *Tyrians make final stand at Shrine of Agenor but are overwhelmed.*

The siege lasted for seven months. 8,000 Tyrians were killed and 30,000 sold into slavery. During the various assaults, 400 Macedonians were killed.

ALEXANDER'S BATTLES–continued

⑤ Battle of Arbela (Gaugamela) 331 B.C.

PERSIAN KEY

Cavalry Infantry
⊏ ⊐ Asiatic levies
○ ○ ○ ○ ○ Chariots (total: 200)
● ● ● ● ● Elephants (total: 15)

1 Sacesinians.	*10* Cappadocians.	*19* Carians.
2 Albanians.	*11* Armenians.	*20* Cadusians.
3 Hyrcanians.	*12* Mardians (archers).	*21* Susians.
4 Tapurians.	*13* Indians.	*22* Persians.
5 Sacians.	*14* Greeks (mercen's).	*23* Arachosians.
6 Parthians.	*15* Persians (horse).	*24* Dahaeians.
7 Medians.	*16* Persians (foot).	*25* Bactrians.
8 Mesopotamians.	*17* Persians (horse).	*26* Scythians.
9 Coelo-Syrians.	*18* Greeks (mercen's).	*27* Bactrians.

PRE-BATTLE DISPOSITIONS

MACEDONIAN KEY (arranged under commanders)

Cavalry — Infantry

1 Andromachus.	*6* Clearchus.	*11* Polyperchon.	*16* Attalus.	*21* Aretes.
2 Agathon.	*7* Philip.	*12* Meleager.	*17* Briso.	*22* Ariston.
3 Coeranus.	*8* Erigyius.	*13* Perdiccas.	*18* Balacrus.	*23* Attalus.
4 Sitalces.	*9* Craterus.	*14* Coenus.	*19* Philotas.	*24* Briso.
5 (mercenaries).	*10* Simmias.	*15* Nicanor.	*20* Menidas.	*25* Cleander.

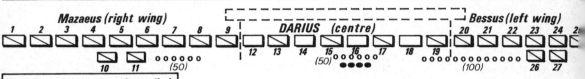

Mazaeus (right wing) — DARIUS (centre) — Bessus (left wing)

The Macedonian strength totalled 47,000 against the Persian total of 250,000. Consequently, Alexander's deployment needed to be flexible to allow for any possible contingency.

hinge — hinge
flap OPEN 'SQUARE' flap

LEFT FLANK-GUARD — Parmenion (left wing) — ALEXANDER (right wing) — RIGHT FLANK-GUARD

Rear Phalanx

Right flank-guard stronger than left.

THE BATTLE–PHASE ONE

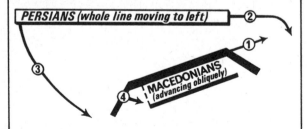

PERSIANS (whole line moving to left)

MACEDONIANS (advancing obliquely)

① *Without physical features (such as hills or rivers) upon which to position his flanks, Alexander moves in an oblique direction towards the Persian line (twice the length of his own) veering to the right.*
② *Persians commence moving to left to keep abreast of Alexander, their left-wing cavalry racing ahead to intercept Macedonian advance.*
③ *Persian right-wing cavalry moves forward to envelop Macedonians from rear.*
④ *Macedonian left flank-guard closes to main body to prevent Persian breakthrough.*

THE BATTLE–PHASE TWO

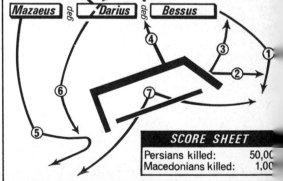

Mazaeus | gap | Darius | gap | Bessus

SCORE SHEET

Persians killed:	50,00
Macedonians killed:	1,00

① *Rapidity of Persian cavalry advance creates gaps Persian main line.* ② *and* ③ *Macedonian right flank guard engages Persian cavalry.* ④ *Alexander advanc into gap between Bessus and Darius; fierce fighting mêlée-style ensues.* ⑤ *Persian right-wing nearly brea through, but* ⑥ *is intercepted by Alexander answering Parmenion's call for help.* ⑦ *Macedonians attack Pers cavalry in strength.* ⑧ *Darius flees.*

© Arthur Banks 1972

❻ Battle of the Hydaspes* 326 B.C.

*Note: modern name is Jhelum.

MACEDONIANS (Alexander)

Companion Cavalry ALEXANDER
Cavalry (Coenus)
Light-armed Infantry
(Seleucus) Phalanx
Hypaspists
Horse-archers

① ② ③ ④ ⑤ ⑥ *feint attack* *(veering)*

PORUS
Chariots o o o o
Cavalry
Elephants
Infantry
Chariots o o o o
Cavalry

INDIANS (Porus)

KEY — Main attacks, numbered in sequence.

STRENGTHS		CASUALTIES	
MACEDONIANS		**MACEDONIANS (killed)**	
Infantry:	10,000	Infantry:	700
Cavalry:	5,000	Cavalry:	280
Horse-archers:	1,000	Horse-archers:	10
INDIANS		**INDIANS**	
Infantry:	30,000	Killed:	12,000
Cavalry:	4,000	Captured:	9,000
Chariots:	200	Elephants captured:	80
Elephants:	200		

Prior to the main battle, Alexander fought an Indian delaying-action with the son of Porus (who was killed). Following this, he undertook a massive task in transporting his army across the River Hydaspes.

ALEXANDER'S TACTICS
In his major battles, Alexander positioned himself on the right wing and opened his attack from that side. This avoided a 'centre' confrontation at the outset and compelled his foes to rearrange their dispositions.

ALEXANDER'S "ALEXANDRIAS"

Note: there is no evidence of an Alexandria at Kandahar.

Alexander founded at least seventeen "Alexandrias" and promised an eighteenth (Alexandria Troas) which was never built. Six are "certain," in that they are represented by modern towns. A further seven existed well down into Greek history. The remaining four were built but the precise location of Alexandria in Babylonia is unknown.

Alexandria Eschate (CHODJEND)
Alexandria on the Oxus (TERMEZ)
Alexandria Bactra
Alexandria in Margiane (MERV)
Alexandria of the Caucasus
Alexandria Nicaea
Alexandria Iomousa
Alexandria Bucephala
Alexandria in Aria (HERAT)
Alexandria in Arachosia (GHAZNI)
Alexandria by Issus
Alexandria in Babylonia (site unknown) ?
Alexandria Prophthasia
Alexandria by Egypt (ALEXANDRIA)
Alexandria in Susiana
Alexandria in Carmania
Alexandria in Makarene

Oxus, Indus, Tigris, Euphrates, Nile

332 B.C., first Alexandria is founded here.

0 — 400 Miles

KEY
● The six foundations where towns remain.
⊙ The seven foundations confirmed in the writings of Greek historians.
• The four foundations agreed by scholars.

THE EFFECT ON WORLD HISTORY OF AN ARMY 'MUTINY' IN 326 B.C.

② Two Rivers and Two Civilizations

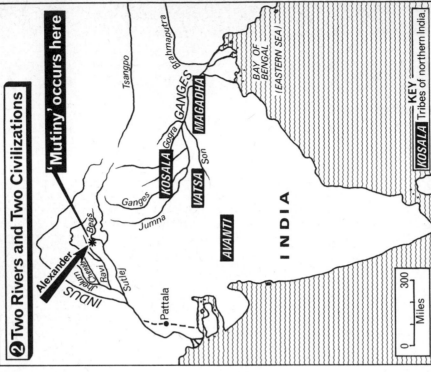

KEY
KOSALA Tribes of northern India.

Alexander knew of the existence of the River Ganges and wished it to be the line of his eastern frontier. If the 'mutiny' had not occurred, he could not have failed to collide with the tribes of northern India, consequently affecting future world events. Sandracottus (Chandragupta), India's first great military leader, was in Alexander's camp at this particular period.

① Alexander's Campaigns in North-West India

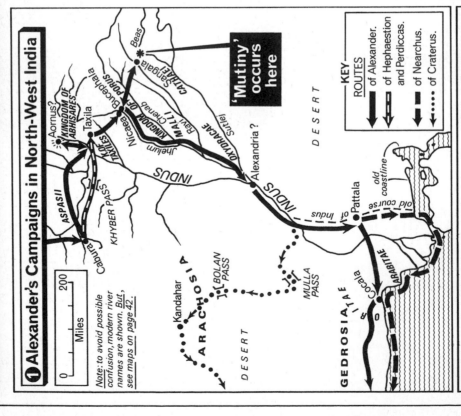

Note: to avoid possible confusion, modern river names are shown. But, see maps on page 42.

KEY —
ROUTES
→ of Alexander.
⇒ of Hephaestion and Perdiccas.
⇛ of Nearchus.
····· of Craterus.

Following his victory over Porus at the river Hydaspes (Jhelum), Alexander built Nicaea and Bucephala, stormed Sangala (capital of the Cathaei), and then advanced to the river Hyphasis (Beas). At this point his army staged a 'mutiny'. Exhausted and homesick after eight years of campaigning, during which they had marched 17,000 miles, the troops refused to go on, and returned to Nicaea.

PROBLEMS OF CHANGING NOMENCLATURE IN HISTORY: THE "LAND OF THE FIVE RIVERS"

❶ Greek Historians' Versions of Indian Names

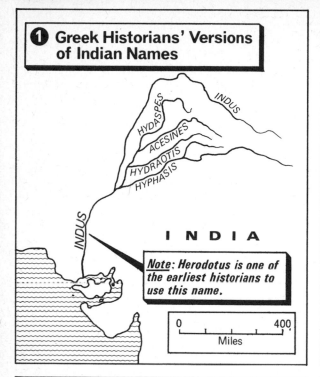

Note: Herodotus is one of the earliest historians to use this name.

0 — 400 Miles

❷ Ancient Indian Names

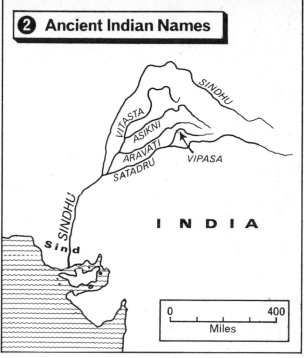

0 — 400 Miles

❸ Names Current in Medieval and Modern History

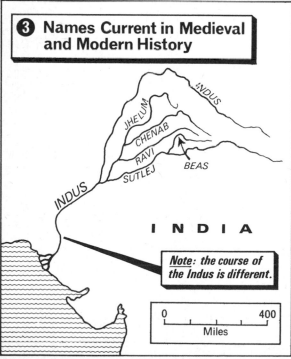

Note: the course of the Indus is different.

0 — 400 Miles

Just as one city may be famous in history under different names (for example, Byzantium - Constantinople - Istanbul), so other changes of name at different periods present a problem to historical cartographers.

The area of north-west India shown on these three sections illustrates this problem, and touches upon another: rivers may change their courses (for example, the Yellow River or Huang Ho in China), and coastlines alter at different periods of history. Often, as at Thermopylae, these changes affect the tactical characteristics of an area.

Side by side with changing nomenclature, goes the additional problem of transliteration (for example, Rheims - Reims).

The Indus (Sindhu in Sanskrit) is the origin of the name India, as well as of Sind.

© Arthur Banks 1972

43

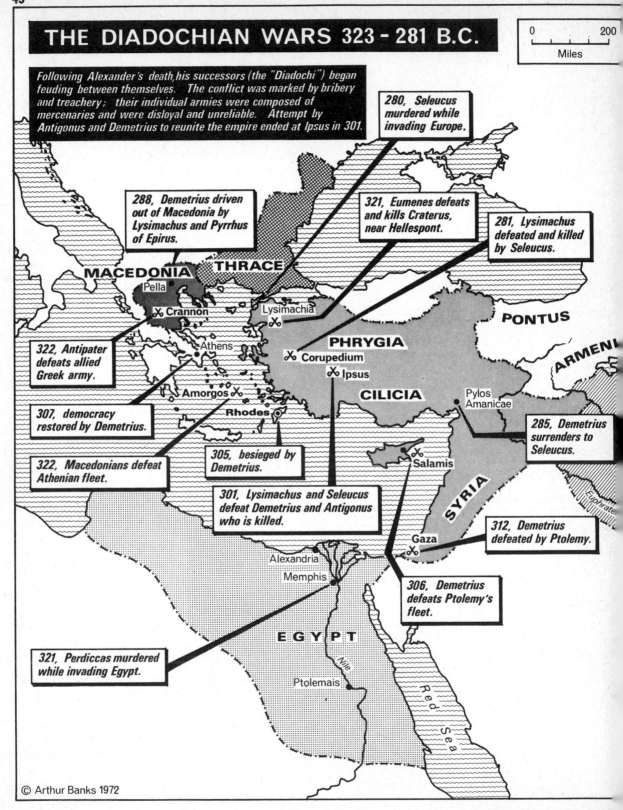

THE DIADOCHIAN WARS 323 - 281 B.C.

0   200
Miles

Following Alexander's death, his successors (the "Diadochi") began feuding between themselves. The conflict was marked by bribery and treachery; their individual armies were composed of mercenaries and were disloyal and unreliable. Attempt by Antigonus and Demetrius to reunite the empire ended at Ipsus in 301.

280, Seleucus murdered while invading Europe.

288, Demetrius driven out of Macedonia by Lysimachus and Pyrrhus of Epirus.

321, Eumenes defeats and kills Craterus, near Hellespont.

281, Lysimachus defeated and killed by Seleucus.

MACEDONIA

THRACE

Pella

PONTUS

Crannon

Lysimachia

ARMENI

322, Antipater defeats allied Greek army.

PHRYGIA

Athens

Corupedium

Ipsus

CILICIA

Pylos
Amanicae

307, democracy restored by Demetrius.

Amorgos

Rhodes

285, Demetrius surrenders to Seleucus.

305, besieged by Demetrius.

Salamis

322, Macedonians defeat Athenian fleet.

SYRIA

301, Lysimachus and Seleucus defeat Demetrius and Antigonus who is killed.

312, Demetrius defeated by Ptolemy.

Gaza

Alexandria

Memphis

306, Demetrius defeats Ptolemy's fleet.

E G Y P T

Nile

321, Perdiccas murdered while invading Egypt.

Ptolemais

Red Sea

Euphrates

© Arthur Banks 1972

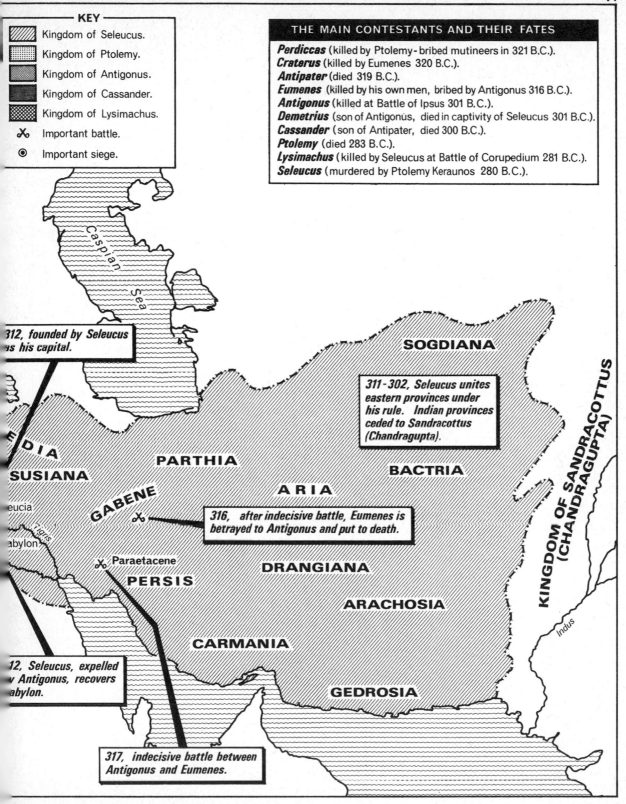

KEY

▨	Kingdom of Seleucus.
▦	Kingdom of Ptolemy.
▩	Kingdom of Antigonus.
▦	Kingdom of Cassander.
▩	Kingdom of Lysimachus.
✄	Important battle.
◉	Important siege.

THE MAIN CONTESTANTS AND THEIR FATES

Perdiccas (killed by Ptolemy-bribed mutineers in 321 B.C.).
Craterus (killed by Eumenes 320 B.C.).
Antipater (died 319 B.C.).
Eumenes (killed by his own men, bribed by Antigonus 316 B.C.).
Antigonus (killed at Battle of Ipsus 301 B.C.).
Demetrius (son of Antigonus, died in captivity of Seleucus 301 B.C.).
Cassander (son of Antipater, died 300 B.C.).
Ptolemy (died 283 B.C.).
Lysimachus (killed by Seleucus at Battle of Corupedium 281 B.C.).
Seleucus (murdered by Ptolemy Keraunos 280 B.C.).

312, founded by Seleucus as his capital.

Caspian Sea

SOGDIANA

311-302, Seleucus unites eastern provinces under his rule. Indian provinces ceded to Sandracottus (Chandragupta).

MEDIA

SUSIANA

PARTHIA

BACTRIA

Seleucia

ARIA

GABENE

Tigris

Babylon

316, after indecisive battle, Eumenes is betrayed to Antigonus and put to death.

KINGDOM OF SANDRACOTTUS (CHANDRAGUPTA)

Paraetacene

PERSIS

DRANGIANA

ARACHOSIA

Indus

CARMANIA

12, Seleucus, expelled by Antigonus, recovers Babylon.

GEDROSIA

317, indecisive battle between Antigonus and Eumenes.

45

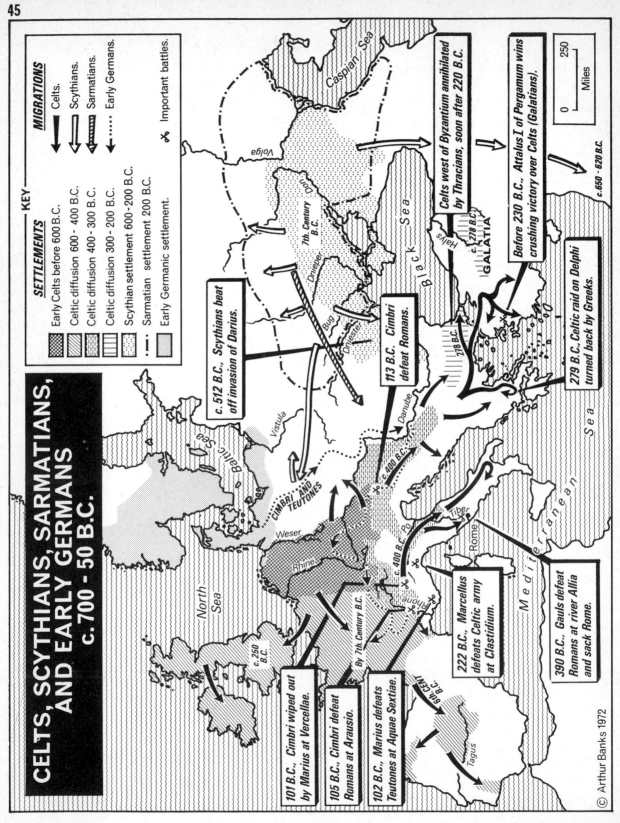

CELTS, SCYTHIANS, SARMATIANS, AND EARLY GERMANS c. 700 - 50 B.C.

KEY

SETTLEMENTS

- Early Celts before 600 B.C.
- Celtic diffusion 600 - 400 B.C.
- Celtic diffusion 400 - 300 B.C.
- Celtic diffusion 300 - 200 B.C.
- Scythian settlement 600 - 200 B.C.
- Sarmatian settlement 200 B.C.
- Early Germanic settlement.

MIGRATIONS

- Celts.
- Scythians.
- Sarmatians.
- Early Germans.
- Important battles.

c. 512 B.C.. Scythians beat off invasion of Darius.

113 B.C. Cimbri defeat Romans.

Celts west of Byzantium annihilated by Thracians, soon after 220 B.C.

Before 230 B.C.. Attalus I of Pergamum wins crushing victory over Celts (Galatians).

279 B.C. Celtic raid on Delphi turned back by Greeks.

101 B.C.. Cimbri wiped out by Marius at Vercellae.

105 B.C. Cimbri defeat Romans at Arausio.

102 B.C. Marius defeats Teutones at Aquae Sextiae.

222 B.C.. Marcellus defeats Celtic army at Clastidium.

390 B.C. Gauls defeat Romans at river Allia and sack Rome.

North Sea · Baltic Sea · Caspian Sea · Black Sea · Mediterranean Sea · Volga · Dnieper · Dniester · Bug · Vistula · Danube · Rhine · Weser · Rhone · Tiber · Rome · Tagus · GALATIA · CIMBRI AND TEUTONES

© Arthur Banks 1972

0   250 Miles

THE WARRING STATES IN CHINA 481-221 B.C.

KEY TO STATES

- CHOU
- CH'U
- CHAO
- CH'I
- WEI
- CH'IN
- HAN
- YEN
- SUNG
- T'ENG
- T'SOU
- LU

Although the main bulk of the Great Wall was not constructed until the period immediately following the Warring States, it is shown on this map because sections of walls were built between 450 - 221 B.C. in efforts to prevent raids into central China by the Asiatic Huns (Hsiung - nu). Also, Cheng (ruler of Ch'in 247 - 222 B.C.) was responsible for the Great Wall's construction when, in 221 B.C., he became Shih Huang Ti and commenced to link together parts of earlier walls.

BARREN WASTE

HSIUNG - NU (HUNS)

TUNG - HU

CHAO-HSIEN

SECTIONS BUILT c.300

SECTIONS BUILT c.290

300

HU

353

BUILT 360

Tai

396

Chi

Chin-yang

Han-tan

HO

Lin-tzu

JUNG

SECTIONS BUILT c.300

300

Yeh

Wei

c.450

237 HO

353 HO

An-i

Hsien-yang

Lo-yang

Yang-cho

Yung

Nan-cheng

Wan

Ts'ai

Huai

333

H

316

Ying

Chiang

E

Wu

Yu-fu-ch'eng

SHU PA

Chiang

Kuei-chi

NOMADS

NOMADS

U (481-334 B.C.)

Y

MILITARY KEY

- ← Chinese inter-state conquests.
- ⇐ Attacks by nomads.
- ⌐⌐⌐ Fortifications.

0 — 200
Miles

© Arthur Banks 1972

This period marked an increase in feudal anarchy. The Ch'in and Ch'u emerged as leading military powers.

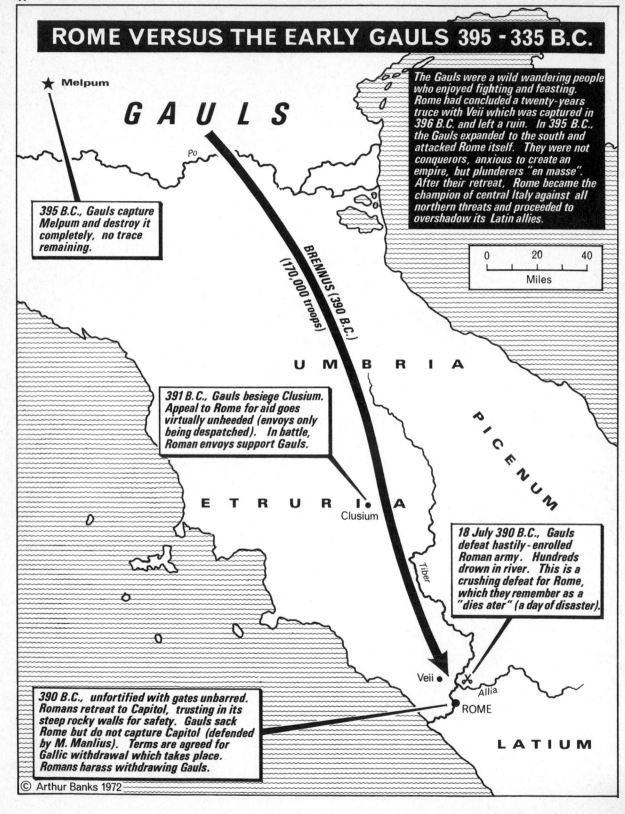

ROME VERSUS THE EARLY GAULS 395 - 335 B.C.

Melpum

GAULS

Po

The Gauls were a wild wandering people who enjoyed fighting and feasting. Rome had concluded a twenty-years truce with Veii which was captured in 396 B.C. and left a ruin. In 395 B.C., the Gauls expanded to the south and attacked Rome itself. They were not conquerors, anxious to create an empire, but plunderers "en masse". After their retreat, Rome became the champion of central Italy against all northern threats and proceeded to overshadow its Latin allies.

395 B.C., Gauls capture Melpum and destroy it completely, no trace remaining.

BRENNUS (390 B.C.) (170,000 troops)

0   20   40
Miles

U M B R I A

P I C E N U M

391 B.C., Gauls besiege Clusium. Appeal to Rome for aid goes virtually unheeded (envoys only being despatched). In battle, Roman envoys support Gauls.

E T R U R I A

Clusium

Tiber

18 July 390 B.C., Gauls defeat hastily-enrolled Roman army. Hundreds drown in river. This is a crushing defeat for Rome, which they remember as a "dies ater" (a day of disaster).

Veii

Allia

ROME

390 B.C., unfortified with gates unbarred. Romans retreat to Capitol, trusting in its steep rocky walls for safety. Gauls sack Rome but do not capture Capitol (defended by M. Manlius). Terms are agreed for Gallic withdrawal which takes place. Romans harass withdrawing Gauls.

L A T I U M

© Arthur Banks 1972

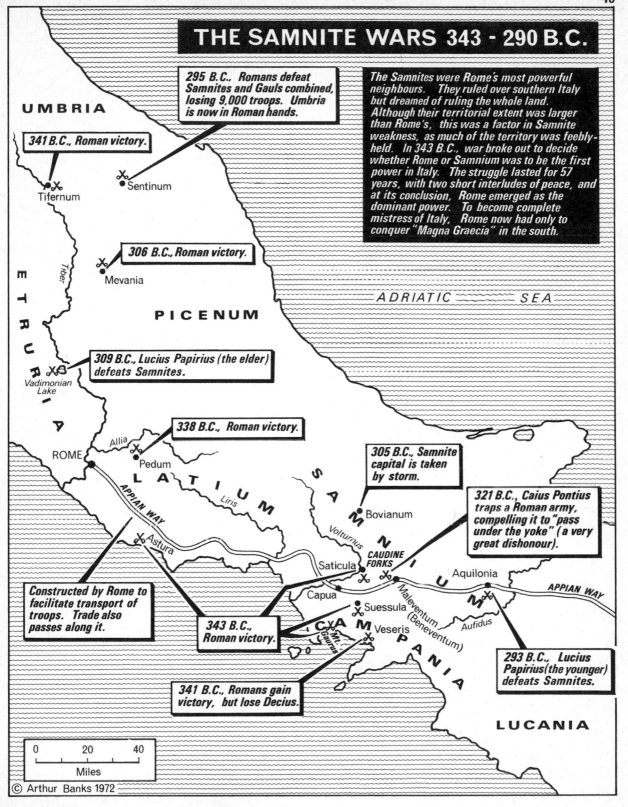

THE SAMNITE WARS 343 - 290 B.C.

295 B.C., Romans defeat Samnites and Gauls combined, losing 9,000 troops. Umbria is now in Roman hands.

The Samnites were Rome's most powerful neighbours. They ruled over southern Italy but dreamed of ruling the whole land. Although their territorial extent was larger than Rome's, this was a factor in Samnite weakness, as much of the territory was feebly-held. In 343 B.C., war broke out to decide whether Rome or Samnium was to be the first power in Italy. The struggle lasted for 57 years, with two short interludes of peace, and at its conclusion, Rome emerged as the dominant power. To become complete mistress of Italy, Rome now had only to conquer "Magna Graecia" in the south.

341 B.C., Roman victory.

UMBRIA

Tifernum

Sentinum

306 B.C., Roman victory.

Mevania

PICENUM

ADRIATIC SEA

ETRURIA

Tiber

309 B.C., Lucius Papirius (the elder) defeats Samnites.

Vadimonian Lake

338 B.C., Roman victory.

Allia

Pedum

ROME

305 B.C., Samnite capital is taken by storm.

321 B.C., Caius Pontius traps a Roman army, compelling it to "pass under the yoke" (a very great dishonour).

LATIUM

Liris

SAMNIUM

Bovianum

Volturnus

APPIAN WAY

Astura

CAUDINE FORKS

Saticula

Aquilonia

APPIAN WAY

Capua

Maleventum (Beneventum)

Aufidus

Constructed by Rome to facilitate transport of troops. Trade also passes along it.

343 B.C., Roman victory.

Suessula

CAMPANIA

Mt. Gaurus

Veseris

293 B.C., Lucius Papirius (the younger) defeats Samnites.

341 B.C., Romans gain victory, but lose Decius.

LUCANIA

0   20   40
Miles

© Arthur Banks 1972

49

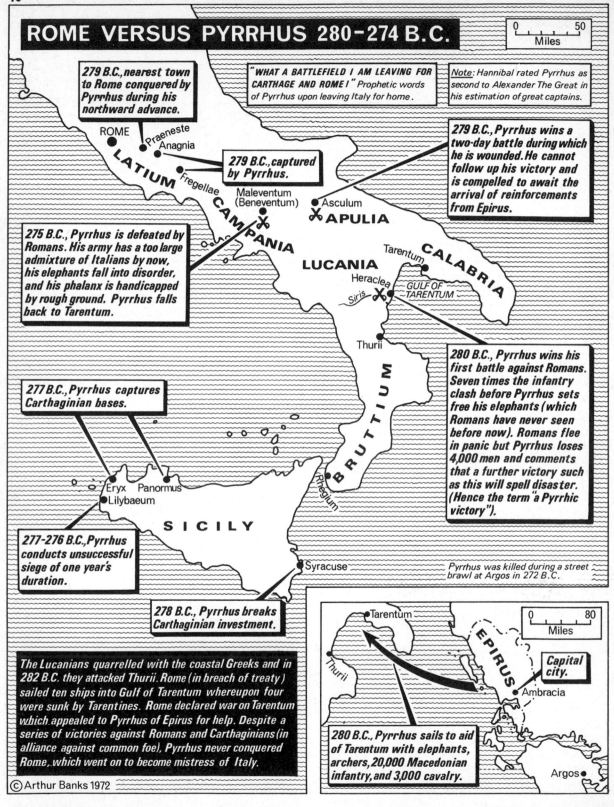

ROME VERSUS PYRRHUS 280-274 B.C.

0 — 50 Miles

279 B.C., nearest town to Rome conquered by Pyrrhus during his northward advance.

"WHAT A BATTLEFIELD I AM LEAVING FOR CARTHAGE AND ROME!" Prophetic words of Pyrrhus upon leaving Italy for home.

Note: Hannibal rated Pyrrhus as second to Alexander The Great in his estimation of great captains.

ROME
Praeneste
Anagnia
LATIUM
Fregellae
CAMPANIA
Maleventum (Beneventum)
Asculum
APULIA
LUCANIA
Tarentum
CALABRIA
Heraclea
Siris
GULF OF TARENTUM
Thurii
BRUTTIUM
Rhegium
Eryx Panormus
Lilybaeum
SICILY
Syracuse

279 B.C., captured by Pyrrhus.

279 B.C., Pyrrhus wins a two-day battle during which he is wounded. He cannot follow up his victory and is compelled to await the arrival of reinforcements from Epirus.

275 B.C., Pyrrhus is defeated by Romans. His army has a too large admixture of Italians by now, his elephants fall into disorder, and his phalanx is handicapped by rough ground. Pyrrhus falls back to Tarentum.

280 B.C., Pyrrhus wins his first battle against Romans. Seven times the infantry clash before Pyrrhus sets free his elephants (which Romans have never seen before now). Romans flee in panic but Pyrrhus loses 4,000 men and comments that a further victory such as this will spell disaster. (Hence the term "a Pyrrhic victory").

277 B.C., Pyrrhus captures Carthaginian bases.

277-276 B.C., Pyrrhus conducts unsuccessful siege of one year's duration.

278 B.C., Pyrrhus breaks Carthaginian investment.

Pyrrhus was killed during a street brawl at Argos in 272 B.C.

The Lucanians quarrelled with the coastal Greeks and in 282 B.C. they attacked Thurii. Rome (in breach of treaty) sailed ten ships into Gulf of Tarentum whereupon four were sunk by Tarentines. Rome declared war on Tarentum which appealed to Pyrrhus of Epirus for help. Despite a series of victories against Romans and Carthaginians (in alliance against common foe), Pyrrhus never conquered Rome, which went on to become mistress of Italy.

© Arthur Banks 1972

0 — 80 Miles
Tarentum
EPIRUS
Capital city.
Thurii
Ambracia
Argos

280 B.C., Pyrrhus sails to aid of Tarentum with elephants, archers, 20,000 Macedonian infantry, and 3,000 cavalry.

CARTHAGINIAN POWER IN THE WESTERN MEDITERRANEAN

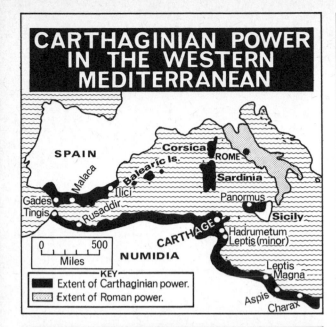

SPAIN

Malaca
Gādes
Tingis
Rusaddir
Ilici
Balearic Is.
Corsica
ROME
Sardinia
Panormus
Sicily
CARTHAGE
Hadrumetum
Leptis (minor)
NUMIDIA
Leptis Magna
Aspis
Charax

0   500
Miles

KEY
■ Extent of Carthaginian power.
▨ Extent of Roman power.

The forthcoming struggle between Rome and Carthage (the "Punic city") was to decide which power was to rule the world. In the event, Rome emerged victorious, with its subsequent influence on history. Two great commanders were involved: Hannibal (for Carthage) and Scipio (for Rome).

ROMAN ITALY

0   80
Miles

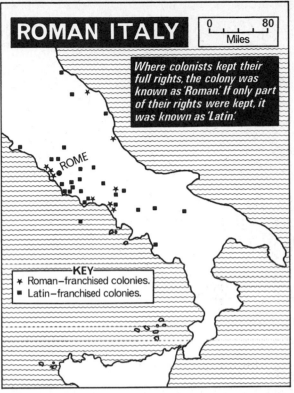

Where colonists kept their full rights, the colony was known as 'Roman'. If only part of their rights were kept, it was known as 'Latin'.

ROME

KEY
✴ Roman-franchised colonies.
■ Latin-franchised colonies.

THE TWO GIANTS COMPARED

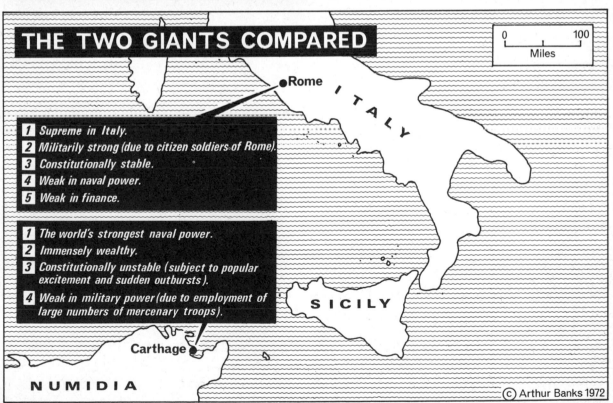

0   100
Miles

●Rome

ITALY

1 *Supreme in Italy.*
2 *Militarily strong (due to citizen soldiers of Rome).*
3 *Constitutionally stable.*
4 *Weak in naval power.*
5 *Weak in finance.*

1 *The world's strongest naval power.*
2 *Immensely wealthy.*
3 *Constitutionally unstable (subject to popular excitement and sudden outbursts).*
4 *Weak in military power (due to employment of large numbers of mercenary troops).*

Carthage

SICILY

NUMIDIA

© Arthur Banks 1972

THE FIRST PUNIC WAR 264 - 242 B.C.

① The General Scene

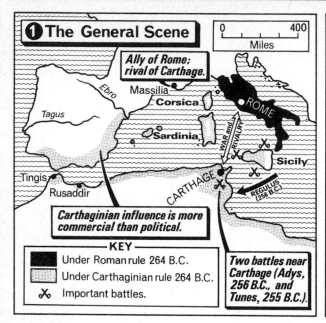

0 — 400
Miles

Ally of Rome; rival of Carthage.

Massilia
Corsica
Ebro
Tagus
ROME
Sardinia
WAR and RIVALRY
Tingis
Rusaddir
CARTHAGE
Sicily
REGULUS (256 B.C.)

Carthaginian influence is more commercial than political.

Two battles near Carthage (Adys, 256 B.C., and Tunes, 255 B.C.).

—KEY—

- ■ Under Roman rule 264 B.C.
- ▨ Under Carthaginian rule 264 B.C.
- ✕ Important battles.

CAUSES OF THE WAR

1 The Mamertines (Campanian mercenaries) seized Messana but were defeated by Hiero II of Syracuse at Mylae (270 B.C.), whereupon they appealed to Carthage for help.

2 Hanno arrived from Carthage and occupied citadel at Messana.

3 Romans ousted Hanno and made treaty with Hiero II.

4 Thus, the war was to decide whether Rome or Carthage was to be paramount in Sicily.

THE NAVAL WAR

1 The Carthaginians were supreme at the outset, so the Romans started a programme of naval construction.

2 Battles apart, the Romans unfortunately lost 700 ships and 200,000 troops in four sudden storms during war.

3 Roman tactics were to row their vessels next to the enemy crafts, secure them together with 'corvi' (crows), and fight a semi land–battle across the decks.

② Sicily: Main Area of Operations

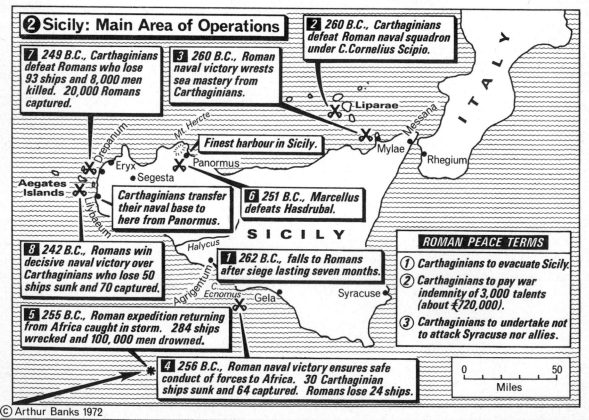

2 260 B.C., Carthaginians defeat Roman naval squadron under C. Cornelius Scipio.

7 249 B.C., Carthaginians defeat Romans who lose 93 ships and 8,000 men killed. 20,000 Romans captured.

3 260 B.C., Roman naval victory wrests sea mastery from Carthaginians.

Finest harbour in Sicily.

Liparae
Mt. Hercte
Drepanum
Eryx
Panormus
Mylae
Messana
ITALY
Rhegium
Aegates Islands
• Segesta
Lilybaeum

Carthaginians transfer their naval base to here from Panormus.

6 251 B.C., Marcellus defeats Hasdrubal.

S I C I L Y

Halycus

8 242 B.C., Romans win decisive naval victory over Carthaginians who lose 50 ships sunk and 70 captured.

1 262 B.C., falls to Romans after siege lasting seven months.

ROMAN PEACE TERMS

① Carthaginians to evacuate Sicily.

② Carthaginians to pay war indemnity of 3,000 talents (about £720,000).

③ Carthaginians to undertake not to attack Syracuse nor allies.

5 255 B.C., Roman expedition returning from Africa caught in storm. 284 ships wrecked and 100,000 men drowned.

Agrigentum
C. Ecnomus
Gela
Syracuse

4 256 B.C., Roman naval victory ensures safe conduct of forces to Africa. 30 Carthaginian ships sunk and 64 captured. Romans lose 24 ships.

0 — 50
Miles

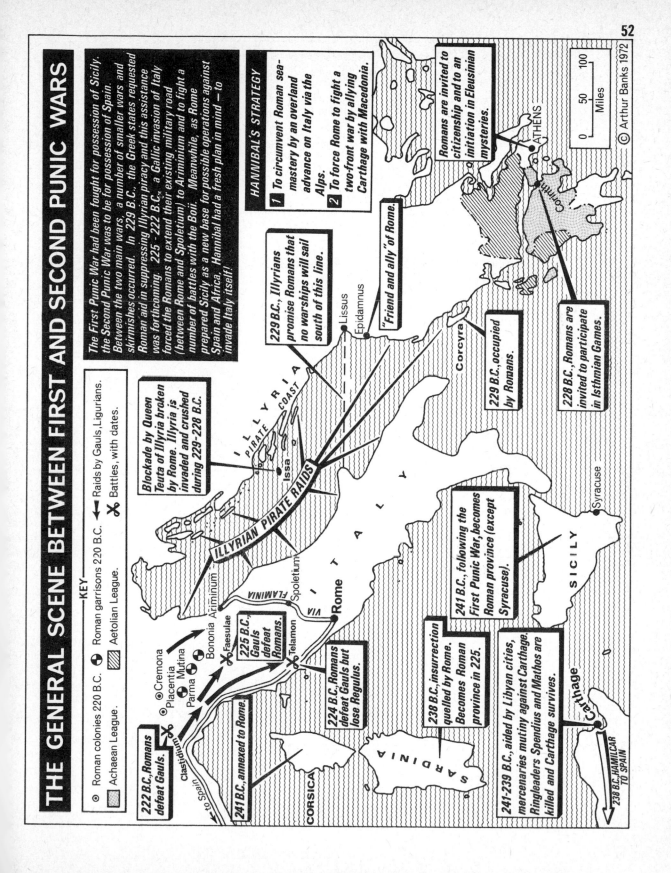

THE GENERAL SCENE BETWEEN FIRST AND SECOND PUNIC WARS

52

The First Punic War had been fought for possession of Sicily. The Second Punic War was to be for possession of Spain. Between the two main wars, a number of smaller wars and skirmishes occurred. In 229 B.C., the Greek states requested Roman aid in suppressing Illyrian piracy and this assistance was forthcoming. 225–222 B.C., a Gallic invasion of Italy forced the Romans to extend their existing military road (between Rome and Spoletium) to Ariminium and to fight a number of battles with the Boii. Meanwhile, as Rome prepared Sicily as a new base for possible operations against Spain and Africa, Hannibal had a fresh plan in mind — to invade Italy itself!

HANNIBAL'S STRATEGY

1 To circumvent Roman sea-mastery by an overland advance on Italy via the Alps.

2 To force Rome to fight a two-front war by allying Carthage with Macedonia.

KEY

⊙ Roman colonies 220 B.C.   ⊕ Roman garrisons 220 B.C.   ↓ Raids by Gauls, Ligurians.

▨ Achaean League.   ▨ Aetolian League.   ✗ Battles, with dates.

229 B.C., Illyrians promise Romans that no warships will sail south of this line.

Blockade by Queen Teuta of Illyria broken by Rome. Illyria is invaded and crushed during 229–228 B.C.

"Friend and ally" of Rome.

Romans are invited to citizenship and to an initiation in Eleusinian mysteries.

228 B.C., Romans are invited to participate in Isthmian Games.

229 B.C., occupied by Romans.

222 B.C., Romans defeat Gauls.

241 B.C., annexed to Rome.

225 B.C., Gauls defeat Romans.

224 B.C., Romans defeat Gauls but lose Regulus.

241 B.C., following the First Punic War, becomes Roman province (except Syracuse).

238 B.C., insurrection quelled by Rome. Becomes Roman province in 225.

241–239 B.C., aided by Libyan cities, mercenaries mutiny against Carthage. Ringleaders Spendius and Mathos are killed and Carthage survives.

238 B.C., HAMILCAR TO SPAIN

© Arthur Banks 1972

0   50   100
Miles

ATHENS

Corcyra

Lissus

Epidamnus

ILLYRIA

PIRATE COAST

ILLYRIAN PIRATE RAIDS

Issa

Cremona

Placentia

Mutina

Parma

Bononia

Clastidium

Faesulae

Telamon

Ariminium

VIA FLAMINIA

Spoletium

Rome

ITALY

Syracuse

SICILY

SARDINIA

CORSICA

Carthage

to Spain

HANNIBAL AND THE SECOND PUNIC WAR 218-201 B.C.

Son of Hamilcar, at the age of nine Hannibal was made to swear undying hatred of Rome, Carthage's rival in the Mediterranean. He trained as a soldier in Carthaginian Spain, and at the age of 26 he commanded the entire army in that territory. His greatest feat was to attack the Romans on their home ground by transporting a huge army (including elephants) by an overland route across the southern Alps, and then down in to Italy itself where he defeated large enemy armies, one after the other. His weakness was at sea; reinforcements could not reach him due to Roman naval supremacy in the western Mediterranean. He refrained from a direct attack upon Rome itself, and the defeat of brother Hasdrubal's reinforcing army at Metaurus (207 B.C.) meant that he was isolated without help in southern Italy.

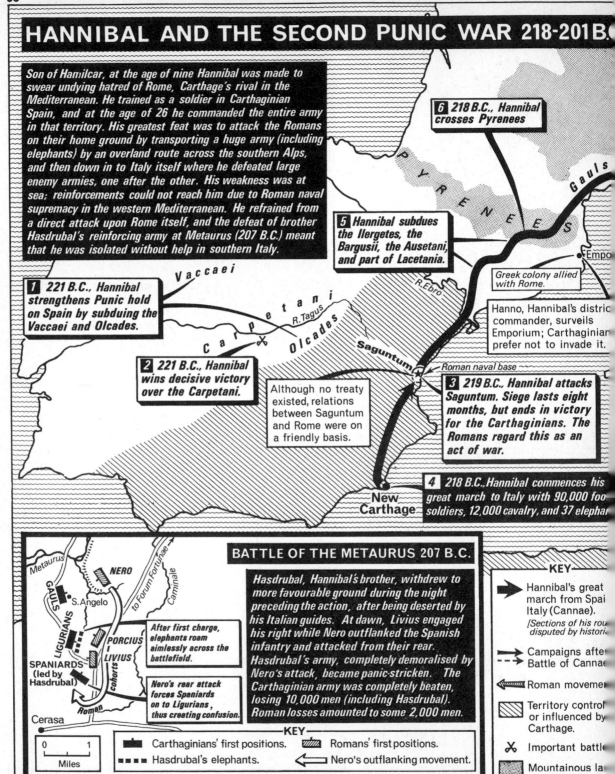

PYRENEES

Gauls

6 218 B.C., Hannibal crosses Pyrenees

5 Hannibal subdues the Ilergetes, the Bargusii, the Ausetani, and part of Lacetania.

Empo

Greek colony allied with Rome.

Vaccaei

1 221 B.C., Hannibal strengthens Punic hold on Spain by subduing the Vaccaei and Olcades.

R. Tagus

Carpetani

Olcades

R. Ebro

Saguntum

Hanno, Hannibal's distric commander, surveils Emporium; Carthaginian prefer not to invade it.

Roman naval base

2 221 B.C., Hannibal wins decisive victory over the Carpetani.

Although no treaty existed, relations between Saguntum and Rome were on a friendly basis.

3 219 B.C., Hannibal attacks Saguntum. Siege lasts eight months, but ends in victory for the Carthaginians. The Romans regard this as an act of war.

4 218 B.C., Hannibal commences his great march to Italy with 90,000 foo soldiers, 12,000 cavalry, and 37 elephar

New Carthage

BATTLE OF THE METAURUS 207 B.C.

Metaurus

NERO

GAULS

S. Angelo

to Forum Fortunae

Carminale

LIGURIANS

PORCIUS

LIVIUS

cohorts

SPANIARDS (led by Hasdrubal)

Roman

Cerasa

After first charge, elephants roam aimlessly across the battlefield.

Nero's rear attack forces Spaniards on to Ligurians, thus creating confusion.

Hasdrubal, Hannibal's brother, withdrew to more favourable ground during the night preceding the action, after being deserted by his Italian guides. At dawn, Livius engaged his right while Nero outflanked the Spanish infantry and attacked from their rear. Hasdrubal's army, completely demoralised by Nero's attack, became panic-stricken. The Carthaginian army was completely beaten, losing 10,000 men (including Hasdrubal). Roman losses amounted to some 2,000 men.

0   1
Miles

KEY

- ▆▆ Carthaginians' first positions.
- ▨ Romans' first positions.
- ▪▪▪ Hasdrubal's elephants.
- ⬅ Nero's outflanking movement.

KEY

- ➡ Hannibal's great march from Spai Italy (Cannae). [Sections of his rou disputed by historie
- ⇒ Campaigns afte Battle of Canna
- ⬅ Roman moveme
- ▨ Territory control or influenced by Carthage.
- ✂ Important battle
- ▨ Mountainous la

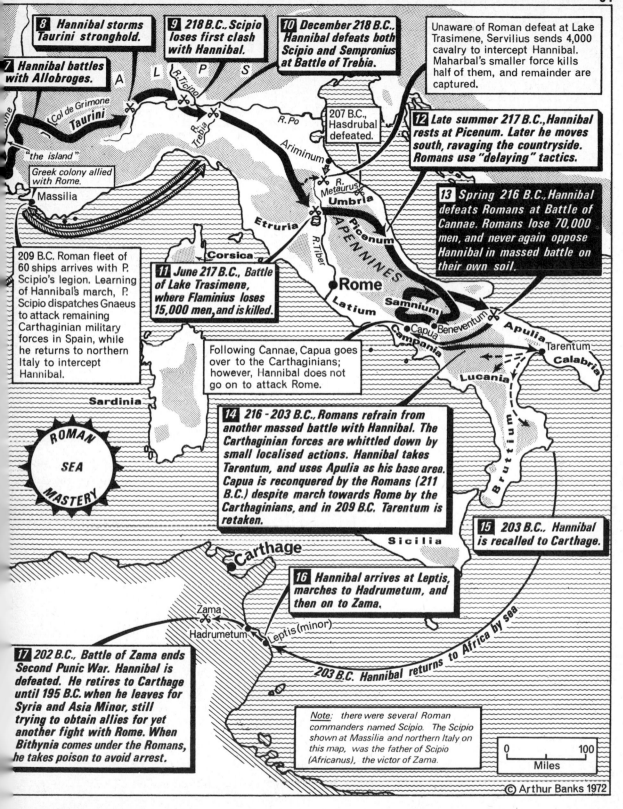

7 Hannibal battles with Allobroges.

8 Hannibal storms Taurini stronghold.

9 218 B.C., Scipio loses first clash with Hannibal.

10 December 218 B.C., Hannibal defeats both Scipio and Sempronius at Battle of Trebia.

Unaware of Roman defeat at Lake Trasimene, Servilius sends 4,000 cavalry to intercept Hannibal. Maharbal's smaller force kills half of them, and remainder are captured.

207 B.C., Hasdrubal defeated.

12 Late summer 217 B.C., Hannibal rests at Picenum. Later he moves south, ravaging the countryside. Romans use "delaying" tactics.

13 Spring 216 B.C., Hannibal defeats Romans at Battle of Cannae. Romans lose 70,000 men, and never again oppose Hannibal in massed battle on their own soil.

209 B.C. Roman fleet of 60 ships arrives with P. Scipio's legion. Learning of Hannibal's march, P. Scipio dispatches Gnaeus to attack remaining Carthaginian military forces in Spain, while he returns to northern Italy to intercept Hannibal.

11 June 217 B.C., Battle of Lake Trasimene, where Flaminius loses 15,000 men, and is killed.

Following Cannae, Capua goes over to the Carthaginians; however, Hannibal does not go on to attack Rome.

14 216 - 203 B.C., Romans refrain from another massed battle with Hannibal. The Carthaginian forces are whittled down by small localised actions. Hannibal takes Tarentum, and uses Apulia as his base area. Capua is reconquered by the Romans (211 B.C.) despite march towards Rome by the Carthaginians, and in 209 B.C. Tarentum is retaken.

15 203 B.C., Hannibal is recalled to Carthage.

16 Hannibal arrives at Leptis, marches to Hadrumetum, and then on to Zama.

17 202 B.C., Battle of Zama ends Second Punic War. Hannibal is defeated. He retires to Carthage until 195 B.C. when he leaves for Syria and Asia Minor, still trying to obtain allies for yet another fight with Rome. When Bithynia comes under the Romans, he takes poison to avoid arrest.

203 B.C. Hannibal returns to Africa by sea

Note: there were several Roman commanders named Scipio. The Scipio shown at Massilia and northern Italy on this map, was the father of Scipio (Africanus), the victor of Zama.

ROMAN SEA MASTERY

"the island"
Greek colony allied with Rome.
Massilia

Col de Grimone
Taurini

R. Ticino
R. Trebia
R. Po
Ariminum
R. Metaurus
Umbria
Etruria
Corsica
R. Tiber
APENNINES
Picenum
Rome
Latium
Samnium
Capua
Campania
Beneventum
Apulia
Tarentum
Calabria
Lucania
Bruttium
Sardinia
Sicilia
Carthage
Zama
Hadrumetum
Leptis (minor)

0   100
Miles

© Arthur Banks 1972

HANNIBAL'S GREAT BATTLES

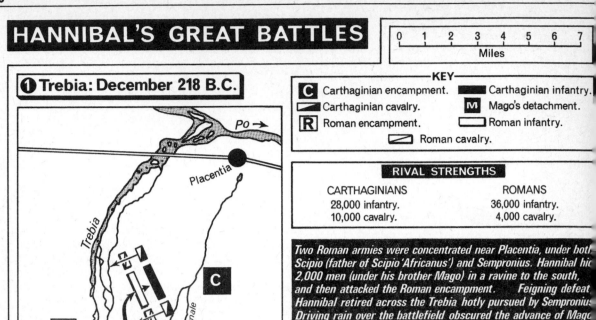

0 1 2 3 4 5 6 7
Miles

❶ Trebia: December 218 B.C.

KEY

C Carthaginian encampment. ▮ Carthaginian infantry.
◣ Carthaginian cavalry. M Mago's detachment.
R Roman encampment. ▯ Roman infantry.
◪ Roman cavalry.

RIVAL STRENGTHS

CARTHAGINIANS	ROMANS
28,000 infantry.	36,000 infantry.
10,000 cavalry.	4,000 cavalry.

Two Roman armies were concentrated near Placentia, under both
Scipio (father of Scipio 'Africanus') and Sempronius. Hannibal hid
2,000 men (under his brother Mago) in a ravine to the south,
and then attacked the Roman encampment. Feigning defeat
Hannibal retired across the Trebia hotly pursued by Sempronius
Driving rain over the battlefield obscured the advance of Mago
who attacked the Romans from their rear. Thus, the Roman
forces were trapped between the two Carthaginian positions
and virtually annihilated. As a result of this victory, 60,000
previously "uncommitted" tribesmen (mainly Gauls) flocked to
join Hannibal, swelling his ranks.

❷ Lake Trasimene: April 217 B.C.

In an ambush north of Lake Trasimen
Hannibal surprised Flaminius (who ha
not adequately reconnoitred the way
ahead). 40,000 Romans were trappe
in a four-mile defile and attacked fro
three directions simultaneously.
15,000 Romans were killed (including
Flaminius and another 15,000 capture
A 4,000-strong cavalry force sent o
by Servilius was likewise annihilate

KEY

◤ Carthaginian cavalry.
▮ Carthaginian heavy infantry.
▨ Carthaginian light infantry.
▯ Roman troops (under Flaminius).
◪ Roman cavalry (sent by Servilius).

0 1 2 3
Miles

©Arthur Banks 1972

❸ Cannae: 2 August 216 B.C. (Hannibal's greatest victory)

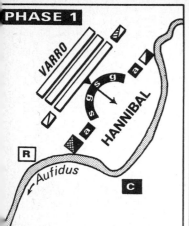

PHASE 1 — VARRO, HANNIBAL, R, Aufidus, C

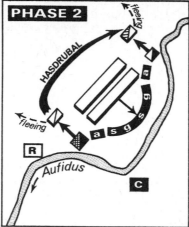

PHASE 2 — HASDRUBAL, fleeing, R, Aufidus, C

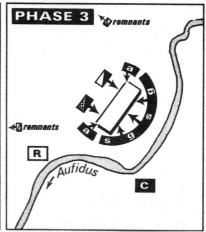

PHASE 3 — remnants, R, Aufidus, C

KEY

CARTHAGINIANS

- **C** Carthaginian encampment.
- Spanish and Gallic heavy cavalry.
- Numidian light cavalry.
- **a** African infantry.
- **s g** Spanish and Gallic infantry.

ROMANS

- **R** Roman encampment.
- Roman cavalry.
- Allied horsemen.
- Allied infantry.

Phase 1 Hannibal's infantry was drawn up in convex formation with cavalry on the wings. As the Romans advanced, the centre was withdrawn to a concave line.
Phase 2 Hannibal's cavalry defeated the Roman cavalry.
Phase 3 Roman front and flanks were now engulfed and encirclement was completed by Hannibal's cavalry units. Of Roman army of 89,600, 70,000 were killed (according to Polybius). Carthaginian losses were only 5,700.

❹ Zama: 19 October 202 B.C. (Hannibal's defeat by Scipio)*

* Later known as 'Africanus' by the Romans. (Full name: PUBLIUS CORNELIUS SCIPIO AFRICANUS).

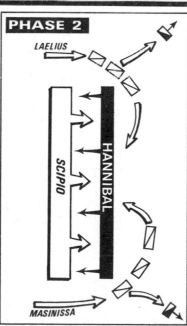

PHASE 1 — Italians, Carthaginians, HANNIBAL, Numidians

PHASE 2 — LAELIUS, SCIPIO, HANNIBAL, MASINISSA

KEY

HANNIBAL

- Main Carthaginian force (Bruttians).
- Ligurian and Gallic infantry.
- Carthaginian and African infantry.
- Cavalry.
- ●●● 80 elephants (disposed in advance).
- Advances and retreats.

SCIPIO

- Main Roman force (triarii).
- First line of velites (hastati).
- Second line of velites (principes).
- Cavalry.
- Advances.

Phase 1 Hannibal advanced his elephants; most were diverted by Roman horn blasts. Masinissa advanced his Numidian cavalry.
Phase 2 Scipio's infantry engaged Hannibal and initially the Carthaginians held firm. Cavalry attacks by Laelius and Masinissa on the rear ultimately proved decisive. Carthaginian losses were 20,000; Romans lost 1,500. Hannibal fled to Hadrumentum.

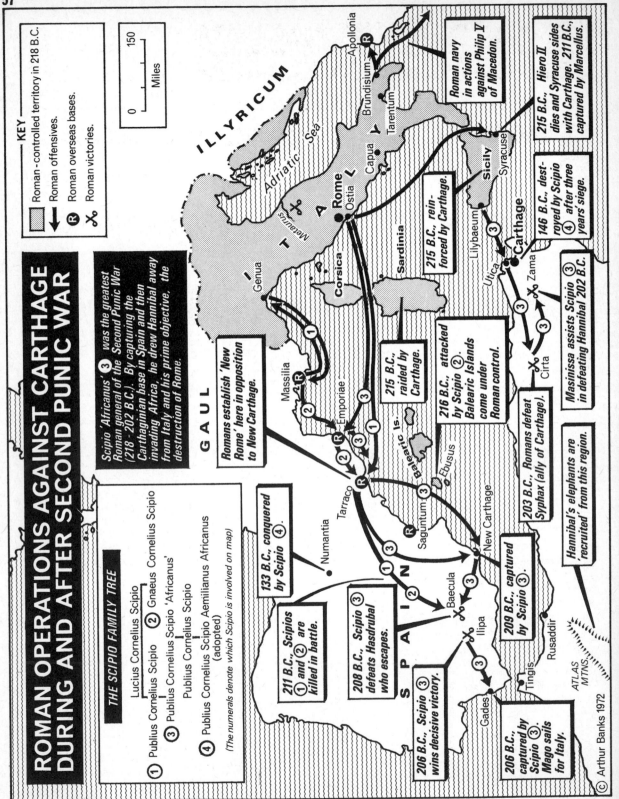

ROMAN CONSULAR ARMY IN THE TIME OF HANNIBAL c. 220 B.C.

KEY
Infantry.
Cavalry.

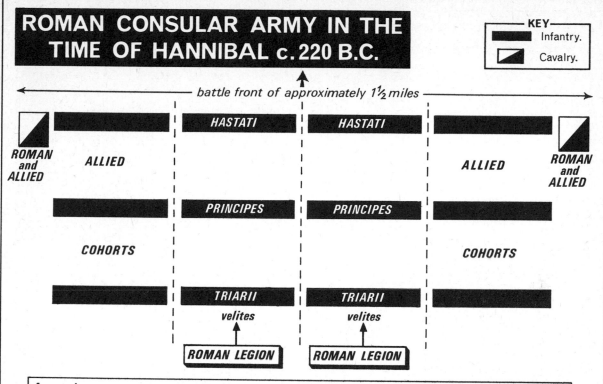

battle front of approximately 1½ miles

ROMAN and ALLIED — ALLIED — HASTATI — HASTATI — ALLIED — ROMAN and ALLIED

PRINCIPES — PRINCIPES

COHORTS — COHORTS

TRIARII — TRIARII
velites — *velites*

ROMAN LEGION — ROMAN LEGION

A consular army comprised some 17,500 men of Romans and "auxilia". A Roman legion contained some 3,000 heavy infantrymen arranged in three main classifications or groupings according to experience and age. The hastati (20-30 age range) were the front line troops; the principes (30-35 age range) were veterans and the backbone of the legion; the triarii were the oldest men. In addition, velites (young light infantry) and cavalry were utilised. Each legion contained ten cohorts of 300 heavy infantry and these were broken down in to manipuli (maniples). In battle, the principes covered gaps in the ranks of the hastati and the triarii covered gaps in the ranks of the principes. The cavalry (total 600) was positioned on the wings and the velites, initially skirmishing in front, withdrew to take up a rear position.

ROMAN LEGION

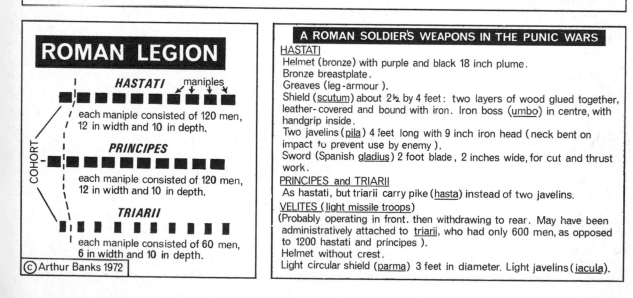

HASTATI maniples
each maniple consisted of 120 men, 12 in width and 10 in depth.

PRINCIPES
each maniple consisted of 120 men, 12 in width and 10 in depth.

COHORT

TRIARII
each maniple consisted of 60 men, 6 in width and 10 in depth.

© Arthur Banks 1972

A ROMAN SOLDIER'S WEAPONS IN THE PUNIC WARS

HASTATI
Helmet (bronze) with purple and black 18 inch plume.
Bronze breastplate.
Greaves (leg-armour).
Shield (scutum) about 2½ by 4 feet: two layers of wood glued together, leather-covered and bound with iron. Iron boss (umbo) in centre, with handgrip inside.
Two javelins (pila) 4 feet long with 9 inch iron head (neck bent on impact to prevent use by enemy).
Sword (Spanish gladius) 2 foot blade, 2 inches wide, for cut and thrust work.
PRINCIPES and TRIARII
As hastati, but triarii carry pike (hasta) instead of two javelins.
VELITES (light missile troops)
(Probably operating in front, then withdrawing to rear. May have been administratively attached to triarii, who had only 600 men, as opposed to 1200 hastati and principes).
Helmet without crest.
Light circular shield (parma) 3 feet in diameter. Light javelins (iacula).

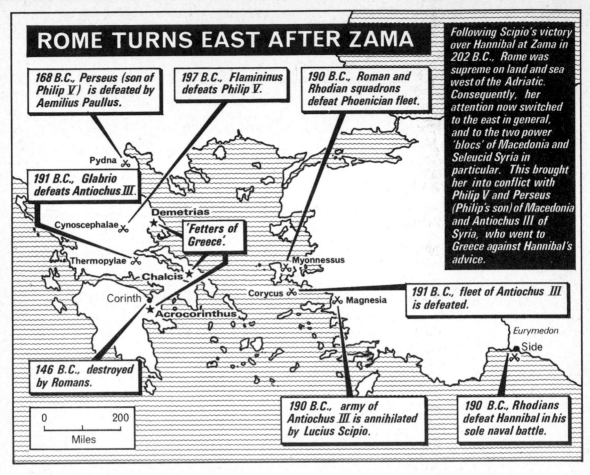

ROME TURNS EAST AFTER ZAMA

168 B.C., Perseus (son of Philip V) is defeated by Aemilius Paullus.

197 B.C., Flamininus defeats Philip V.

190 B.C., Roman and Rhodian squadrons defeat Phoenician fleet.

191 B.C., Glabrio defeats Antiochus III.

Pydna ⚔

Demetrias ★

Cynoscephalae ⚔

'Fetters of Greece'.

Thermopylae ⚔

Chalcis ★

Corinth

Myonnessus ⚔

★ Acrocorinthus

Corycus ⚔

✗ Magnesia

191 B.C., fleet of Antiochus III is defeated.

Eurymedon

● Side
⚔

146 B.C., destroyed by Romans.

0 ———— 200
Miles

190 B.C., army of Antiochus III is annihilated by Lucius Scipio.

190 B.C., Rhodians defeat Hannibal in his sole naval battle.

Following Scipio's victory over Hannibal at Zama in 202 B.C., Rome was supreme on land and sea west of the Adriatic. Consequently, her attention now switched to the east in general, and to the two power 'blocs' of Macedonia and Seleucid Syria in particular. This brought her into conflict with Philip V and Perseus (Philip's son) of Macedonia and Antiochus III of Syria, who went to Greece against Hannibal's advice.

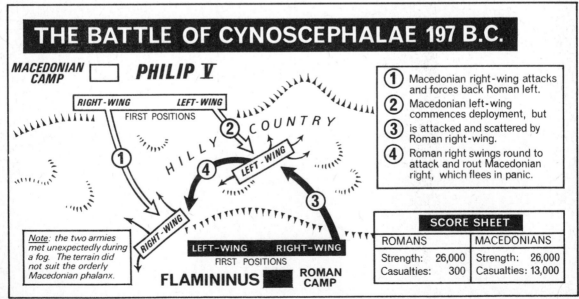

THE BATTLE OF CYNOSCEPHALAE 197 B.C.

MACEDONIAN CAMP ☐ **PHILIP V**

RIGHT-WING   LEFT-WING
FIRST POSITIONS

HILLY COUNTRY

① ② ③ ④

LEFT-WING

RIGHT-WING

LEFT-WING   RIGHT-WING
FIRST POSITIONS

FLAMININUS ■ **ROMAN CAMP**

Note: the two armies met unexpectedly during a fog. The terrain did not suit the orderly Macedonian phalanx.

① Macedonian right-wing attacks and forces back Roman left.
② Macedonian left-wing commences deployment, but
③ is attacked and scattered by Roman right-wing.
④ Roman right swings round to attack and rout Macedonian right, which flees in panic.

SCORE SHEET	
ROMANS	**MACEDONIANS**
Strength: 26,000	Strength: 26,000
Casualties: 300	Casualties: 13,000

THE NEAR EAST IN CONFLICT c.200 – 125 B.C.

This period was marked by a number of wars and struggles involving Seleucid Syria, Ptolemaic Egypt, and the Maccabees in Palestine. Meanwhile, Rome (heavily engaged in Greece) became increasingly involved as her power continued to expand eastwards.

KEY

⚔ Important battles.

⬇ Antiochus IV's two invasions of Egypt, 171 and 168 B.C.

⬆ Broad lines of Roman expansion and involvement.

◉ Victories of Judas 166 - 161 B.C.

200
Miles
0

129 B.C., Phraates II of Parthia defeats and kills Antiochus VII.

141 B.C., Mithridates I of Parthia captures city.

145 B.C., Ptolemy VI of Egypt defeats Alexander Balas of Syria but is killed.

198 B.C., Antiochus III wins victory, making Palestine a dependency of the Seleucids.

160 B.C., Bacchides of Syria defeats and kills Judas.

165 B.C., Judas captures most of city including temple. Seleucid garrison holds out in citadel.

143 B.C., Jonathan is ambushed and captured by Syrians and some dissident Jews. Later, killed.

168 B.C., Antiochus IV is warned by Rome to restore Egypt to the Ptolemies.

SELEUCID SYRIA

ASIA MINOR

PTOLEMAIC EGYPT

Caspian Sea

Black Sea

Mediterranean Sea

Araxes

Tigris

Euphrates

Babylon

Ecbatana ⚔

Oerobarus ⚔

Orontes

Halys

Pergamum

Alexandria

Ptolemais

Paneion ⚔

Elasa ⚔

Adasa 161 B.C.

Jerusalem

Beth Horon 166 B.C.

Emmaus 166 B.C.

Beth Zur 165 B.C.

© Arthur Banks 1972

ROMAN EXPANSION IN THE NEAR EAST

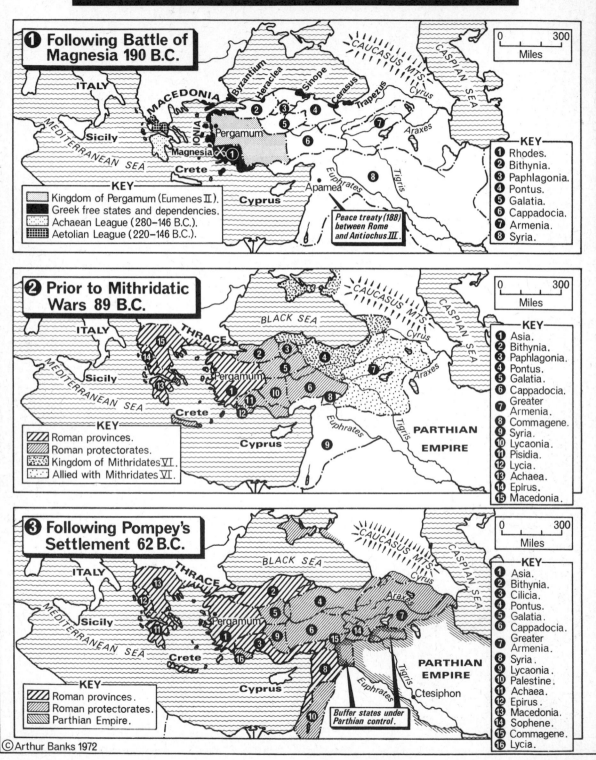

❶ Following Battle of Magnesia 190 B.C.

ITALY
MACEDONIA
IONIA
Pergamum
Magnesia ✕ ①
Sicily
MEDITERRANEAN SEA
Crete
Cyprus
Byzantium
Heraclea
Sinope
Cerasus
Trapezus
CAUCASUS MTS.
CASPIAN SEA
Cyrus
Araxes
Euphrates
Tigris
Apamea

② ③ ⑦ ④ ⑤ ⑥ ⑧

0　300
Miles

Peace treaty (188) between Rome and Antiochus III.

KEY
- Kingdom of Pergamum (Eumenes II).
- Greek free states and dependencies.
- Achaean League (280–146 B.C.).
- Aetolian League (220–146 B.C.).

KEY
❶ Rhodes.
❷ Bithynia.
❸ Paphlagonia.
❹ Pontus.
❺ Galatia.
❻ Cappadocia.
❼ Armenia.
❽ Syria.

❷ Prior to Mithridatic Wars 89 B.C.

ITALY
THRACE
BLACK SEA
CAUCASUS MTS.
CASPIAN SEA
Cyrus
Araxes
Sicily
MEDITERRANEAN SEA
Pergamum
Crete
Cyprus
Euphrates
Tigris
PARTHIAN EMPIRE

⑮ ⑭ ⑬ ① ⑪ ⑫ ② ③ ④ ⑤ ⑩ ⑥ ⑧ ⑦ ⑨

0　300
Miles

KEY
- Roman provinces.
- Roman protectorates.
- Kingdom of Mithridates VI.
- Allied with Mithridates VI.

KEY
❶ Asia.
❷ Bithynia.
❸ Paphlagonia.
❹ Pontus.
❺ Galatia.
❻ Cappadocia.
❼ Greater Armenia.
❽ Commagene.
❾ Syria.
❿ Lycaonia.
⓫ Pisidia.
⓬ Lycia.
⓭ Achaea.
⓮ Epirus.
⓯ Macedonia.

❸ Following Pompey's Settlement 62 B.C.

ITALY
THRACE
BLACK SEA
CAUCASUS MTS.
CASPIAN SEA
Cyrus
Araxes
Sicily
MEDITERRANEAN SEA
Pergamum
Crete
Cyprus
Euphrates
Tigris
Ctesiphon
PARTHIAN EMPIRE

⑬ ⑫ ⑪ ① ⑯ ③ ② ⑤ ⑨ ④ ⑥ ⑮ ⑭ ⑦ ⑧ ⑩

0　300
Miles

Buffer states under Parthian control.

KEY
- Roman provinces.
- Roman protectorates.
- Parthian Empire.

KEY
❶ Asia.
❷ Bithynia.
❸ Cilicia.
❹ Pontus.
❺ Galatia.
❻ Cappadocia.
❼ Greater Armenia.
❽ Syria.
❾ Lycaonia.
❿ Palestine.
⓫ Achaea.
⓬ Epirus.
⓭ Macedonia.
⓮ Sophene.
⓯ Commagene.
⓰ Lycia.

© Arthur Banks 1972

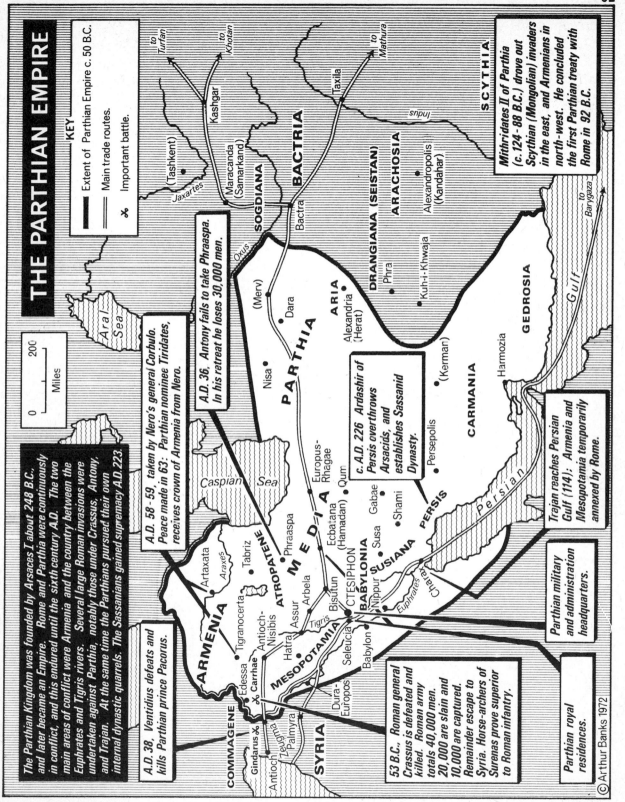

62

THE PARTHIAN EMPIRE

KEY

—— Extent of Parthian Empire c. 50 B.C.

⚌ Main trade routes.

⚔ Important battle.

0 ___ 200

Miles

The Parthian Kingdom was founded by Arsaces I about 248 B.C. and later became an Empire. Rome and Parthia were continuously in conflict, and this endured until the sixth century A.D. The two main areas of conflict were Armenia and the country between the Euphrates and Tigris rivers. Several large Roman invasions were undertaken against Parthia, notably those under Crassus, Antony, and Trajan. At the same time the Parthians pursued their own internal dynastic quarrels. The Sassanians gained supremacy A.D. 223.

A.D. 58 - 59, taken by Nero's general Corbulo. Peace made in 63: Parthian nominee Tiridates, receives crown of Armenia from Nero.

A.D. 36. Antony fails to take Phraaspa. In his retreat he loses 30,000 men.

Mithridates II of Parthia (c.124 - 88 B.C.) drove out Scythian (Mongolian) invaders in the east, and Armenians in north-west. He concluded the first Parthian treaty with Rome in 92 B.C.

A.D. 38, Ventidius defeats and kills Parthian prince Pacorus.

c. A.D. 226 Ardashir of Persis overthrows Arsacids, and establishes Sassanid Dynasty.

Trajan reaches Persian Gulf (114): Armenia and Mesopotamia temporarily annexed by Rome.

Parthian military and administration headquarters.

53 B.C., Roman general Crassus is defeated and killed. Roman army totals 40,000 men. 20,000 are slain and 10,000 are captured. Remainder escape to Syria. Horse-archers of Surenas prove superior to Roman infantry.

Parthian royal residences.

© Arthur Banks 1972

THE EXPANSION OF CH'IN POWER AND INFLUENCE

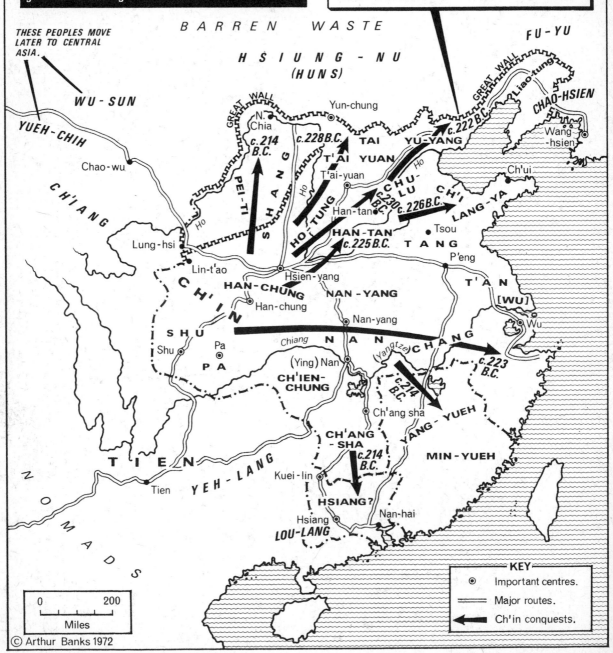

Cheng took the title of Shih Huang Ti, proclaiming himself Emperor of China. (The name China is derived from Ch'in). He built the Great Wall to prevent raids into China by northern nomads, and made military expeditions south of the Yangtze. His two main generals were Ming T'ien and Chao T'o.

The Great Wall of China (constructed from brick, stone, and earth), was 1,500 miles in length, with watchtowers every few hundred yards. Along the top ran a 12 feet - wide roadway, and at irregular intervals there were gatehouses. Moats protected vulnerable sections of the wall on its northern side.

BARREN WASTE

HSIUNG - NU (HUNS)

FU - YU

THESE PEOPLES MOVE LATER TO CENTRAL ASIA.

WU - SUN

YUEH - CHIH

Chao-wu

CH'IANG

Lung-hsi

Lin-t'ao

GREAT WALL

N. Chia

c.214 B.C.

PEI-TI

SHANG

Ho

c.228 B.C.

T'AI YUAN

T'ai-yuan

Ho

Yun-chung

TAI

YU-YANG

c.222 B.C.

Liao-tung

CHAO-HSIEN

Wang -hsien

HO-TUNG

CHU-LU

c.230 B.C.

Han-tan

c.226 B.C.

Ch'ui

Ho

LANG-YA

CH'I

Tsou

T'ANG

P'eng

HAN-TAN

c.225 B.C.

Hsien-yang

HAN-CHUNG

Han-chung

NAN - YANG

Nan-yang

T'AN

[WU]

Wu

CH'IN

SHU

Shu

Pa

PA

Chiang

(Ying) Nan

NAN

(Yangtze)

CHANG

c.223 B.C.

CH'IEN-CHUNG

c.214 B.C.

Ch'ang sha

YANG - YUEH

MIN-YUEH

TIEN

NOMADS

Tien

YEH - LANG

CH'ANG -SHA

c.214 B.C.

Kuei-lin

HSIANG?

Hsiang

LOU-LANG

Nan-hai

0   200
Miles

© Arthur Banks 1972

KEY
- ⊙ Important centres.
- ═══ Major routes.
- ◀━━ Ch'in conquests.

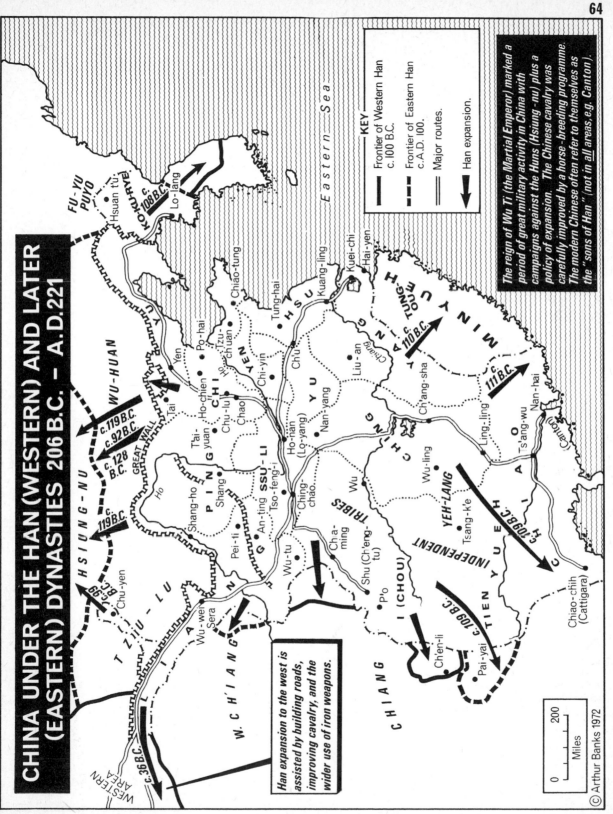

64

CHINA UNDER THE HAN (WESTERN) AND LATER (EASTERN) DYNASTIES 206 B.C. – A.D.221

KEY

— Frontier of Western Han c.100 B.C.

-·- Frontier of Eastern Han c.A.D. 100.

═ Major routes.

➤ Han expansion.

The reign of Wu Ti (the Martial Emperor) marked a period of great military activity in China with campaigns against the Huns (Hsiung-nu) plus a policy of expansion. The Chinese cavalry was carefully improved by a horse-breeding programme. The modern Chinese often refer to themselves as the "sons of Han" (not in all areas, e.g. Canton).

Han expansion to the west is assisted by building roads, improving cavalry, and the wider use of iron weapons.

FU-YU PUYO

Hsuan t'u

KO-KURYEI

c.108 B.C.

Lo-lang

Eastern Sea

WU-HUAN

c.119 B.C.
c.92 B.C.
c.128 B.C.

GREAT WALL

HSIUNG-NU

c.119 B.C.

c.99 B.C.

Chu-yen

T ZIU-LU

Wu-wei

Sera

W. CH'IANG

WESTERN AREA

c.36 B.C.

Tai

Yen

Po-hai

Ho-chien

Tzu-chuan

Chiao-tung

Tung-hai

HSU

Kuang-ling

Kuei-chi

Hai-yen

TUNG-O

c.110 B.C.

MIN-YUEH

c.111 B.C.

Nan-hai

(Canton)

Ts'ang-wu

Ling-ling

Ch'ang-sha

Chiang

Liu-an

Chu

YU

Chi-yin

Ho-nan (Lo-yang)

Nan-yang

CHING

Wu-ling

YEH-LANG

Tsang-ke

c.106 B.C.

TIEN YUEH

Pai-yai

Ch'en-li

Chiao-chih (Cattigara)

Tai-yuan

Chu-lu

Chao

PING

CHI

YEN

Shang-ho

Shang

SSU-LI

Tso-feng-i

An-ting

Ching-chao

Cha-ming

Wu-tu

Shu (Ch'eng-tu)

P'o

I (CHOU)

INDEPENDENT

CHIANG TRIBES

Wu

0 200 Miles

© Arthur Banks 1972

Antonine Wall.

Hadrian's Wall.

Baltic Sea

BRITAIN

Londinium

(G E R M A N Y)

LOWER GERMANY

'Limes' (fortified line).

Durocortorum

Danube   Vindobona

Rhine

B E L G I C A

LUGDUNENSIS

UPPER GERMANY

RAETIA

NORICUM

PANNONIA

Bay of Biscay

GAUL

AQUITANIA

NARBONENSIS

I T A L Y

I L L Y R I C U M

D A L M A T I A

Adriatic Sea

GALACIA

TARRACONENSIS

Ebro

LUSITANIA

SPAIN

Corsica

Rome

Ostia

Port of Rome.

Tarraco

Saguntum

BAETICA

Sardinia

New Carthage

M e d i t e r r a n e a n

Carthage

Sicily

Syracuse

M A U R E T A N I A

NUMIDIA

AFRICA
Earlier Province

A F R I C A

Leptis Magna

KEY TO ROADS IN ITALY

❶ Via Valeria.	❽ Via Salaria.
❷ Via Postumia.	❾ Via Popillia.
❸ Via Latina.	❿ Via Cassia.
❹ Via Flaminia.	⓫ Via Trajana.
❺ Via Aurelia.	⓬ Via Domitiana.
❻ Via Appia.	⓭ Via Julia Augusta.
❼ Via Aemilia.	

In the late Third Century A.D., a rampart, ditch, and wall (?) was constructed. It was known as "fossatum Africae".

KEY TO ALPINE AREAS
1. PENNINE, 2. COTTIAN, 3. MARITIME

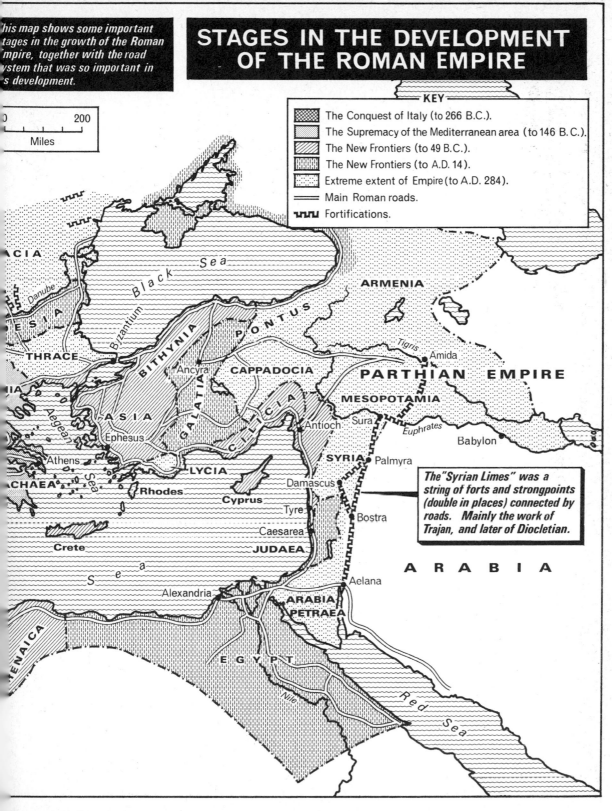

This map shows some important stages in the growth of the Roman Empire, together with the road system that was so important in its development.

STAGES IN THE DEVELOPMENT OF THE ROMAN EMPIRE

200

Miles

KEY

	The Conquest of Italy (to 266 B.C.).
	The Supremacy of the Mediterranean area (to 146 B.C.).
	The New Frontiers (to 49 B.C.).
	The New Frontiers (to A.D. 14).
	Extreme extent of Empire (to A.D. 284).
	Main Roman roads.
	Fortifications.

ACIA

Danube

Black   Sea

MESIA

Byzantium

ARMENIA

THRACE

PONTUS

Ancyra

CAPPADOCIA

Tigris

Amida

BITHYNIA

PARTHIAN   EMPIRE

IA

MESOPOTAMIA

Aegean

ASIA

GALATIA

CILICIA

Antioch

Sura

Euphrates

Ephesus

Babylon

Athens

SYRIA

Palmyra

CHAEA

Sea

LYCIA

Damascus

The "Syrian Limes" was a string of forts and strongpoints (double in places) connected by roads. Mainly the work of Trajan, and later of Diocletian.

Rhodes

Cyprus

Cyprus

Tyre

Bostra

Caesarea

Crete

S e a

JUDAEA

ARABIA

Alexandria

Aelana

ENAICA

ARABIA PETRAEA

E G Y P T

Nile

Red   Sea

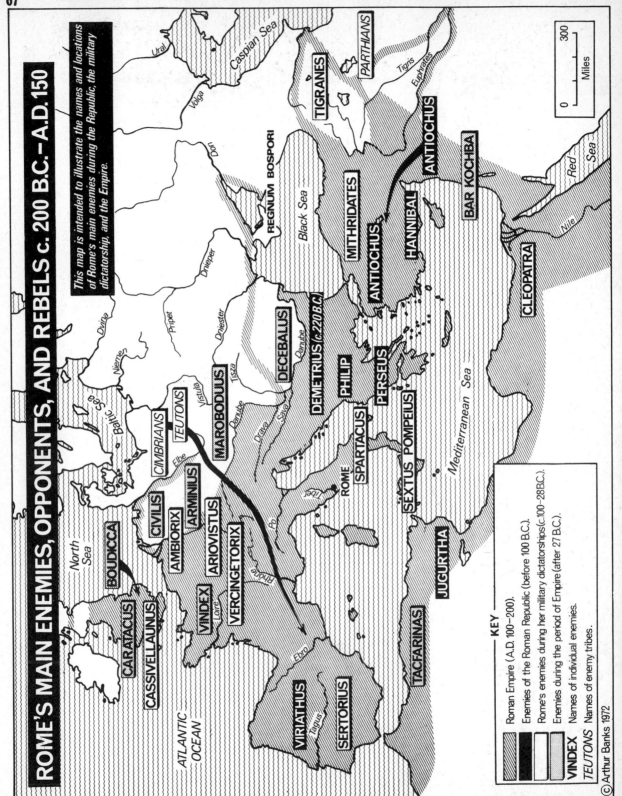

ROME'S MAIN ENEMIES, OPPONENTS, AND REBELS c. 200 B.C.–A.D.150

This map is intended to illustrate the names and locations of Rome's main enemies during the Republic, the military dictatorship, and the Empire.

Ural

Caspian Sea

Volga

PARTHIANS

Tigris

Euphrates

TIGRANES

Don

REGNUM BOSPORI

ANTIOCHUS

Dnieper

Black Sea

MITHRIDATES

ANTIOCHUS

HANNIBAL

BAR KOCHBA

Red Sea

Dvina

Pripet

Dniester

DECEBALUS

DEMETRIUS (c.220 B.C.)

PHILIP

PERSEUS

CLEOPATRA

Nile

Niemen

Vistula

Tisza

MAROBODUS

Danube

Drava

Sava

SPARTACUS

Mediterranean Sea

Baltic Sea

Elbe

CIMBRIANS

TEUTONS

ROME

SEXTUS POMPEIUS

North Sea

BOUDICCA

CIVILIS

AMBIORIX

ARMINIUS

ARIOVISTUS

VINDEX

VERCINGETORIX

Rhone

Loire

Tiber

Po

JUGURTHA

CARATACUS

CASSIVELLAUNUS

Ebro

ATLANTIC OCEAN

VIRIATHUS

Tagus

SERTORIUS

TACFARINAS

0   300

Miles

KEY

Roman Empire (A.D. 100–200).

Enemies of the Roman Republic (before 100 B.C.).

Rome's enemies during her military dictatorships (c.100–28B.C.).

Enemies during the period of Empire (after 27 B.C.).

VINDEX   Names of individual enemies.

TEUTONS   Names of enemy tribes.

© Arthur Banks 1972

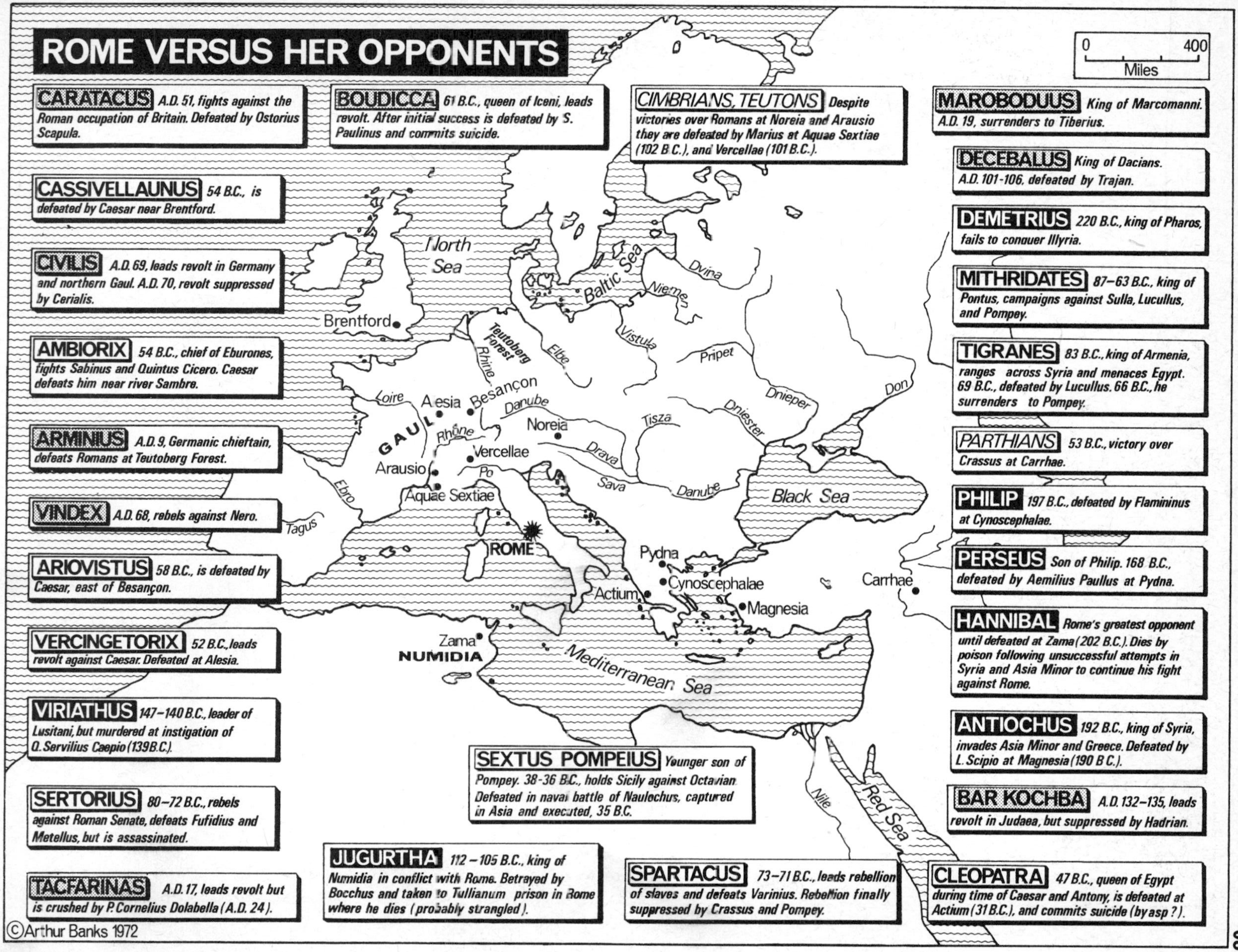

ROME VERSUS HER OPPONENTS

© Arthur Banks 1972

0 — 400 Miles

MAROBODUUS King of Marcomanni. A.D. 19, surrenders to Tiberius.

DECEBALUS King of Dacians. A.D. 101-106, defeated by Trajan.

DEMETRIUS 220 B.C., king of Pharos, fails to conquer Illyria.

MITHRIDATES 87-63 B.C. king of Pontus, campaigns against Sulla, Lucullus, and Pompey.

TIGRANES 83 B.C. king of Armenia, ranges across Syria and menaces Egypt. 69 B.C., defeated by Lucullus. 66 B.C., he surrenders to Pompey.

PARTHIANS 53 B.C., victory over Crassus at Carrhae.

PHILIP 197 B.C. defeated by Flaminius at Cynoscephalae.

PERSEUS Son of Philip. 168 B.C., defeated by Aemilius Paullus at Pydna.

HANNIBAL Rome's greatest opponent until defeated at Zama (202 B.C.). Dies by poison following unsuccessful attempts in Syria and Asia Minor to continue his fight against Rome.

ANTIOCHUS 192 B.C., king of Syria, invades Asia Minor and Greece. Defeated by L. Scipio at Magnesia (190 B.C.).

BAR KOCHBA A.D. 132-135, leads revolt in Judaea, but suppressed by Hadrian.

CLEOPATRA 47 B.C., queen of Egypt during time of Caesar and Antony, is defeated at Actium (31 B.C.), and commits suicide (by asp?).

CARATACUS A.D. 51, fights against the Roman occupation of Britain. Defeated by Ostorius Scapula.

BOUDICCA 61 B.C., queen of Iceni, leads revolt. After initial success is defeated by S. Paulinus and commits suicide.

CIMBRIANS, TEUTONS Despite victories over Romans at Noreia and Arausio they are defeated by Marius at Aquae Sextiae (102 B.C.) and Vercellae (101 B.C.).

CASSIVELLAUNUS 54 B.C., is defeated by Caesar near Brentford.

CIVILIS A.D. 69, leads revolt in Germany and northern Gaul. A.D. 70, revolt suppressed by Cerialis.

AMBIORIX 54 B.C., chief of Eburones, fights Sabinus and Quintus Cicero. Caesar defeats him near river Sambre.

ARMINIUS A.D. 9, Germanic chieftain, defeats Romans at Teutoberg Forest.

VINDEX A.D. 68, rebels against Nero.

ARIOVISTUS 58 B.C., is defeated by Caesar, east of Besançon.

VERCINGETORIX 52 B.C., leads revolt against Caesar. Defeated at Alesia.

VIRIATHUS 147-140 B.C., leader of Lusitani, but murdered at instigation of Q. Servilius Caepio (139 B.C.).

SERTORIUS 80-72 B.C., rebels against Roman Senate, defeats Fufidius and Metellus, but is assassinated.

TACFARINAS A.D. 17, leads revolt but is crushed by P. Cornelius Dolabella (A.D. 24).

JUGURTHA 112-105 B.C., king of Numidia in conflict with Rome. Betrayed by Bocchus and taken to Tullianum prison in Rome where he dies (probably strangled).

SEXTUS POMPEIUS Younger son of Pompey. 38-36 B.C., holds Sicily against Octavian. Defeated in naval battle of Naulochus, captured in Asia and executed, 35 B.C.

SPARTACUS 73-71 B.C., leads rebellion of slaves and defeats Varinius. Rebellion finally suppressed by Crassus and Pompey.

Map labels: Don, Black Sea, Carrhae, Red Sea, Nile, Dnieper, Dniester, Pripet, Tisza, Danube, Vistula, Dvina, Niemen, Baltic Sea, Elbe, Drava, Sava, Po, Magnesia, Pydna, Cynoscephalae, Actium, Mediterranean Sea, Zama, NUMIDIA, North Sea, Teutoberg Forest, Rhine, Noreia, Vercellae, ROME, Aesia, Besançon, Loire, Rhône, Aquae Sextiae, GAUL, Arausio, Ebro, Tagus, Brentford.

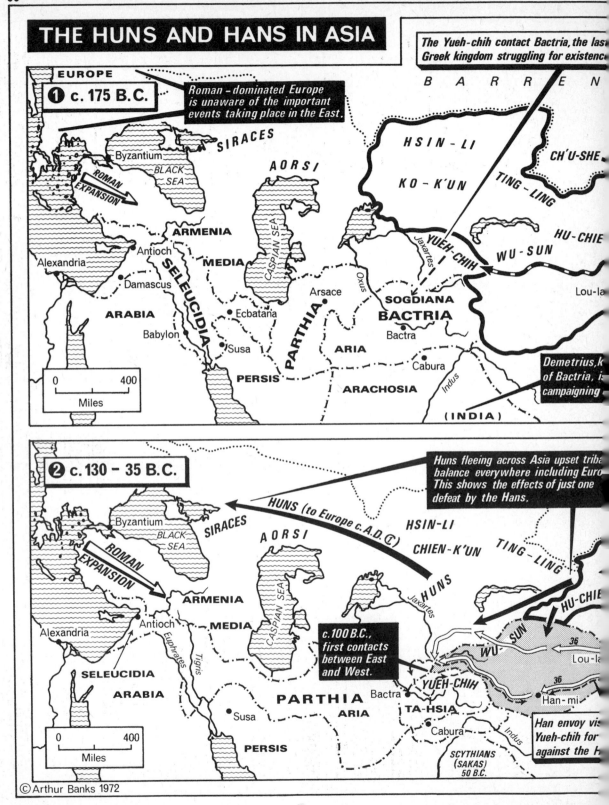

THE HUNS AND HANS IN ASIA

① c. 175 B.C.

The Yueh-chih contact Bactria, the las[t]
Greek kingdom struggling for existenc[e]

EUROPE

Roman-dominated Europe
is unaware of the important
events taking place in the East.

BARREN

SIRACES

AORSI

HSIN-LI

KO-K'UN

CH'U-SHE

TING-LING

HU-CHIE

Byzantium

BLACK SEA

ROMAN EXPANSION

ARMENIA

MEDIA

CASPIAN SEA

YUEH-CHIH

WU-SUN

Antioch

Alexandria

Damascus

SELEUCIDIA

Arsace

Oxus

SOGDIANA
BACTRIA

Lou-la

ARABIA

Ecbatana

PARTHIA

Bactra

Babylon

Susa

ARIA

Cabura

Demetrius, k[ing]
of Bactria, i[s]
campaigning

0 — 400 Miles

PERSIS

ARACHOSIA

Indus

(INDIA)

② c. 130 – 35 B.C.

Huns fleeing across Asia upset triba[l]
balance everywhere including Euro[pe.]
This shows the effects of just one
defeat by the Hans.

Byzantium

BLACK SEA

SIRACES

AORSI

HSIN-LI

CHIEN-K'UN

TING-LING

HUNS (to Europe c.A.D. ①)

ROMAN EXPANSION

ARMENIA

MEDIA

CASPIAN SEA

Jaxartes

HUNS

HU-CHIE

Alexandria

Antioch

Euphrates

Tigris

WU-SUN

36

Lou-la

c.100 B.C.,
first contacts
between East
and West.

SELEUCIDIA

ARABIA

PARTHIA

Susa

Bactra

ARIA

YUEH-CHIH

36

Han-mi

TA-HSIA

Cabura

Indus

Han envoy vis[its]
Yueh-chih for [?]
against the H[uns]

0 — 400 Miles

PERSIS

SCYTHIANS
(SAKAS)
50 B.C.

© Arthur Banks 1972

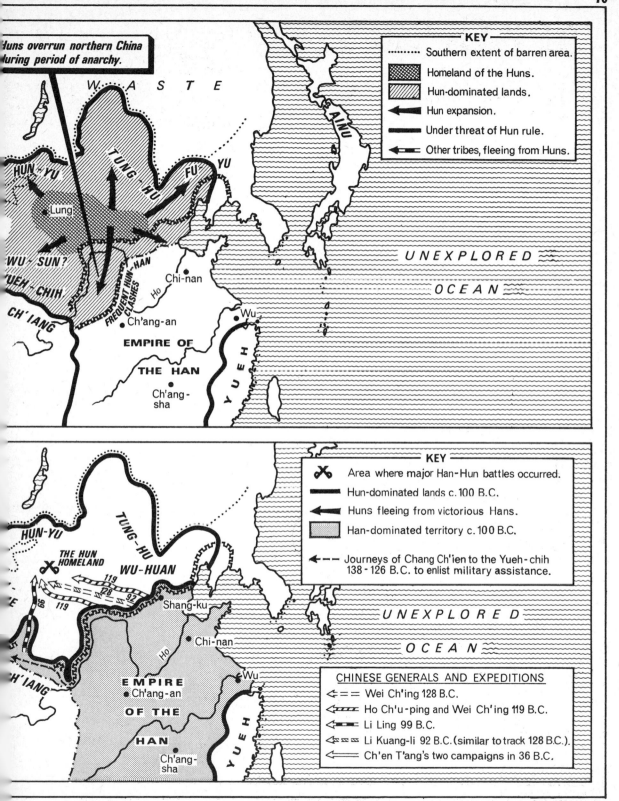

Huns overrun northern China during period of anarchy.

W A S T E

TUNG-HU

FU-YU

AINU

HUN-YU

Lung

WU-SUN?

YUEH-CHIH

CH'IANG

FREQUENT HUN CLASHES

Ho

Chi-nan

Ch'ang-an

Wu

EMPIRE OF

THE HAN

Ch'ang-sha

YUEH

UNEXPLORED

OCEAN

---KEY---
.... Southern extent of barren area.
▨ Homeland of the Huns.
▧ Hun-dominated lands.
◄━━ Hun expansion.
━━━ Under threat of Hun rule.
◄┅┅ Other tribes, fleeing from Huns.

HUN-YU

TUNG-HU

THE HUN HOMELAND

WU-HUAN

119

128

92

99

119

Shang-ku

CH'IANG

Ho

Chi-nan

EMPIRE

Ch'ang-an

OF THE

Wu

HAN

Ch'ang-sha

YUEH

UNEXPLORED

OCEAN

---KEY---
⚔ Area where major Han-Hun battles occurred.
━━━ Hun-dominated lands c. 100 B.C.
◄━━ Huns fleeing from victorious Hans.
░ Han-dominated territory c. 100 B.C.
◄┅┅ Journeys of Chang Ch'ien to the Yueh-chih 138-126 B.C. to enlist military assistance.

CHINESE GENERALS AND EXPEDITIONS
◄═══ Wei Ch'ing 128 B.C.
◄▭▭▭ Ho Ch'u-ping and Wei Ch'ing 119 B.C.
◄▬▬▬ Li Ling 99 B.C.
◄▭▭▭ Li Kuang-li 92 B.C. (similar to track 128 B.C.).
◄─── Ch'en T'ang's two campaigns in 36 B.C.

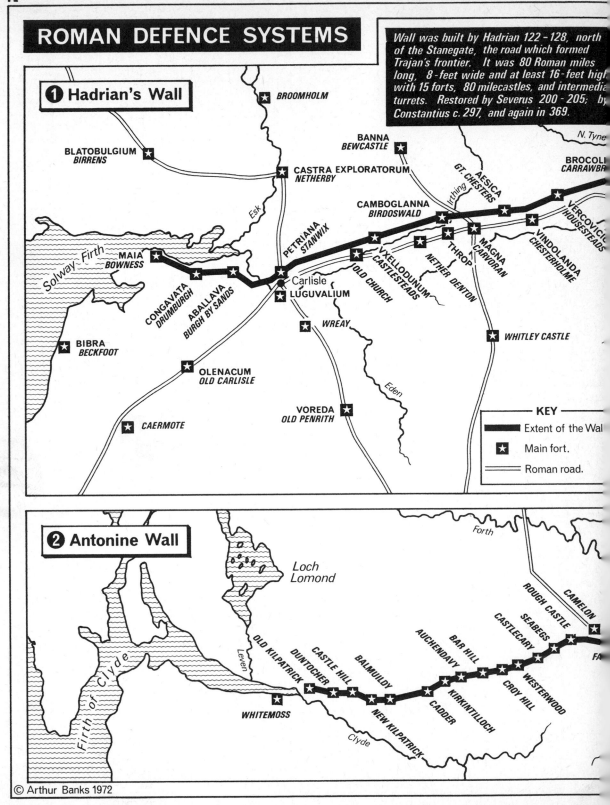

ROMAN DEFENCE SYSTEMS

① Hadrian's Wall

Wall was built by Hadrian 122 - 128, north of the Stanegate, the road which formed Trajan's frontier. It was 80 Roman miles long, 8 - feet wide and at least 16 - feet high, with 15 forts, 80 milecastles, and intermediate turrets. Restored by Severus 200 - 205; by Constantius c. 297, and again in 369.

N. Tyne

BROOMHOLM

BANNA
BEWCASTLE

BLATOBULGIUM
BIRRENS

GT. CHESTERS
AESICA

BROCOLI
CARRAWBR

CASTRA EXPLORATORUM
NETHERBY

CAMBOGLANNA
BIRDOSWALD

VERCOVICI
HOUSESTEADS

Irthing

Esk

PETRIANA
STANWIX

VXELLODUNUM
CASTLESTEADS

THROP

MAGNA
CARVORAN

VINDOLANDA
CHESTERHOLME

MAIA
BOWNESS

NETHER DENTON

Solway Firth

CONGAVATA
DRUMBURGH

ABALLAVA
BURGH BY SANDS

Carlisle
LUGUVALIUM

OLD
CHURCH

WREAY

BIBRA
BECKFOOT

WHITLEY CASTLE

OLENACUM
OLD CARLISLE

Eden

VOREDA
OLD PENRITH

CAERMOTE

KEY

■ Extent of the Wall
★ Main fort.
— Roman road.

② Antonine Wall

Forth

Loch Lomond

ROUGH CASTLE

CAMELON

CASTLECARY

SEABEGS

Leven

OLD KILPATRICK

DUNTOCHER

CASTLE HILL

BALMUILDY

AUCHENDAVY

BAR HILL

WESTERWOOD

Firth of Clyde

WHITEMOSS

NEW KILPATRICK

CADDER

KIRKINTILLOCH

CROY HILL

Clyde

FA

© Arthur Banks 1972

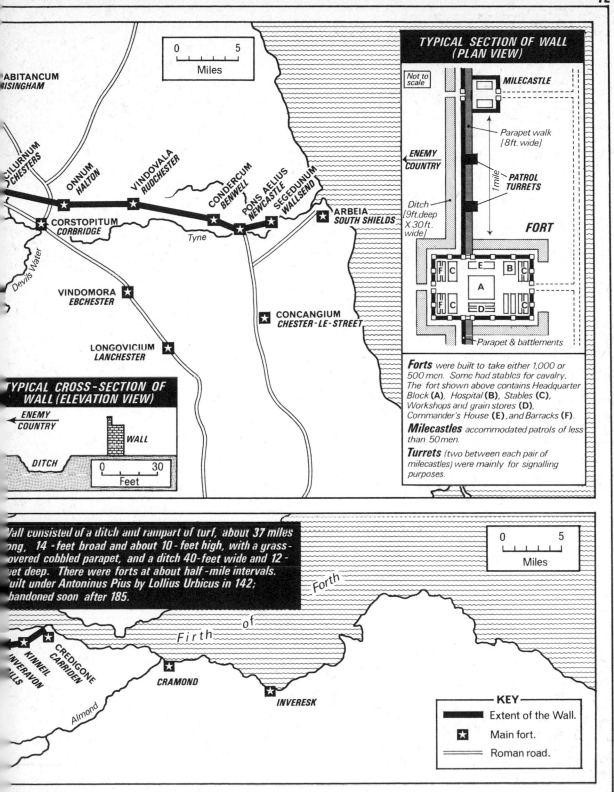

ABITANCUM
RISINGHAM

CILURNUM
CHESTERS

ONNUM
HALTON

VINDOVALA
RUDCHESTER

CONDERCUM
BENWELL

PONS AELIUS
NEWCASTLE

SEGEDUNUM
WALLSEND

ARBEIA
SOUTH SHIELDS

Tyne

CORSTOPITUM
CORBRIDGE

Devils Water

VINDOMORA
EBCHESTER

CONCANGIUM
CHESTER-LE-STREET

LONGOVICIUM
LANCHESTER

0 — 5
Miles

TYPICAL SECTION OF WALL (PLAN VIEW)

Not to scale

MILECASTLE

ENEMY COUNTRY

Parapet walk [8ft. wide]

1 mile

PATROL TURRETS

Ditch [9ft.deep X 30ft. wide]

FORT

F C E B C
A
F C D F

Parapet & battlements

Forts were built to take either 1,000 or 500 men. Some had stables for cavalry. The fort shown above contains Headquarter Block **(A)**, Hospital **(B)**, Stables **(C)**, Workshops and grain stores **(D)**, Commander's House **(E)**, and Barracks **(F)**.

Milecastles accommodated patrols of less than 50 men.

Turrets (two between each pair of milecastles) were mainly for signalling purposes.

TYPICAL CROSS-SECTION OF WALL (ELEVATION VIEW)

ENEMY COUNTRY

WALL

DITCH

0 — 30
Feet

Wall consisted of a ditch and rampart of turf, about 37 miles long, 14-feet broad and about 10-feet high, with a grass-covered cobbled parapet, and a ditch 40-feet wide and 12-feet deep. There were forts at about half-mile intervals. Built under Antoninus Pius by Lollius Urbicus in 142; abandoned soon after 185.

Forth

Firth of

CREDIGONE
CARRIDEN

KINNEIL
INVERAVON

CRAMOND

INVERESK

Almond

0 — 5
Miles

KEY

▬▬▬ Extent of the Wall.

⋆ Main fort.

═══ Roman road.

ROMAN DEFENCE SYSTEMS - continued

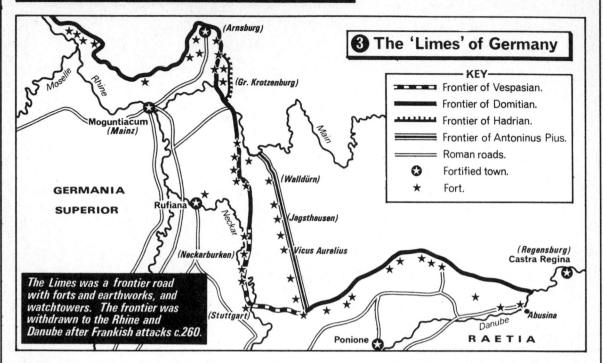

❸ The 'Limes' of Germany

KEY
- ▨▨▨▨ Frontier of Vespasian.
- ▬▬▬ Frontier of Domitian.
- ▥▥▥▥ Frontier of Hadrian.
- ≡≡≡ Frontier of Antoninus Pius.
- ══ Roman roads.
- ✪ Fortified town.
- ★ Fort.

(Arnsburg)
(Gr. Krotzenburg)
Moguntiacum (Mainz)
Moselle
Rhine
GERMANIA SUPERIOR
Rufiana
Neckar
Main
(Walldürn)
(Jagsthausen)
Vicus Aurelius
(Neckarburken)
(Stuttgart)
Ponione
(Regensburg) Castra Regina
Danube
Abusina
RAETIA

The Limes was a frontier road with forts and earthworks, and watchtowers. The frontier was withdrawn to the Rhine and Danube after Frankish attacks c.260.

❹ The 'Limes' of Syria

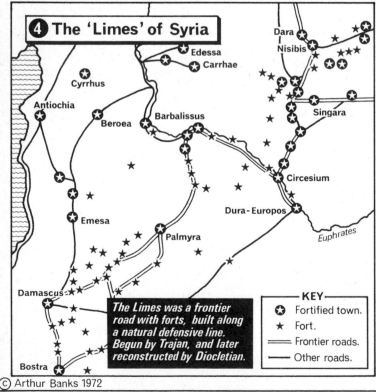

Dara
Nisibis
Edessa
Carrhae
Cyrrhus
Antiochia
Beroea
Barbalissus
Singara
Circesium
Emesa
Palmyra
Dura-Europos
Euphrates
Damascus
Bostra

The Limes was a frontier road with forts, built along a natural defensive line. Begun by Trajan, and later reconstructed by Diocletian.

KEY
- ✪ Fortified town.
- ★ Fort.
- ══ Frontier roads.
- ── Other roads.

© Arthur Banks 1972

❺ A Typical Roman Camp

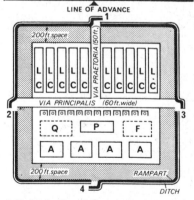

LINE OF ADVANCE
1
200 ft. space
VIA PRAETORIA (50 ft.)
L L L L L   L L L L L L
C C C C C   C C C C C C
VIA PRINCIPALIS (60 ft. wide)
2   3
Q   P   F
A   A   A   A
200 ft. space   RAMPART
4
DITCH

- **L** Legionaries' lines, in 8-men leather tents.
- **C** Centurions' tents, at end of men's lines.
- **P** Praetorium: Commander's tent and HQ area.
- **Q** Quaestorium: Quartermaster's area.
- **F** Forum: Market-place or parade-ground.
- **A** Lines of allied troops.
- ▣ Tents of officers (legionary tribunes & praefecti). allied

Area required for one legion's camp: about 20 acres.

1 *PORTA PRAETORIA.*
2 *PORTA PRINCIPALIS SINISTRA.*
3 *PORTA PRINCIPALIS DEXTRA.*
4 *PORTA DECUMANA.*

6 Camp Entrances

To prevent direct enemy assaults on the gates of camps, the following methods of construction were used:

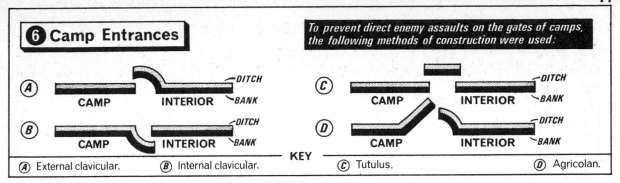

KEY

(A) External clavicular. (B) Internal clavicular. (C) Tutulus. (D) Agricolan.

7 The 'Limes' of Africa

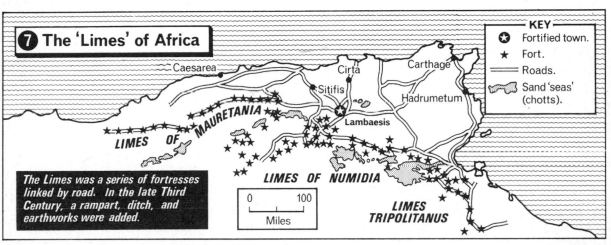

KEY
- Fortified town.
- Fort.
- Roads.
- Sand 'seas' (chotts).

The Limes was a series of fortresses linked by road. In the late Third Century, a rampart, ditch, and earthworks were added.

8 The 'Limes' of Dacia and the Danube

In 80, Domitian constructed fortifications north of the Danube, and in 106, Trajan established a Limes in Dacia. In 271, Aurelian abandoned Dacia to the barbarians, and the frontier fell back to the river Danube.

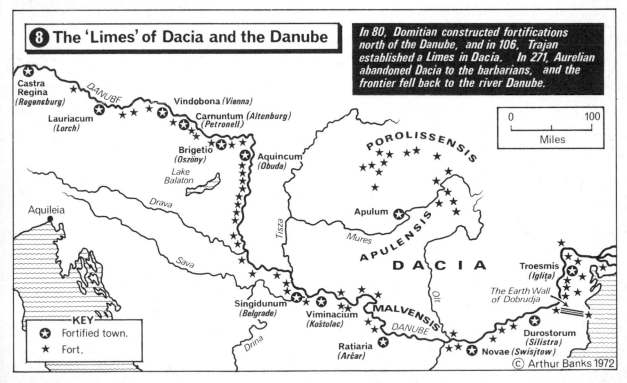

KEY
- Fortified town.
- Fort.

© Arthur Banks 1972

BASIC ORGANIZATION OF THE ROMAN LEGION

8 MEN = 1 TENT (CONTUBERNIUM)

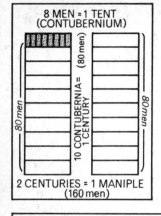

80 men

10 CONTUBERNIA = 1 CENTURY (80 men)

80 men

2 CENTURIES = 1 MANIPLE (160 men)

6 CENTURIES = 1 COHORT (480 men)

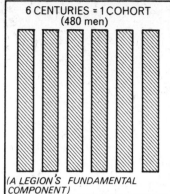

(A LEGION'S FUNDAMENTAL COMPONENT)

5	4	3	2
9	8	7	6

COHORT **1** HAD 5 DOUBLE CENTURIES

10

10 COHORTS = 1 LEGION (about 5,120 men)

ROMAN LEGION IN BATTLE ORDER

↑ *DIRECTION OF ADVANCE*

COHORTS

5	4	3	2		1

10	9	8	7	6

COHORTS

(Note: strongest cohorts shown ▨ *)*

Allies (auxilia) stationed where required.

Cavalry often positioned on the wings.

Least experienced soldiers in cohorts **7** and **9**. Cohort **1** could be a useful independent sub-unit.

(above arrangement according to Vegetius)

OFFICERS
1 Commander (legatus);   1 senior tribune;
1 Praefectus castrorum;   5 junior tribunes.

60 Centurions (senior one is _primipilus_).
120 horsemen per legion (scouts and despatch riders).

IMPORTANT ROMAN NAVAL BASES

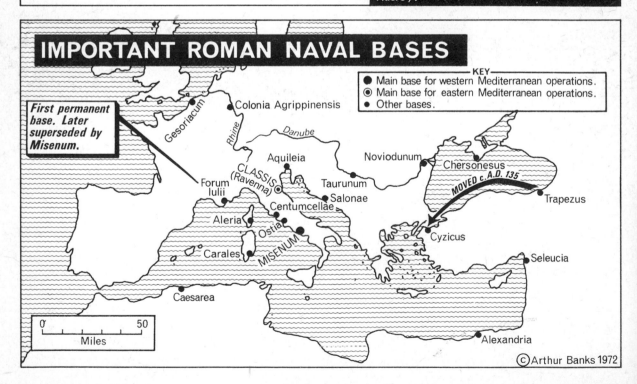

KEY
● Main base for western Mediterranean operations.
◉ Main base for eastern Mediterranean operations.
• Other bases.

First permanent base. Later superseded by Misenum.

Gesoriacum
Colonia Agrippinensis
Rhine
Danube
Aquileia
Noviodunum
Chersonesus
MOVED c. A.D. 135
CLASSIS (Ravenna)
Forum Iulii
Taurunum
Salonae
Centumcellae
Trapezus
Aleria
Ostia
MISENUM
Carales
Cyzicus
Seleucia
Caesarea
Alexandria

0   50
Miles

© Arthur Banks 1972

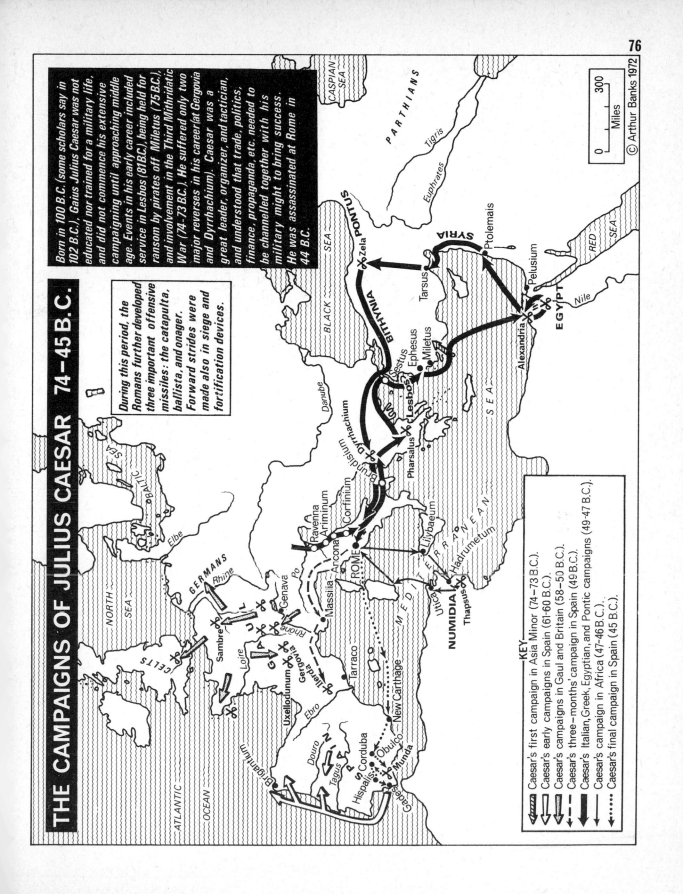

THE CAMPAIGNS OF JULIUS CAESAR 74–45 B.C.

Born in 100 B.C. (some scholars say in 102 B.C.), Gaius Julius Caesar was not educated nor trained for a military life, and did not commence his extensive campaigning until approaching middle age. Events in his early career included service in Lesbos (81 B.C.), being held for ransom by pirates off Miletus (75 B.C.), and involvement in the Third Mithridatic War (74–73 B.C.). He suffered only two major reverses in his career (at Gergovia and Dyrrhachium). Caesar was a great leader, organizer, and tactician, and understood that trade, politics, finance, propaganda, etc. needed to be channelled together with his military might to bring success. He was assassinated at Rome in 44 B.C.

During this period, the Romans further developed three important offensive missiles: the catapulta, ballista, and onager. Forward strides were made also in siege and fortification devices.

© Arthur Banks 1972

0   300
Miles

KEY

Caesar's first campaign in Asia Minor (74–73 B.C.).
Caesar's early campaigns in Spain (61–60 B.C.).
Caesar's campaigns in Gaul and Britain (58–50 B.C.).
Caesar's three–months' campaign in Spain (49 B.C.).
Caesar's Italian, Greek, Egyptian, and Pontic campaigns (49–47 B.C.).
Caesar's campaign in Africa (47–46 B.C.).
Caesar's final campaign in Spain (45 B.C.).

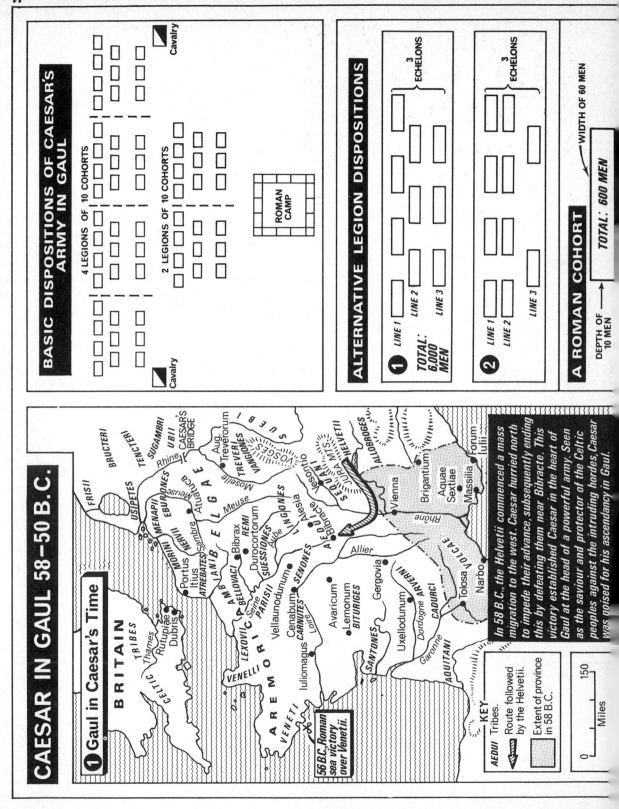

BASIC DISPOSITIONS OF CAESAR'S ARMY IN GAUL

Cavalry

4 LEGIONS OF 10 COHORTS

2 LEGIONS OF 10 COHORTS

ROMAN CAMP

Cavalry

ALTERNATIVE LEGION DISPOSITIONS

1 LINE 1 LINE 2 LINE 3 — 3 ECHELONS

TOTAL: 6,000 MEN

2 LINE 1 LINE 2 LINE 3 — 3 ECHELONS

A ROMAN COHORT

DEPTH OF 10 MEN

WIDTH OF 60 MEN

TOTAL: 600 MEN

CAESAR IN GAUL 58–50 B.C.

1 Gaul in Caesar's Time

BRITAIN

CELTIC TRIBES

Thames

Rutupiae
Dubris

Portus Itius
ATREBATES
MORINI
MENAPII
EBURONES
NERVII
AMBIANI
BELLOVACI
LEXOVII
Seine
PARISII
Vellaunodunum
Cenabum
CARNUTES
Loire
Iuliomagus
VENELLI
A R E M O R I C A
VENETI

FRISII
BRUCTERI
TENCTERI
USIPETES
SUGAMBRI
UBII
CAESAR'S BRIDGE
Rhine
Aug. Treverorum
TREVERI
VANGIONES
Moselle
Meuse
Sambre
Atuatuca
B E L G A E
Duocortorum
SUESSIONES
REMI
Bibrax
Aube
LINGONES
Alesia
Bibracte
AEDUI
Vesontio
S U E B I
VOSGES MTS.
SEQUANI
JURA MTS.
HELVETII
ALLOBROGES
Vienna
Rhône
Brigantium
Aquae Sextiae
Massilia
Forum Iulii
VOLCAE
Tolosa
Narbo
Garonne
AQUITANI
CADURCI
ARVERNI
Dordogne
Uxellodunum
SANTONES
Gergovia
BITURIGES
Lemonum
Avaricum
Allier

56 B.C. Roman sea victory over Veneti.

In 58 B.C., the Helvetii commenced a mass migration to the west. Caesar hurried north to impede their advance, subsequently ending this by defeating them near Bibracte. This victory established Caesar in the heart of Gaul at the head of a powerful army. Seen as the saviour and protector of the Celtic peoples against the intruding hordes, Caesar was poised for his ascendancy in Gaul.

KEY
AEDUI Tribes.
Route followed by the Helvetii.
Extent of province in 58 B.C.

0 — 150
Miles

③ Victory over the Belgae 57 B.C.

PHASE 1

ROMAN RIGHT IS HEAVILY ATTACKED

Sambre
ATREBATES
BELGIC CAMP
B
ROMAN CAMP
R
VIROMANDUI
NERVII

KEY
■ Roman legions (numbered).
▭ Roman cavalry.
→ Movements, in sequence.
▭ Belgic dispositions.
⇨ Belgic retreats.
♀♀♀ Woods.

PHASE 2

Sambre
B *Captured by Romans*.
R
NERVII
③ *arriving*

KEY
■ Roman legions (numbered).
R Roman camp.
B Belgic camp.
→ Movements, in sequence.
♀♀♀ Woods.

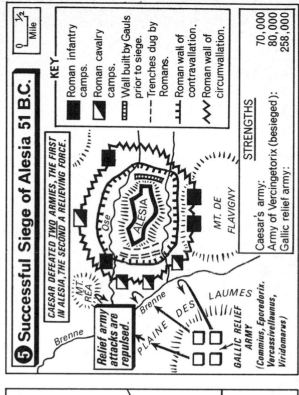

② Victory over the Helvetii 58 B.C.

↑ to Augustodunum

KEY
R Roman camp.
(H) Helvetian 'laager' (camp encircled by wagons).
▨ Roman first positions.
⊟ Helvetian first position.
■ Roman second position.
▲ Helvetian flank attack from 'laager'.
▭ Helvetian second position.
⇧ Helvetian advance from high ground.
⇦ Helvetian retreat into 'laager'.
⬛⬇ Final Roman attack.
• Toulon-sur-Arroux

Miles 0 1 2

Arroux
Armecy •
Montmort •
Auzon Brook
R
(H)

↑ to Bibracte

The loss of their camp compelled the Helvetii to surrender. Caesar ordered them to return home.

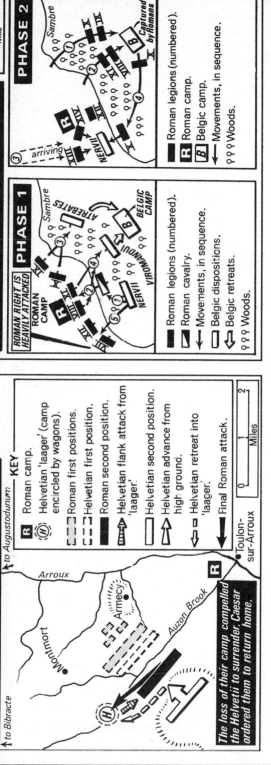

⑤ Successful Siege of Alesia 51 B.C.

CAESAR DEFEATED TWO ARMIES, THE FIRST IN ALESIA, THE SECOND A RELIEVING FORCE.

KEY
■ Roman infantry camps.
◨ Roman cavalry camps.
▭▭ Wall built by Gauls prior to siege.
--- Trenches dug by Romans.
╨╨ Roman wall of contravallation.
〰 Roman wall of circumvallation.

0 ½ Mile

Ose
ALESIA
MT. DE FLAVIGNY
MT. RÉA
Brenne
Brenne
PLAINE DES LAUMES

Relief army attacks are repulsed.

GALLIC RELIEF ARMY
(Commius, Eporedorix. Vercassivellaunus, Viridomarus)

STRENGTHS
Caesar's army: 70,000
Army of Vercingetorix (besieged): 80,000
Gallic relief army: 258,000

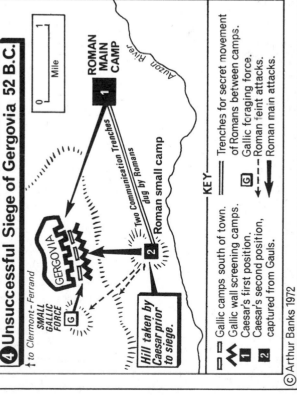

④ Unsuccessful Siege of Gergovia 52 B.C.

↑ to Clermont–Ferrand

0 1 Mile

ROMAN MAIN CAMP 1
Two Communication Trenches dug by Romans
2 Roman small camp
Auzon River
GERGOVIA
SMALL GALLIC FORCE
G

Hill taken by Caesar prior to siege.

KEY
⬚ Gallic camps south of town.
〰 Gallic wall screening camps.
1 Caesar's first position.
2 Caesar's second position, captured from Gauls.
═══ Trenches for secret movement of Romans between camps.
G Gallic forarging force.
⇠ Roman feint attacks.
⬇ Roman main attacks.

© Arthur Banks 1972

CAESAR VERSUS POMPEY

① Rival Strengths

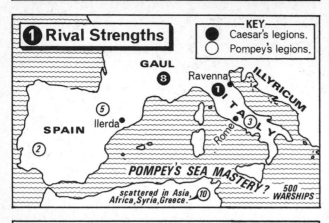

KEY
● Caesar's legions.
○ Pompey's legions.

GAUL ⑧
Ravenna ● ①
ILLYRICUM
⑤
ITALY
SPAIN
Ilerda ●
② Rome ③
POMPEY'S SEA MASTERY?
scattered in Asia, Africa, Syria, Greece. ⑩
500 WARSHIPS

③ Operations in Greece 48 B.C.

February, Antony lands with 12,800 troops.

Nymphaeum ● LISSUS
Pompey's base, besieged by Caesar. Pompey breaks siege.
Dyrrhachium
Heraclea
POMPEY Egnatian Way
Apollonia
ADRIATIC SEA
CAESAR POMPEY
CAESAR
Palaeste
THESSALY
January, Caesar lands with 25,000 troops.
Aeginium ● Larissa
Gomphi ●
Ambracia ● Pharsalus ✂
Corcyra
Both Caesar and Antony pierce Pompey's sea screen.

After Caesar crossed the Rubicon and moved to the south, Pompey gradually retired, eventually crossing the Adriatic to Dyrrhachium. Caesar saw that pursuit was unwise until Pompey's legions in Spain were immobilized. He accomplished this between May - July 49 B.C. near Ilerda. Returning to Italy, Caesar evaded Pompey's naval patrols and crossing to Greece, invested Dyrrhachium. Pompey broke the siege but his army was defeated at Pharsalus, 15,000 being killed and 24,000 being captured. He escaped to Egypt, only to be murdered.

② Ilerda Operations 49 B.C.

not to scale

CAESAR'S FIRST TASK WAS TO CONQUER POMPEY'S LEGIONS IN SPAIN.

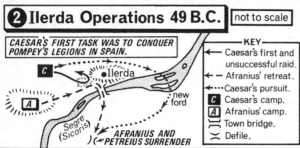

C Caesar's camp
Ilerda ●
A Afranius' camp
new ford
Segre (Sicoris)
AFRANIUS AND PETREIUS SURRENDER

KEY
→ Caesar's first and unsuccessful raid.
⇢ Afranius' retreat.
⋯⋯ Caesar's pursuit.
C Caesar's camp.
A Afranius' camp.
)(Town bridge.
⋈ Defile.

④ Pharsalus: the decisive battle 48 B.C.

PHASE 1

Note: Caesar's infantry lines equalled Pompey's in length but not in density.

Enipeus
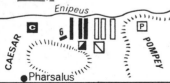
CAESAR C 6 P POMPEY
Pharsalus ●

CAESAR'S DISPOSITIONS

C Encampment.
◪ Cavalry (1,000).
▬ Infantry, in three lines (18,000).
🔳 Line of six cohorts in reserve (3,000).

POMPEY'S DISPOSITIONS

P Encampment.
◻ Cavalry (6,700).
▭ Infantry, in three lines (38,000).

PHASE 2

Enipeus
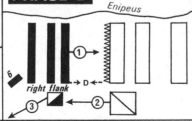
right flank
→ D ←

OPENING MOVES

Opening gesture: a champion from each side advances to fight a duel →D← (object, to inspire their respective front lines).

① Caesar's infantry moves forward, hurling 'pila' (javelins) at enemy.

② Pompey's cavalry charges Caesar's cavalry (numerically inferior).

③ Caesar's cavalry moves back, thus (apparently) exposing his right flank. Caesar's reserves 🔳 alerted.

PHASE 3

Enipeus
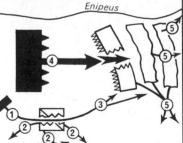

CAESAR'S ATTACKS

① Caesar's reserve line of six cohorts engages Pompey's cavalry who panic and flee ②.

③ Cohorts advance to attack left wing of Pompey's infantry, while Caesar's three lines close up to form one concerted unit ◤.

④ Caesar orders general advance.

⑤ Attacked from two directions at same time, Pompey's army flees.

CAESAR'S LATER CAMPAIGNS 48-45 B.C.

0   1
Mile

❶ Siege of Alexandria

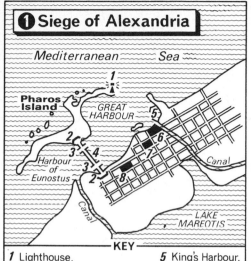

Mediterranean   Sea

Pharos Island

GREAT HARBOUR

1

5

6

2

3

4

3

2

8

Harbour of Eunostus

Canal

Canal

LAKE MAREOTIS

KEY

1 Lighthouse.
2 Redoubts.
3 Archways.
4 Mole.
5 King's Harbour.
6 Royal Palace.
7 Theatre.
8 Library.

Caesar pursued Pompey to Egypt where he was informed of the latter's death. At Alexandria, he was besieged by Ptolemy XII and former Pompey supporters. Mithridates of Pergamum marched to Caesar's aid and together they defeated Ptolemy at the Battle of the Nile (47 B.C.). Later, Caesar went on to fight successful campaigns against Pharnaces in Pontus, and against other units of Pompey's forces in Africa (main battle was at Thapsus). His final campaign was in Spain where he defeated the sons of Pompey, Gnaeus and Sextus, plus Labienus.

❷ Battle of Thapsus 46 B.C.

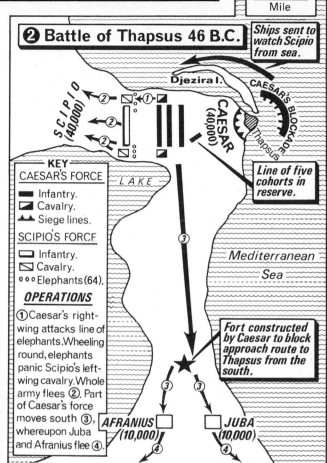

Ships sent to watch Scipio from sea.

Djezira I.

SCIPIO (40,000)

CAESAR (40,000)

CAESAR'S BLOCKADE

Thapsus

Line of five cohorts in reserve.

LAKE

Mediterranean Sea

Fort constructed by Caesar to block approach route to Thapsus from the south.

AFRANIUS (10,000)

JUBA (10,000)

KEY

CAESAR'S FORCE

▬ Infantry.
◨ Cavalry.
⛰ Siege lines.

SCIPIO'S FORCE

☐ Infantry.
◪ Cavalry.
ooo Elephants (64).

OPERATIONS

① Caesar's right-wing attacks line of elephants. Wheeling round, elephants panic Scipio's left-wing cavalry. Whole army flees ②. Part of Caesar's force moves south ③, whereupon Juba and Afranius flee ④.

❸ Caesar's Final Campaign in Spain 45 B.C.

0   10   20
Miles

Sextus with two legions.

Corduba

Guadalquivir

Obulco

1

2

9

Ategua

5

3

4

Soricaria

Ulia

Ucubi

Guadajoz

6

7

In minor battle, Gnaeus loses 500.

8

Carmo

Hispalis

Peinado

Ventipo

Genil

Munda

10

Gnaeus loses 30,000, Caesar loses 1,000.

to Gades

RIVAL FORCES

Caesar's strength: 40,000.
Gnaeus' strength: 50,000.

OPERATIONS

⬅ Caesar's movements.
⬅--- Gnaeus' movements.

① Caesar arrives at Obulco to learn that Ulia ✳ is besieged by Gnaeus. ② Caesar advances to Corduba to entice Gnaeus to aid brother Sextus. Ruse succeeds ③ but Gnaeus refuses a direct clash. Caesar moves to capture fresh grain at Ategua, following which Gnaeus advances ④ to Ucubi, and then to Soricaria. ⑤ Caesar pursues Gnaeus to Munda ⑥ & ⑦, wins victory, deals with Sextus ⑧, and ends tour ⑨ & ⑩. *(Gnaeus and Labienus are killed; Sextus escapes).*

© Arthur Banks 1972

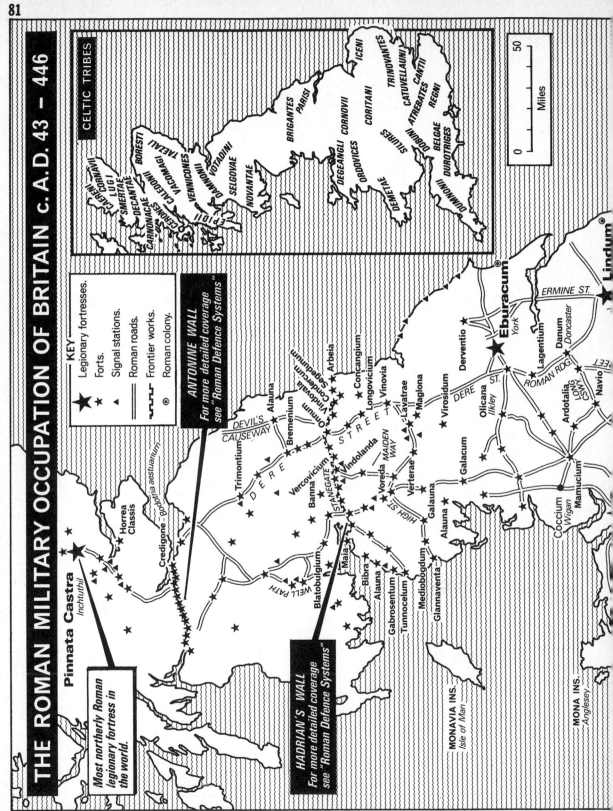

THE ROMAN MILITARY OCCUPATION OF BRITAIN c. A.D. 43 – 446

CELTIC TRIBES

ICENI
TRINOVANTES
PARISI
CANTII
BRIGANTES
CATUVELLAUNI
ATREBATES
REGNI
CORITANI
CORNOVII
BELGAE
DUROTRIGES
DEGEANGLI
ORDOVICES
SILURES
DUMNONII
DEMETAE
DOBUNNI
NOVANTAE
SELGOVAE
VOTADINI
DAMNONII
VENNICONES
EPIDII
VACOMAGI
CALEDONII
DECANTAE
TAEZALI
BORESTI
SMERTAE
LUGI
CORNAVII
CAERENI
GERONES
CARNONACAE

KEY

★ Legionary fortresses.
★ Forts.
▲ Signal stations.
══ Roman roads.
⊢⊣ Frontier works.
® Roman colony.

ANTONINE WALL
For more detailed coverage see "Roman Defence Systems"

HADRIAN'S WALL
For more detailed coverage see "Roman Defence Systems"

Pinnata Castra
Inchtuthil

Most northerly Roman legionary fortress in the world.

Horrea Classis

Credigone – Bodotria aestuarium

Trimontium

DEVIL'S CAUSEWAY

DERE STREET

Bremenium
Alauna
Ornum
Vindovala Condercum
Segedunum
Arbeia
Concangium
Longovicium
Vinovia
Lavatrae
Maglona
Virosidum
Derventio

Eburacum
York

ERMINE ST.

Lagentium
Danum
Doncaster

Vercovicium
Banna
Vindolanda
STANEGATE
Voreda
MAIDEN WAY
Verterae
Galauna
Galacum
Olicana
Ilkley
ROMAN RDG.
Ardotalia
LONG CSWY.
Navio

Maia
WELL PATH
Blatobulgium
Bibra
Alauna
Gabrosentum
Tunnocelum
Mediobogdum
Glannaventa
Alauna
HIGH ST.
Mediobogdum
Coccium
Wigan
Mamucium

Lindum ®

DERE ST.

MONA INS.
Anglesey

MONAVIA INS.
Isle of Man

Miles
0   50

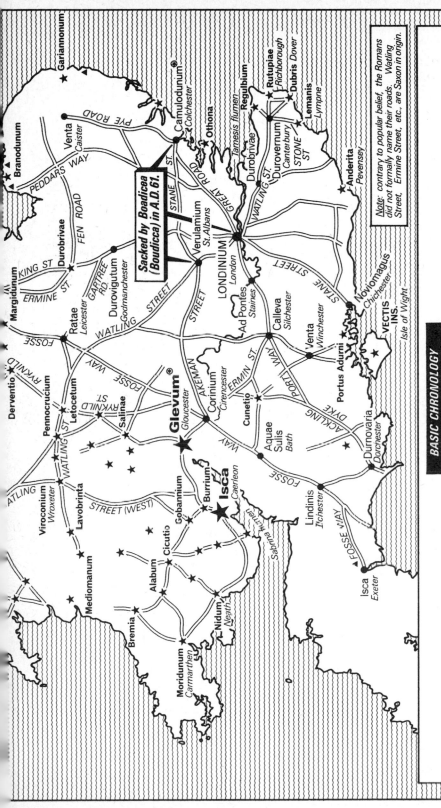

82

Sacked by Boadicea (Boudicca) in A.D. 61.

Note: contrary to popular belief, the Romans did not formally name their roads. Watling Street, Ermine Street, etc., are Saxon in origin.

BASIC CHRONOLOGY

1 55 - 54 B.C., Julius Caesar makes two expeditions to Britain from Gaul.

2 A.D. 43, Claudian invasion under Aulus Plautius. Campaigns in west, midlands, and east undertaken by four legions.

3 51, Caratacus is defeated in northern Wales.

4 61, Anglesey attacked. Revolt of Iceni (under Boudicca) suppressed.

5 71 - 74, Petillius Cerealis moves frontier north from Lincoln to York.

6 78, conquest of Anglesey and north Wales completed.

7 83 - 84, Agricola defeats Caledonians. Roman fleet circumnavigates Britain.

8 122, construction of Hadrian's Wall commenced.

9 139 - 142, construction of Antonine Wall; broken 180 - 184.

10 196 - 197, Hadrian's Wall destroyed by Maeatae.

11 205 - 208, Hadrian's Wall rebuilt by order of Septimius Severus.

12 211, Britain divided into two provinces.

13 288 - 296, Britain breaks away from Empire, under Carausius.

14 360 - 370, Picts, Scots, Attacotti, and Saxons raid Britain.

15 410, civitates instructed by Emperor Honorius to protect themselves.

16 446, final appeal of civitates to Aetius.

© Arthur Banks 1972

83

THE CAMPAIGN OF ACTIUM 31 B.C.

MAIN CAUSES OF THE WAR BETWEEN OCTAVIAN AND ANTONY

1. Antony's marriage to Cleopatra VII of Egypt following his divorce from Octavia, sister of Octavian. Antony's will, formally publicized by Octavian, left some Roman possessions to his children by Cleopatra. This was seen as a future threat to Rome.

2. Antony's naval and army concentrations in Greece. These were regarded in Rome as preliminaries to an invasion of Italy.

② Antony's Raids on Octavian's Camp

KEY
1 Antony's first camp.
2 Antony's second camp.
0 Octavian's camp.

GULF OF AMBRACIA

LONG WALLS BUILT BY OCTAVIAN TO PROTECT SEA ACCESS TO CAMP.

Gomarus

TROOPS BY SEA

APRIL
Actium
AUGUST
LAND ATTACK
CAVALRY RAID

Antony's plans to defeat Octavian by combined land and sea units ended in failure. Many of his troops deserted, including leaders.

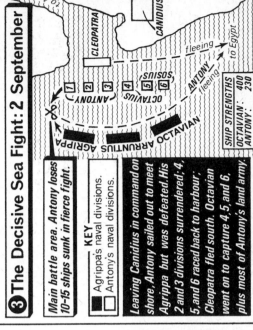

③ The Decisive Sea Fight: 2 September

to Actium
CANIDIUS
CLEOPATRA
fleeing to Egypt
ANTONY 1 2 3 4 5 SOSIUS 6
OCTAVIAN
ANTONY fleeing
ARRUNTIUS AGRIPPA OCTAVIAN

KEY
■ Agrippa's naval divisions.
□ Antony's naval divisions.

SHIP STRENGTHS
OCTAVIAN: 400
ANTONY: 230

Main battle area. Antony loses 10-15 ships sunk in fierce fight.

Leaving Canidius in command on shore, Antony sailed out to meet Agrippa but was defeated. His 2 and 3 divisions surrendered; 4, 5, and 6 raced back to harbour, Cleopatra fled south. Octavian went on to capture 4, 5, and 6, plus most of Antony's land army.

① Strengths, Dispositions, and Early Moves

Note: Agrippa was Octavian's naval commander.

RIVAL STRENGTHS

	OCTAVIAN	ANTONY
Troops:	92,000	Troops: 145,000
Ships:	400	Ships: 500

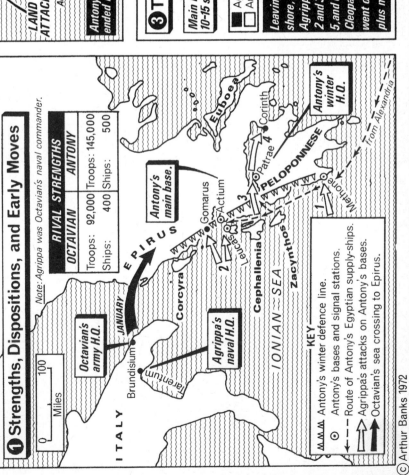

ITALY
Brundisium
Tarentum
Octavian's army H.Q.
JANUARY
Agrippa's naval H.Q.
IONIAN SEA
Corcyra
EPIRUS
Gomarus
Actium
Antony's main base.
Leucas
Cephallenia
Zacynthos
PELOPONNESE
Patrae
Corinth
Euboea
Antony's winter H.Q.
Methone
From Alexandria

KEY
⋀⋀⋀ Antony's winter defence line.
⊙ Antony's bases and signal stations.
--- Route of Antony's Egyptian supply-ships.
⇧ Agrippa's attacks on Antony's bases.
⬆ Octavian's sea crossing to Epirus.

0   100
Miles

© Arthur Banks 1972

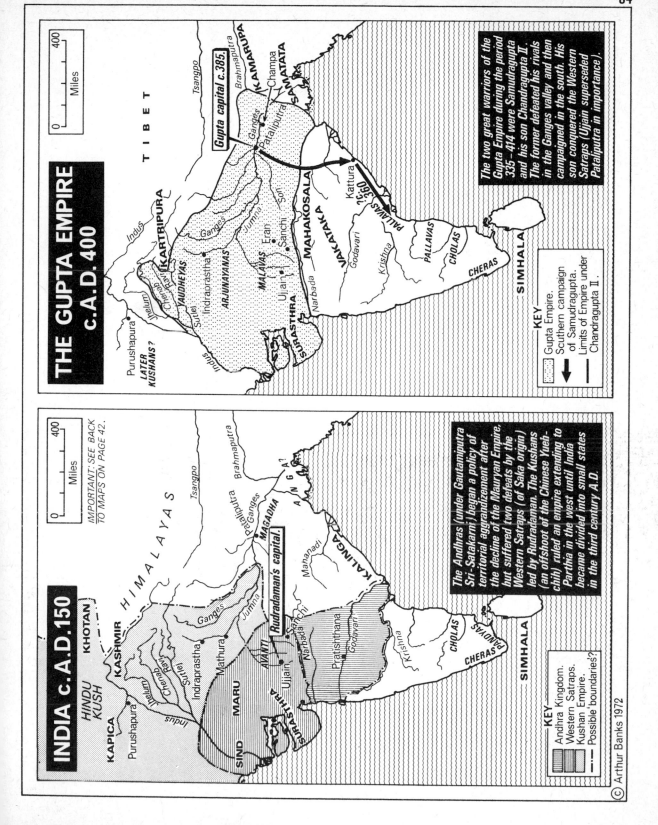

THE GUPTA EMPIRE c.A.D. 400

400
Miles
0

T I B E T

Gupta capital c.385.

KAMARUPA

SAMATATA

Champa

Brahmaputra

Ganges

Pataliputra

Tsangpo

KARTRIPURA

Indus

Chenab
Ravi
Sutlej
Jhelum

Ganges

Jumna
Son?
Sanchi
Eran

MALAVAS
Ujjain

ARJUNAYANAS

Indraprastha

YAUDHEYAS

Purushapura

LATER KUSHANS?

SURASTHA

Narbada

MAHAKOSALA

VAKATAKA

Kattura
c.360?

PALLAVAS

Godavari

Krishna

PALLAVAS

CHOLAS

CHERAS

SIMHALA

The two great warriors of the Gupta Empire during the period 335–414 were Samudragupta and his son Chandragupta II. The former defeated his rivals in the Ganges valley and then campaigned in the south. His son defeated the Western Satraps (Ujjain superseded Pataliputra in importance).

KEY
Gupta Empire.
Southern campaign of Samudragupta.
Limits of Empire under Chandragupta II.

INDIA c.A.D.150

400
Miles
0

IMPORTANT: SEE BACK TO MAPS ON PAGE 42.

KHOTAN

HINDU KUSH

KAPICA

KASHMIR

H I M A L A Y A S

Tsangpo

Brahmaputra

Pataliputra

Ganges

Rudradaman's capital.

MAGADHA

ANGA?

Purushapura

Indus

Jhelum
Chenab
Ravi
Sutlej

Ganges

Jumna

Mathura

Indraprastha

MARU

SIND

SURASTRA

AVANTI

Ujjain

Narbada

Sanchi

Pratisthana

MALWA

Mahanadi

KALINGA

Godavari

Krishna

CHOLAS

PANDYAS

CHERAS

SIMHALA

The Andhras (under Gautamiputra Sri-Satakarni) began a policy of territorial aggrandizement after the decline of the Mauryan Empire, but suffered two defeats by the Western Satraps (of Saka origin) led by Rudradaman. The Kushans (an offshoot of the Chinese Yueh-chih) ruled an empire extending to Parthia in the west until India became divided into small states in the third century A.D.

KEY
Andhra Kingdom.
Western Satraps.
Kushan Empire.
Possible 'boundaries'?

© Arthur Banks 1972

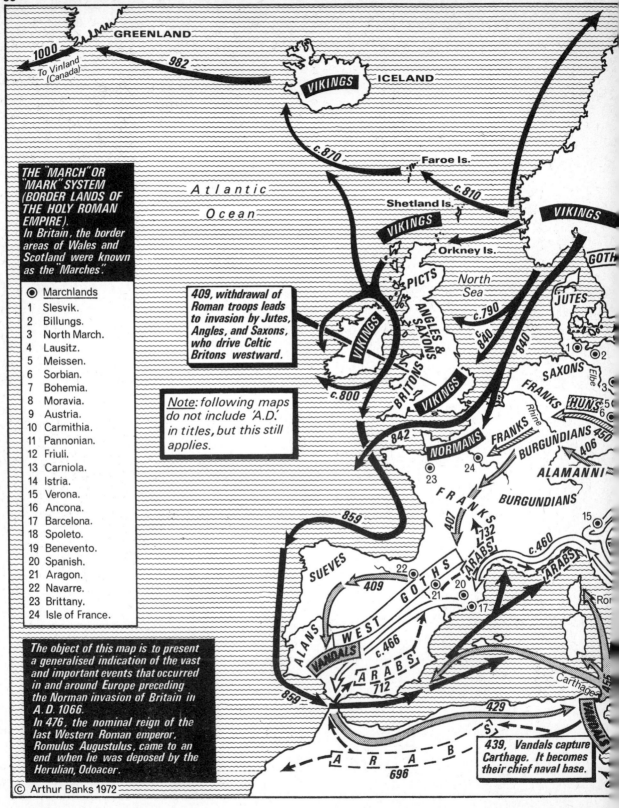

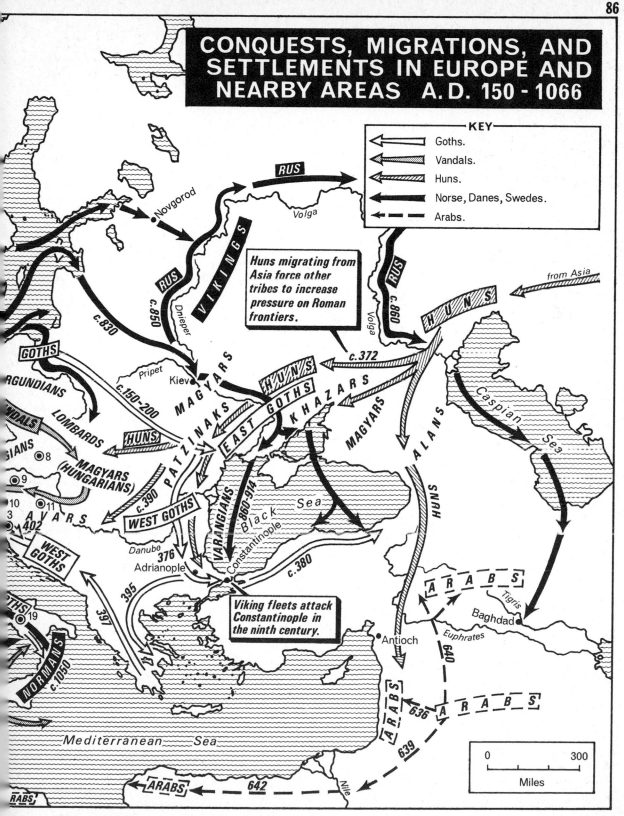

CONQUESTS, MIGRATIONS, AND SETTLEMENTS IN EUROPE AND NEARBY AREAS A.D. 150 - 1066

KEY

⇐	Goths.
⇐	Vandals.
⇐	Huns.
⟸	Norse, Danes, Swedes.
⇠	Arabs.

Huns migrating from Asia force other tribes to increase pressure on Roman frontiers.

Viking fleets attack Constantinople in the ninth century.

RUS

Novgorod

Volga

from Asia

RUS

VIKINGS

c. 850

Dnieper

RUS

c. 860

Volga

HUNS

c. 830

c. 372

GOTHS

Pripet

Kiev

MAGYARS

HUNS

EAST GOTHS

KHAZARS

Caspian Sea

BURGUNDIANS

c. 150-200

PATZINAKS

MAGYARS

ALANS

LOMBARDS

HUNS

MAGYARS (HUNGARIANS)

VARANGIANS

c. 860-914

Black Sea

HUNS

8

9

c. 390

WEST GOTHS

10

11

AVARS

402

Danube

376

Adrianople

Constantinople

c. 380

ARABS

Tigris

Baghdad

WEST GOTHS

395

397

Antioch

Euphrates

640

GOTHS

19

NORMANS

c. 1050

636

ARABS

ARABS

639

Mediterranean Sea

642

Nile

ARABS

0		300

Miles

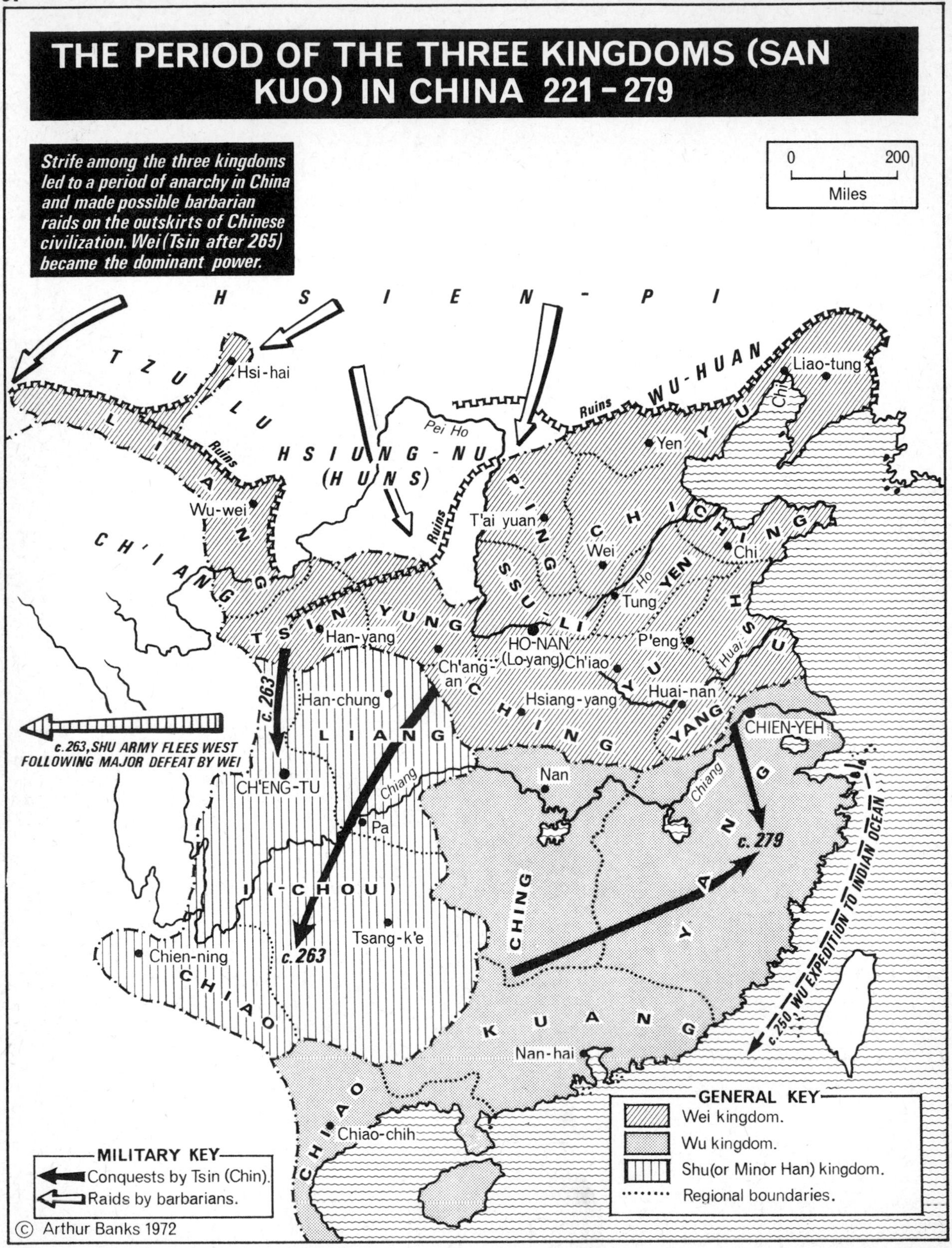

THE PERIOD OF THE THREE KINGDOMS (SAN KUO) IN CHINA 221 - 279

Strife among the three kingdoms led to a period of anarchy in China and made possible barbarian raids on the outskirts of Chinese civilization. Wei (Tsin after 265) became the dominant power.

0   200
Miles

H S I E N - P I

TZU LU
Hsi-hai
Ruins
WU-HUAN
Liao-tung
Chi
PEI HO
HSIUNG-NU (HUNS)
Yen
YU
Wu-wei
Ruins
T'ai yuan
PING
CHI
Wei
Chi
CH'IANG
SSU-LI
Ho
YEN
HSU
Tung
TSIN
YUNG
Han-yang
Ch'ang-an
HO-NAN (Lo-yang)
Ch'iao
YU
P'eng
Huai
Ch'ing
Han-chung
CHING
Hsiang-yang
Huai-nan
YANG
CHIEN-YEH

c.263, SHU ARMY FLEES WEST FOLLOWING MAJOR DEFEAT BY WEI

LIANG
Chiang
Nan
c. 263
CH'ENG-TU
Pa
YANG
c. 279
WU EXPEDITION TO INDIAN OCEAN
c.250,
(K-CHOU)
CHING
Tsang-k'e
c. 263
Chien-ning
CHIAO
KUANG
Nan-hai
CHIAO
Chiao-chih

GENERAL KEY
Wei kingdom.
Wu kingdom.
Shu (or Minor Han) kingdom.
Regional boundaries.

MILITARY KEY
Conquests by Tsin (Chin).
Raids by barbarians.

© Arthur Banks 1972

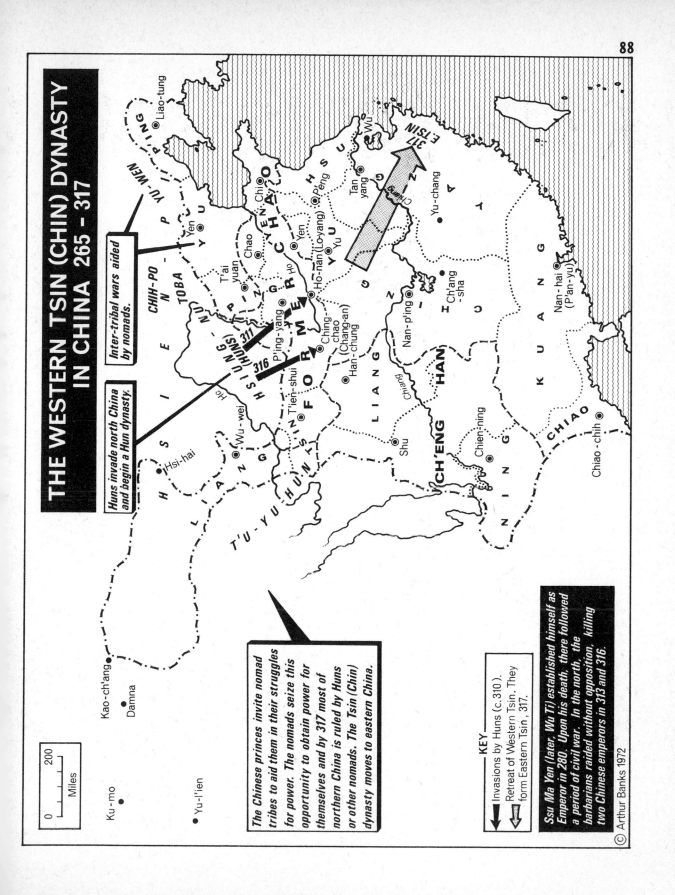

THE WESTERN TSIN (CHIN) DYNASTY IN CHINA 265 - 317

Inter-tribal wars aided by nomads.

Huns invade north China and begin a Hun dynasty.

The Chinese princes invite nomad tribes to aid them in their struggles for power. The nomads seize this opportunity to obtain power for themselves and by 317 most of northern China is ruled by Huns or other nomads. The Tsin (Chin) dynasty moves to eastern China.

— KEY —
Invasions by Huns (c.310).
Retreat of Western Tsin. They form Eastern Tsin, 317.

Ssu Ma Yen (later, Wu Ti) established himself as Emperor in 280. Upon his death, there followed a period of civil war. In the north, the barbarians raided without opposition, killing two Chinese emperors in 313 and 316.

© Arthur Banks 1972

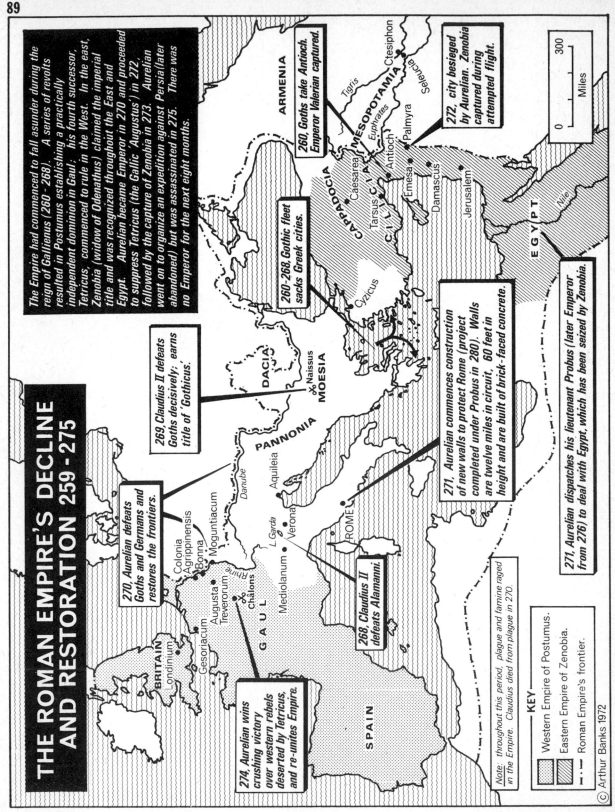

90

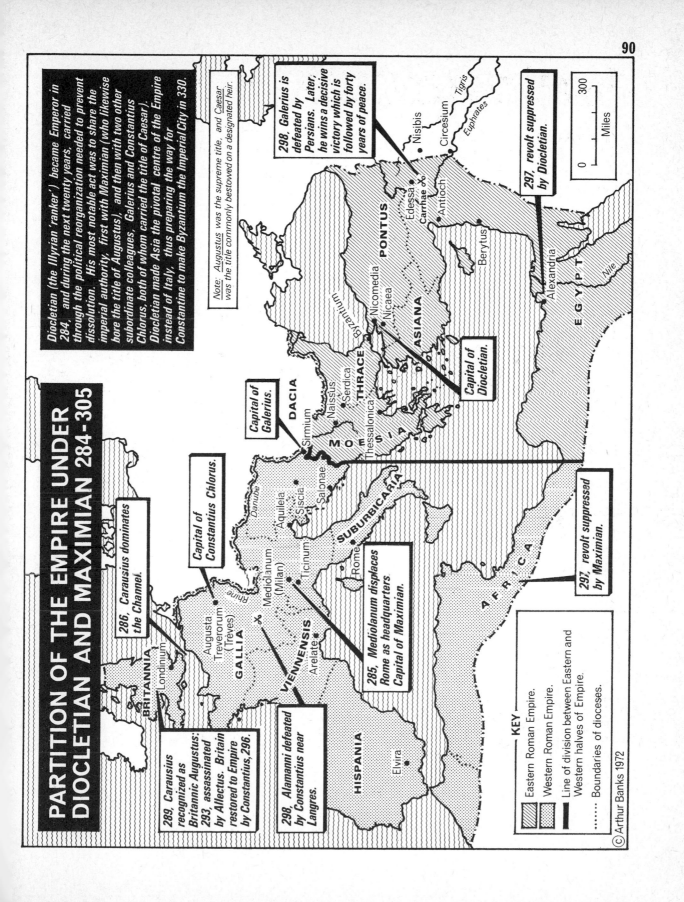

PARTITION OF THE EMPIRE UNDER DIOCLETIAN AND MAXIMIAN 284-305

Diocletian (the Illyrian 'ranker') became Emperor in 284, and during the next twenty years, carried through the political reorganization needed to prevent dissolution. His most notable act was to share the imperial authority, first with Maximian (who likewise bore the title of Augustus), and then with two other subordinate colleagues, Galerius and Constantius Chlorus, both of whom carried the title of Caesar. Diocletian made Asia the pivotal centre of the Empire instead of Italy, thus preparing the way for Constantine to make Byzantium the Imperial City in 330.

Note: Augustus was the supreme title, and Caesar was the title commonly bestowed on a designated heir.

298. Galerius is defeated by Persians. Later, he wins a decisive victory which is followed by forty years of peace.

297, revolt suppressed by Diocletian.

Capital of Diocletian.

Capital of Galerius.

286, Carausius dominates the Channel.

289, Carausius recognized as Britannic Augustus: 293, assassinated by Allectus. Britain restored to Empire by Constantius, 296.

298, Alamanni defeated by Constantius near Langres.

Capital of Constantius Chlorus.

285, Mediolanum displaces Rome as headquarters. Capital of Maximian.

297, revolt suppressed by Maximian.

KEY
Eastern Roman Empire.
Western Roman Empire.
Line of division between Eastern and Western halves of Empire.
Boundaries of dioceses.

© Arthur Banks 1972

NORTHERN CHINA IN CONFLICT 317-534

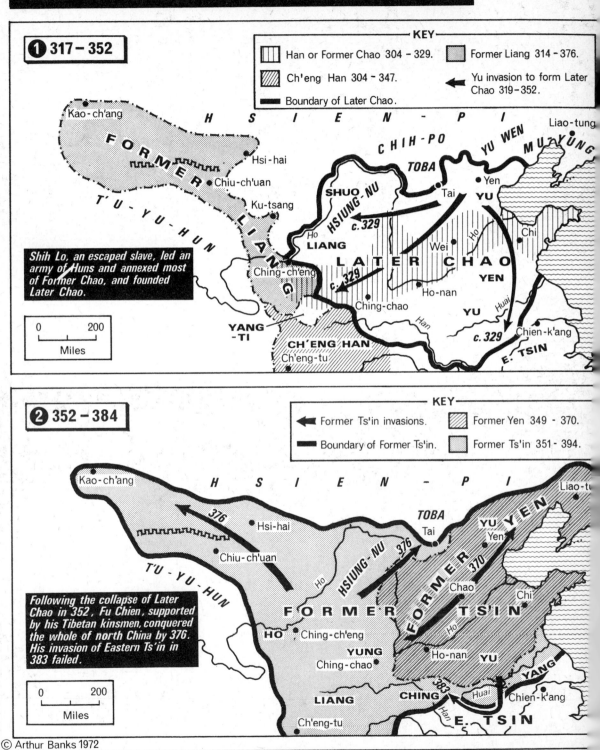

1 317 – 352

KEY

⊞ Han or Former Chao 304 – 329.	▓ Former Liang 314 – 376.
▨ Ch'eng Han 304 – 347.	← Yu invasion to form Later Chao 319 – 352.
▬ Boundary of Later Chao.	

Kao-ch'ang

H S I E N – P I

Liao-tung

F O R M E R   L I A N G

CHIH-PO

TOBA

YU WEN

MU YUNG

Hsi-hai

Chiu-ch'uan

Yen

Tai

YU

T'U-YU-HUN

Ku-tsang

SHUO

HSIUNG-NU

c. 329

Ho

LIANG

Wei

Ho

Chi

Ching-ch'eng

L A T E R   C H A O

c. 329

YEN

Shih Lo, an escaped slave, led an army of Huns and annexed most of Former Chao, and founded Later Chao.

Ho-nan

YU

Huai

Chien-k'ang

YANG -TI

CH'ENG HAN

Ching-chao

c. 329

E. TSIN

0   200
Miles

Ch'eng-tu

---

2 352 – 384

KEY

← Former Ts'in invasions.	▨ Former Yen 349 - 370.
▬ Boundary of Former Ts'in.	▒ Former Ts'in 351 - 394.

Kao-ch'ang

H S I E N – P I

Liao-tu

Hsi-hai

376

TOBA

Tai

YU YEN

Yen

T'U-YU-HUN

Chiu-ch'uan

HSIUNG-NU

376

376

F O R M E R   Y E N

370

Ho

Chao

Chi

Following the collapse of Later Chao in 352, Fu Chien, supported by his Tibetan kinsmen, conquered the whole of north China by 376. His invasion of Eastern Ts'in in 383 failed.

F O R M E R   T S ' I N

HO

Ching-ch'eng

YUNG

Ho-nan

YU

YANG

Ching-chao

383

CHING

Huai

Chien-k'ang

0   200
Miles

LIANG

Han

Ch'eng-tu

E.   T S I N

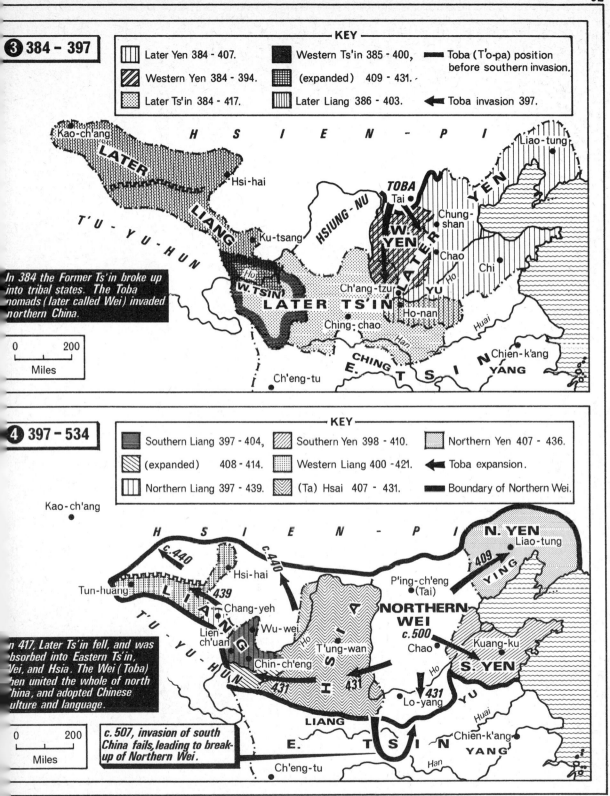

3 **384 – 397**

— KEY —

⊞ Later Yen 384 - 407.	■ Western Ts'in 385 - 400,
⊠ Western Yen 384 - 394.	▦ (expanded) 409 - 431.
⊡ Later Ts'in 384 - 417.	▥ Later Liang 386 - 403.

━ Toba (T'o-pa) position before southern invasion.

◄ Toba invasion 397.

H S I E N - P I

Kao-ch'ang

LATER

Hsi-hai

LIANG

T' U - Y U - H U N

Ku-tsang

HSIUNG-NU

Liao-tung

YEN

TOBA

Tai

Chung-shan

W. YEN

LATER

Chao

Chi

W. TSIN

Ho

YU

Ch'ang-tzu

LATER TS'IN

Ho-nan

Ching-chao

Han

Huai

Chien-k'ang

CHING

YANG

E. TS'IN

Ch'eng-tu

In 384 the Former Ts'in broke up into tribal states. The Toba nomads (later called Wei) invaded northern China.

0   200

Miles

---

4 **397 – 534**

— KEY —

▤ Southern Liang 397 - 404,	⊠ Southern Yen 398 - 410.	⊡ Northern Yen 407 - 436.
⊠ (expanded) 408 - 414.	⊡ Western Liang 400 - 421.	◄ Toba expansion.
⊞ Northern Liang 397 - 439.	⊠ (Ta) Hsai 407 - 431.	━ Boundary of Northern Wei.

Kao-ch'ang

H S I E N - P I

N. YEN

c.440

c.440

Hsi-hai

409

Liao-tung

Tun-huang

LIANG

439

YING

P'ing-ch'eng (Tai)

Chang-yeh

NORTHERN WEI c.500

Wu-wei

Lien-ch'uan

HSIA

T'ung-wan

Chao

Kuang-ku

T' U - Y U - H U N

Chin-ch'eng

431

431

S. YEN

Ho

Lo-yang

431

YU

In 417, Later Ts'in fell, and was absorbed into Eastern Ts'in, Wei, and Hsia. The Wei (Toba) then united the whole of north China, and adopted Chinese culture and language.

LIANG

E. TS'IN

Huai

Chien-k'ang

YANG

c. 507, invasion of south China fails, leading to break-up of Northern Wei.

Han

Ch'eng-tu

0   200

Miles

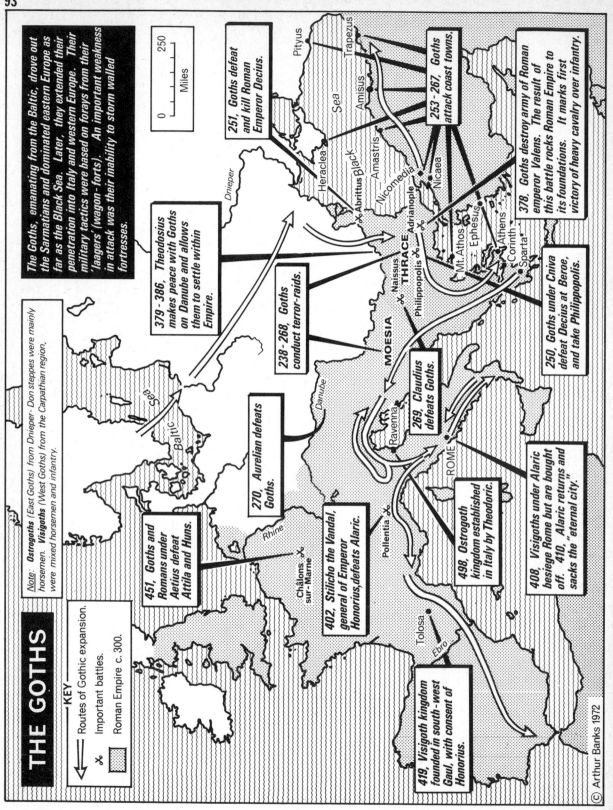

THE GOTHS

KEY

— Routes of Gothic expansion.

✗ Important battles.

▒ Roman Empire c. 300.

Note: **Ostrogoths** (East Goths) from Dnieper-Don steppes were mainly horsemen. **Visigoths** (West Goths) from the Carpathian region, were mixed horsemen and infantry.

The Goths, emanating from the Baltic, drove out the Sarmatians and dominated eastern Europe as far as the Black Sea. Later, they extended their penetration into Italy and western Europe. Their military tactics were based on forays from their 'laagers' (wagon - forts). An important weakness in attack was their inability to storm walled fortresses.

250, Goths under Cniva defeat Decius at Beroe, and take Philippopolis.

251, Goths defeat and kill Roman Emperor Decius.

253 - 267, Goths attack coast towns.

378, Goths destroy army of Roman emperor Valens. The result of this battle rocks Roman Empire to its foundations. It marks first victory of heavy cavalry over infantry.

379 - 386, Theodosius makes peace with Goths on Danube and allows them to settle within Empire.

238 - 268, Goths conduct terror-raids.

269, Claudius defeats Goths.

270, Aurelian defeats Goths.

451, Goths and Romans under Aetius defeat Attila and Huns.

402, Stilicho the Vandal, general of Emperor Honorius, defeats Alaric.

498, Ostrogoth kingdom established in Italy by Theodoric.

408, Visigoths under Alaric besiege Rome but are bought off. 410, Alaric returns and sacks the "eternal city."

419, Visigoth kingdom founded in south-west Gaul, with consent of Honorius.

Pityus

Trapezus

Amisus

Black Sea

Amastris

Heraclea

Abrittus ✗

Nicomedia

Nicaea

Ephesus

Mt. Athos

Athens

Corinth

Sparta

Adrianople ✗

Naissus ✗

THRACE

MOESIA

Philippopolis ✗

Ravenna

Dnieper

Danube

ROME

Pollentia ✗

Châlons-sur-Marne ✗

Rhine

Baltic Sea

Tolosa

Ebro

250 Miles

0

© Arthur Banks 1972

THE HUNNISH ASSAULT ON EUROPE
c. 400 – 455

KEY

THE ROMAN EMPIRE c. 400

- Prefecture of Italy.
- Prefecture of Gaul.
- Prefecture of Illyricum.
- Prefecture of the East.

→ Main advance of the Huns, with dates.

⊙ Cities attacked by the Huns.

1 Arras.	16 Milan.
2 Tournai.	17 Pavia.
3 Amiens.	18 Verona.
4 Cambrai.	19 Vicenza.
5 Cologne.	20 Patavium.
6 Trêves.	21 Altinum.
7 Mainz.	22 Aquileia.
8 Strasbourg.	23 Sirmium.
9 Rheims.	24 Singidunum.
10 Châlons.	25 Viminacium.
11 Metz.	26 Ratiaria.
12 Paris.	27 Naissus.
13 Orléans.	28 Sardica.
14 Bergamo.	29 Philippopolis.
15 Brescia.	30 Constantinople.

BATTLE OF CHÂLONS JUNE 451

AETIUS

ROMANS & FRANKS
ALANS
THEODORIC & VISIGOTHS
① ② ③

GERMANS
HUNS
OSTROGOTHS
ATTILA

Marne
Châlons

Wagon 'laager' (camp)

Strengths and casualties are unknown but are generally accepted as enormous. Had Attila triumphed, Europe would have been ruled by peoples of Asian stock.

372

454, Huns defeated and dispersed by German coalition at Battle of Nedao.

c. 376-400

376

436-450

c. 452

453

451, important Hunnish defeat, by Romans and Goths.

451, Huns fail to overrun this important city.

The most important warrior - leader of the Huns was Attila (died, 453).

Roman naval base.

Caspian Sea
Tigris
Euphrates
0 200 Miles

Black Sea
Heraclea
Adrianople
PONTUS
ASIA
EGYPT

Rhine
Danube
BRITAIN
GAUL
ITALY
ROME
SPAIN
AFRICA
Ebro

© Arthur Banks 1972

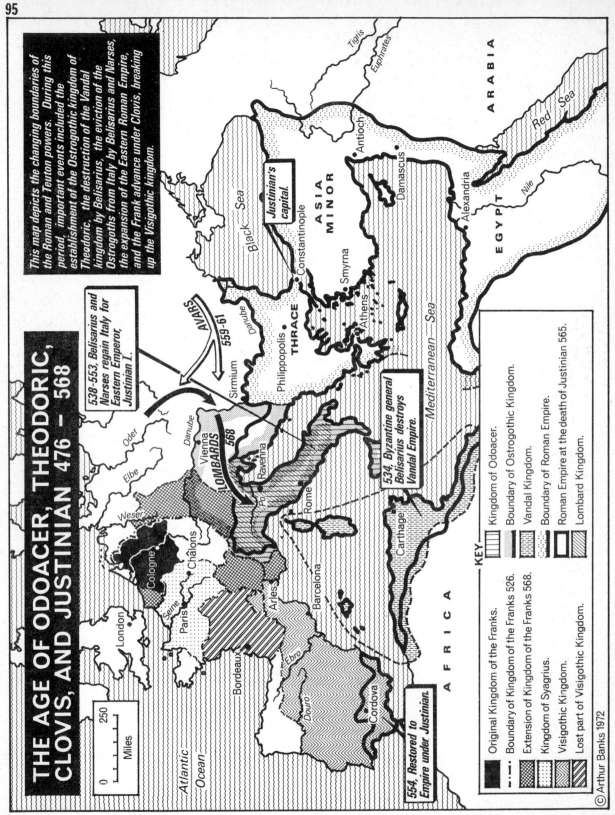

THE AGE OF ODOACER, THEODORIC, CLOVIS, AND JUSTINIAN 476 – 568

This map depicts the changing boundaries of the Roman and Teuton powers. During this period, important events included the establishment of the Ostrogothic kingdom of Theodoric, the destruction of the Vandal kingdom by Belisarius, the eviction of the Ostrogoths from Italy by Belisarius and Narses, the expansion of the Eastern Roman Empire, and the Frank advance under Clovis, breaking up the Visigothic kingdom.

Justinian's capital.

538-553. Belisarius and Narses regain Italy for Eastern Emperor, Justinian I.

AVARS 559-61

534. Byzantine general Belisarius destroys Vandal Empire.

554. Restored to Empire under Justinian.

0 250
Miles

KEY

- Original Kingdom of the Franks.
- Boundary of Kingdom of the Franks 526.
- Extension of Kingdom of the Franks 568.
- Kingdom of Syagrius.
- Visigothic Kingdom.
- Lost part of Visigothic Kingdom.

- Kingdom of Odoacer.
- Boundary of Ostrogothic Kingdom.
- Vandal Kingdom.
- Boundary of Roman Empire.
- Roman Empire at the death of Justinian 565.
- Lombard Kingdom.

ARABIA
Red Sea
Tigris
Euphrates
ASIA MINOR
Antioch
Damascus
Alexandria
Nile
EGYPT
Black Sea
Constantinople
Smyrna
Athens
THRACE
Philippopolis
Danube
Sirmium
Mediterranean Sea
AFRICA
Carthage
Rome
Ravenna
Po
LOMBARDS 568
Vienna
Danube
Oder
Elbe
Weser
Cologne
Châlons
Paris
Seine
London
Atlantic Ocean
Bordeaux
Arles
Barcelona
Ebro
Douro
Cordova

© Arthur Banks 1972

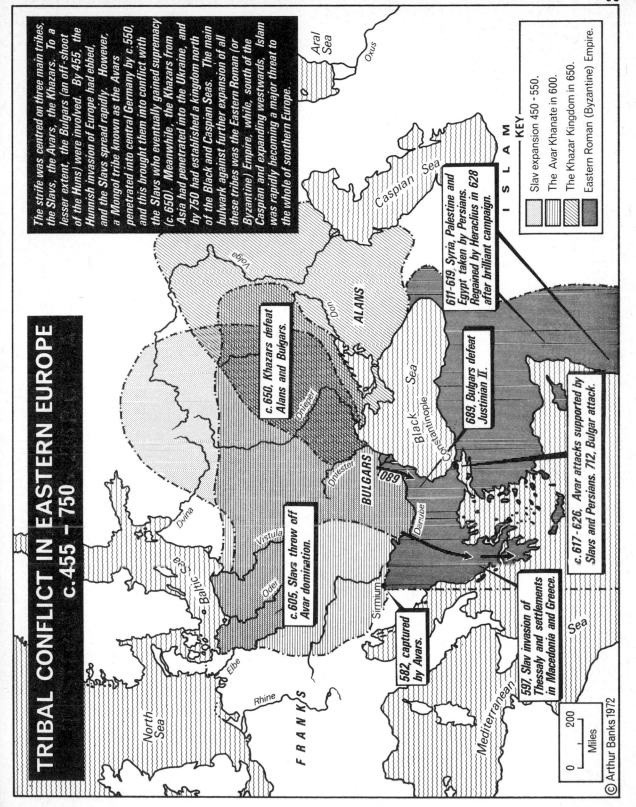

TRIBAL CONFLICT IN EASTERN EUROPE c.455 – 750

The strife was centred on three main tribes, the Slavs, the Avars, the Khazars. To a lesser extent, the Bulgars (an off-shoot of the Huns) were involved. By 455, the Hunnish invasion of Europe had ebbed, and the Slavs spread rapidly. However, a Mongol tribe known as the Avars penetrated into central Germany by c.550, and this brought them into conflict with the Slavs who eventually gained supremacy (c.650). Meanwhile, the Khazars from Asia had penetrated into the Ukraine, and by 750 had established a kingdom north of the Black and Caspian Seas. The main bulwark against further expansion of all these tribes was the Eastern Roman (or Byzantine) Empire, while, south of the Caspian and expanding westwards, Islam was rapidly becoming a major threat to the whole of southern Europe.

KEY

- Slav expansion 450 - 550.
- The Avar Khanate in 600.
- The Khazar Kingdom in 650.
- Eastern Roman (Byzantine) Empire.

c.650, Khazars defeat Alans and Bulgars.

611-619, Syria, Palestine and Egypt taken by Persians. Regained by Heraclius in 628 after brilliant campaign.

689, Bulgars defeat Justinian II.

c.617-626, Avar attacks supported by Slavs and Persians. 712, Bulgar attack.

c.605, Slavs throw off Avar domination.

582, captured by Avars.

597, Slav invasion of Thessaly and settlements in Macedonia and Greece.

Aral Sea

Oxus

Caspian Sea

Volga

ALANS

Don

Dnieper

Black Sea

Constantinople

Dniester

BULGARS

689

Danube

Sirmium

Vistula

Oder

Dvina

Baltic Sea

Elbe

Rhine

North Sea

FRANKS

Mediterranean Sea

ISLAM

200

0

Miles

© Arthur Banks 1972

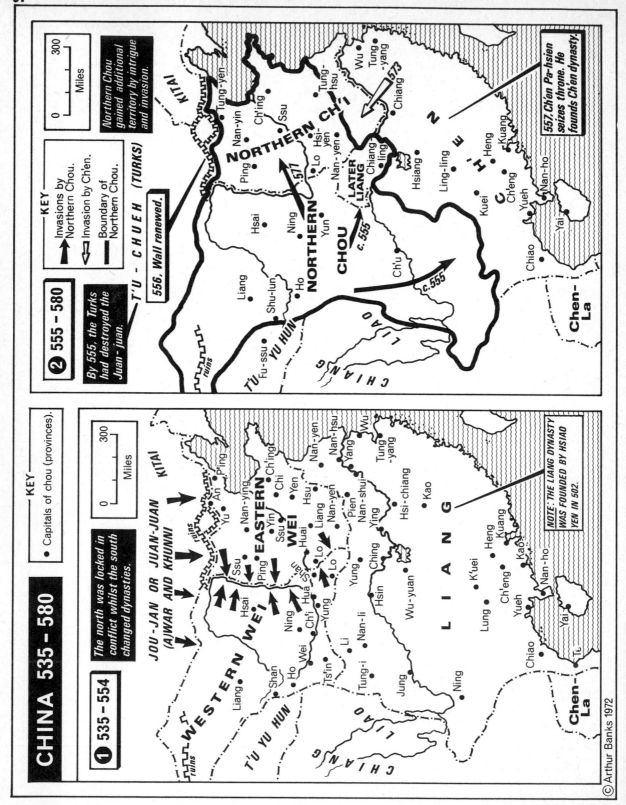

CHINA 535 – 580

KEY
- Capitals of chou (provinces).

① 535 – 554

The north was locked in conflict whilst the south changed dynasties.

JOU-JAN OR JUAN-JUAN (A)WAR AND KHUNNI

KITAI

0 — 300 Miles

WESTERN WEI

EASTERN WEI

An-ping · Nan-ying · Ch'ing · Nan-yen · Nan-hsu · Wu
Yu · Ssu · Chi · Yen · Yang · Tung-yang
Nan-ying · Yin · Hsu · Liang · Nan-yen
Ping · Huai · Lo · Pien · Nan-shui · Kao
Hsai · Hua · Li · Lo · Ying · Hsi-chiang
Ning · Ch'i · Yung · Ching
Shan · Ho · Wei · Ts'in · Li · Nan-li · Hsin · Wu-yuan
Liang · Jung · Tung-i · Ning

LIANG

Lung · Heng · Kuang · Ch'eng · Yueh · Kao
K'uei · Nan-ho

NOTE: THE LIANG DYNASTY WAS FOUNDED BY HSIAO YEN IN 502.

Chiao · Yai · Tt

Chen-La

T'U YU HUN

CHIANG

LIAO

© Arthur Banks 1972

KEY
- Invasions by Northern Chou.
- Invasion by Ch'en.
- Boundary of Northern Chou.

② 555 – 580

By 555, the Turks had destroyed the Juan-juan.

T'U - CHUEH (TURKS)

556. Wall renewed.

0 — 300 Miles

KITAI

NORTHERN CH'I

Tung-yen · Wu · Tung-yang
Nan-yin · Ch'ing · Ssu · Tung-hsu · Chiang · 573
Ping · Ning · Lo · Hsi-yen · Kuang · Heng
Hsai · Yun · Nan-yen · Chiang-ling · Hsiang · Ling-ling
NORTHERN CHOU · LATER LIANG · Ch'eng · Nan-ho
c.555 · CH'EN · Kuei · Yueh
Liang · Shu-lun · Ho · Chu · c.555 · Yai

577

Northern Chou gained additional territory by intrigue and invasion.

557. Ch'en Pa-hsien seizes throne. He founds Ch'en dynasty.

T'U YU HUN · Fu-ssu · ruins

CHIANG · LIAO

Chiao · Chen-La

THE SUI SUPREMACY IN CHINA

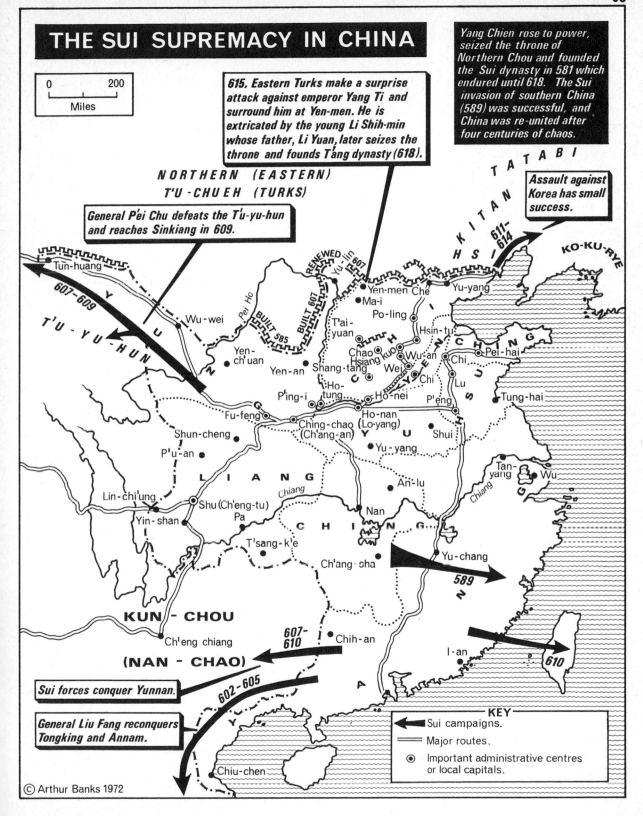

0   200
Miles

615, Eastern Turks make a surprise attack against emperor Yang Ti and surround him at Yen-men. He is extricated by the young Li Shih-min whose father, Li Yuan, later seizes the throne and founds T'ang dynasty (618).

Yang Chien rose to power, seized the throne of Northern Chou and founded the Sui dynasty in 581 which endured until 618. The Sui invasion of southern China (589) was successful, and China was re-united after four centuries of chaos.

Assault against Korea has small success.

NORTHERN (EASTERN)
T'U-CHUEH (TURKS)

General P'ei Chu defeats the T'u-yu-hun and reaches Sinkiang in 609.

KITAN

HSI

611-614

KO-KU-RYE

TATABI

RENEWED 607
Yu-lin 607

Tun-huang

607-609

Y U

Pei Ho

BUILT 585

BUILT 607

Yen-men Che

Yu-yang

T'U-YU-HUN

Wu-wei

Yen-ch'uan

Yen-an

Shang-tang

Ma-i
Po-ling
T'ai-yuan

CH'I
Chao Kuo
Hsiang
Wei
Ho-tung

Hsin-tu
Wu-an
Chi
Lu

Pei-hai

Tung-hai

YEN

HSU

Ho-nei
P'ing-i

P'eng

Fu-feng

Ching-chao
(Ch'ang-an)

Ho-nan
(Lo-yang)

Yu-yang

Shui

Shun-cheng

YU

Tan-yang
Wu

P'u-an

An-lu

Lin-chi'ung

L I A N G

Chiang

Chiang

Shu (Ch'eng-tu)

Yin-shan

Pa

Nan

CHING

T'sang-k'e

Ch'ang-sha

Yu-chang

589
N

KUN - CHOU

Ch'eng chiang

607-610

Chih-an

I-an

610

Sui forces conquer Yunnan.

(NAN - CHAO)

602-605

Y

A

General Liu Fang reconquers Tongking and Annam.

Chiu-chen

KEY

⬅	Sui campaigns.
═	Major routes.
◉	Important administrative centres or local capitals.

© Arthur Banks 1972

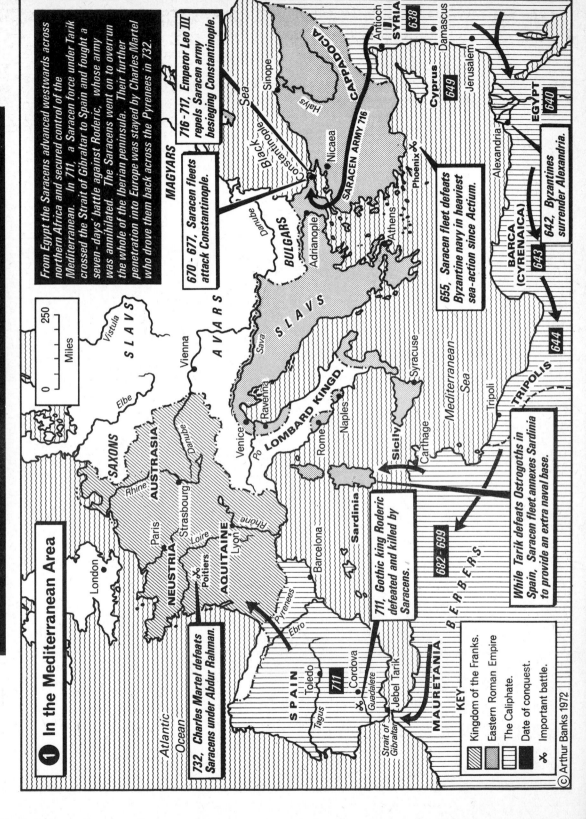

② In Asia

Islam absorbed Syria, Egypt, and Armenia. Following their victory at Nehavend in 642, the Saracens went on to gain the whole of Persia, afterwards extending their dominions to the river Indus.

711

652

711

712, King of Sind defeated and killed by Mohammed bin Kasim.

644

(SASSANID EMPIRE)

KHORASAN

PERSIA

MEDIA

FARS

KERMAN

MEKRAN

S I N D

PUNJAB

Kashgar

Samarkand

Bokhara

Balkh

Kabul

Multan

Herat

Merv

Oxus

Jaxartes

Indus

Aral Sea

Arabian Sea

693, Justinian II defeated by Saracens, who seize Armenia.

693

Caspian Sea

ARMENIA

Tiflis

Istahan

Nehavend

Baghdad

Tigris

Euphrates

Kadesia

MESOPOTAMIA

Edessa

Antioch

Siffin

Damascus

Yermak

S Y R I A

Jerusalem

Persian Gulf

Basra

642, Omar defeats Yezdigird. Omar's force of 30,000 troops shatters Persian army of 150,000.

637, Saracens defeat Persian army under Rustom.

638

c.570, birth of Mohammed.

632

A R A B I A

Mecca

Medina

Red Sea

Nile

EGYPT

640

Alexandria

Black Sea

Constantinople

Sinope

Sebastopolis

CAPPADOCIA

Halys

Nicaea

SARACEN ARMY 716

659, indecisive 2-day civil war between Ali and Muawiya.

Saracen victories over Byzantines (634) and Persians (636).

250

0

Miles

KEY

Eastern Roman Empire.

The Caliphate.

Date of conquest.

Important battle.

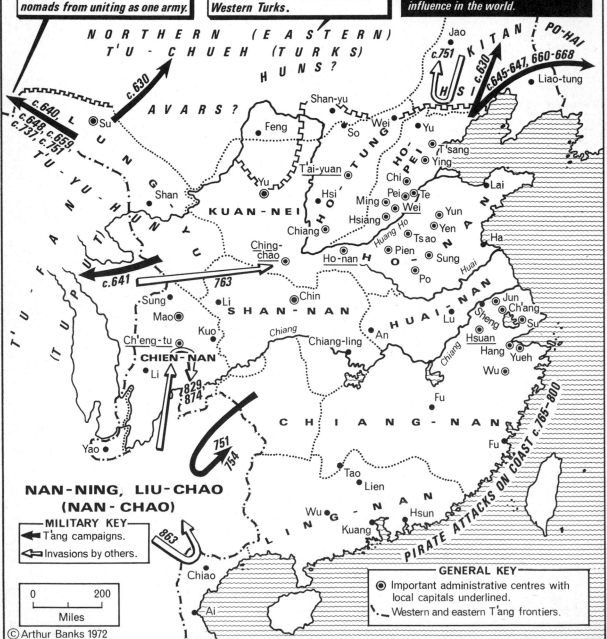

THE T'ANG DYNASTY IN CHINA 618 – 907

EARLY GUNPOWDER
c.850, SOME ELEMENTARY FORM OF FLASH POWDER WAS USED BY THE CHINESE FOR SPECTACULAR EFFECTS (EARLY FIREWORKS?).

The T'ang dynasty was commenced by Li Yuan (later, Kao Tsu), and under it, China became large, prosperous, and powerful. The dominant military figure was T'ai Tsung (Li Shih-min) who built up a large cavalry arm, and fought campaigns against the Eastern and Western Turks. Hsuan Tsung repelled Arab penetration in Central Asia, and strengthened Chinese influence in the world.

The T'ang attacks on Turkestan keep open trade routes and separate Tibetan and Turkish nomads from uniting as one army.

The T'ang win the support of the Uigur cavalry in their fight against the common foe – the Eastern and Western Turks.

U I G U R S

N O R T H E R N   (E A S T E R N)
T'U - C H U E H   (T U R K S)
HUNS?

AVARS?

c.630

c.640
c.648, c.659
c.737, c.751

LUNG

T'U - YU - HUN

TU-FAN

(TUPUT)
(IT

c.641

763

Su

Shan

Sung
Mao

Ch'eng-tu
CHIEN-NAN
Li

Yao

Feng

Yu

T'ai-yuan

KUAN-NEI

Hsi

Chiang

Ching-
chao

Ho-nan

Li
Chin

SHAN-NAN

Kuo

Chiang

Chiang-ling

829
874

751
754

Shan-yu

So

Wei

Yu

HO-TUNG

Chi

Ming
Pei

Hsiang

Huang Ho

Pien

Te
Wei

Yun
Yen

Tsao

Po
Sung

HO-NAN

HO-PEI

T'sang
Ying

Lai

Ha

Huai

Jao
c.751
HSI
KITAN
PO-HAI

c.630
c.645-647, 660-668
Liao-tung

An

HUAI-NAN

Lu

Jun
Ch'ang
Sheng
Su

Hsuan
Hang
Yueh

Wu

Fu

C H I A N G - N A N

Fu

NAN-NING, LIU-CHAO (NAN-CHAO)

751
754

863

Tao
Lien

Wu
Kuang

L I N G - N A N

Hsun

PIRATE ATTACKS ON COAST c.765-800

Chiao

Ai

---MILITARY KEY---
◄ T'ang campaigns.
◄ Invasions by others.

0   200
Miles

© Arthur Banks 1972

---GENERAL KEY---
◉ Important administrative centres with local capitals underlined.
—·— Western and eastern T'ang frontiers.

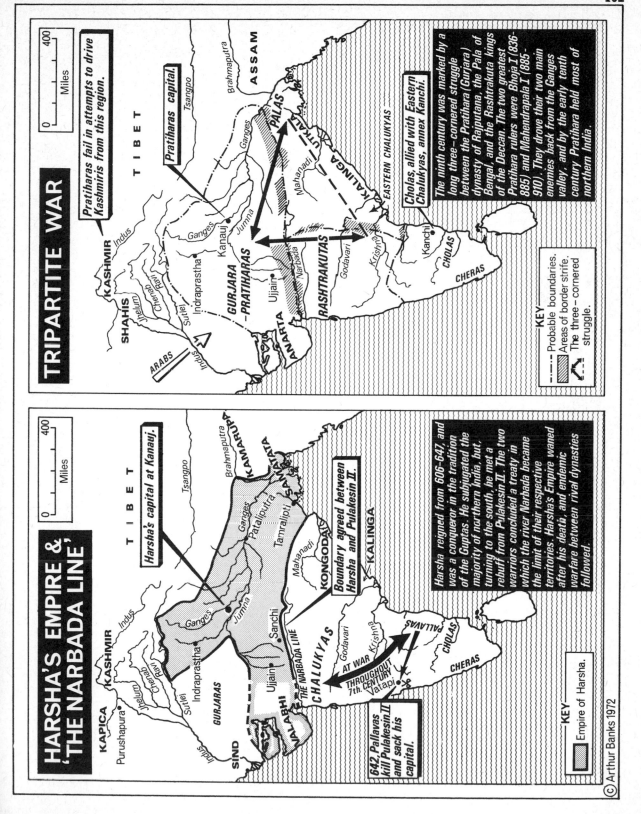

TRIPARTITE WAR

Pratiharas fail in attempts to drive Kashmiris from this region.

Pratiharas capital.

The ninth century was marked by a long three-cornered struggle between the Pratihara (Gurjara) dynasty of Rajputana, the Pala of Bengal, and the Rashtrakuta kings of the Deccan. The two greatest Pratihara rulers were Bhoja I (836-885) and Mahendrapala I (885-910). They drove their two main enemies back from the Ganges valley, and by the early tenth century Pratihara held most of northern India.

Cholas, allied with Eastern Chalukyas, annex Kanchi.

KEY
- Probable boundaries.
- Areas of border strife.
- The three-cornered struggle.

KASHMIR • SHAHIS • ARABS • Indus • Ravi • Chenab • Jhelum • Sutlej • Indraprastha • GURJARA-PRATIHARAS • Kanauj • Ganges • Jumna • Ujjain • ANARTA • Narbada • RASHTRAKUTAS • Godavari • Krishna • CHOLAS • Kanchi • CHERAS • KALINGA • EASTERN CHALUKYAS • Mahanadi • PALAS • ASSAM • Brahmaputra • Tsangpo • TIBET

HARSHA'S EMPIRE & 'THE NARBADA LINE'

Harsha's capital at Kanauj.

Boundary agreed between Harsha and Pulakesin II.

Harsha reigned from 606-647, and was a conqueror in the tradition of the Guptas. He subjugated the majority of northern India, but, turning to the south, he met a rebuff from Pulakesin II. The two warriors concluded a treaty in which the river Narbada became the limit of their respective territories. Harsha's Empire waned after his death, and endemic warfare between rival dynasties followed.

642 Pallavas kill Pulakesin II and sack his capital.

AT WAR THROUGHOUT 7th CENTURY

KEY
- Empire of Harsha.

© Arthur Banks 1972

KAPICA • Purushapura • KASHMIR • SIND • GURJARAS • VALABHI • Ujjain • Sanchi • Indraprastha • Indus • Jhelum • Chenab • Ravi • Sutlej • Ganges • Jumna • Pataliputra • Tamralipti • KAMARUPA • SAMATATA • KONGODA • KALINGA • Mahanadi • THE NARBADA LINE • CHALUKYAS • Vatapi • Godavari • Krishna • PALLAVAS • CHOLAS • CHERAS • TIBET • Tsangpo • Brahmaputra

Miles 0 400

103

STAGES IN THE MAKING OF ENGLAND AND WALES 600 - 886

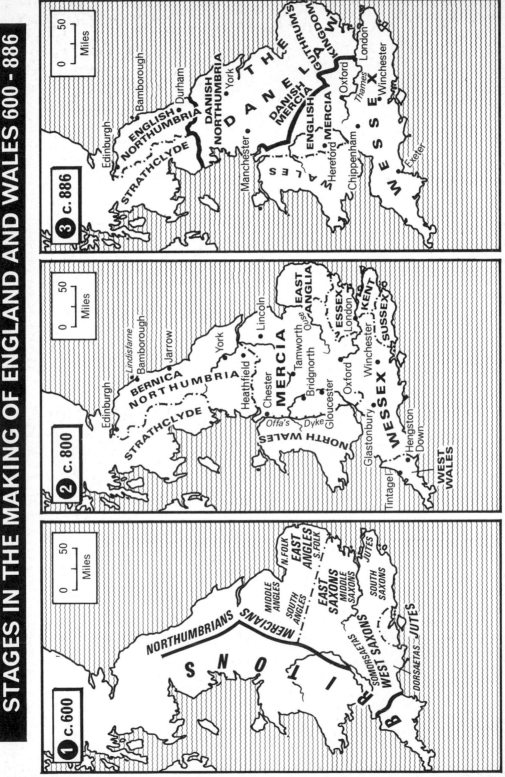

1 c. 600

0 50 Miles

BRITONS

NORTHUMBRIANS

MERCIANS

MIDDLE ANGLES

SOUTH ANGLES

N. FOLK
EAST ANGLES
S. FOLK

EAST SAXONS

MIDDLE SAXONS

SOUTH SAXONS

JUTES

WEST SAXONS

SOMORSAETAS

DORSAETAS — JUTES

2 c. 800

0 50 Miles

Edinburgh

STRATHCLYDE

BERNICA
NORTHUMBRIA

Lindisfarne
Bamborough
Jarrow

York

Lincoln

Heathfield

Chester

MERCIA

Tamworth
Ouse
Bridgnorth
Gloucester

NORTH WALES

Offa's Dyke

Oxford

EAST ANGLIA

ESSEX
London

Winchester
WESSEX

KENT
SUSSEX

Glastonbury

Hengston Down

Tintagel

WEST WALES

3 c. 886

0 50 Miles

Edinburgh

STRATHCLYDE

ENGLISH NORTHUMBRIA

DANISH NORTHUMBRIA

Bamborough
Durham
York

Manchester

WALES

Hereford

ENGLISH MERCIA

DANISH MERCIA

GUTHRUM'S KINGDOM

D A N E L A W

Oxford
Thames
London
Winchester
WESSEX

Chippenham

Exeter

In Britain, the Britons were restricted to an ever more limited area in the west, and Northumbrian supremacy passed, first to Mercia, and thence to Wessex. Egbert's "peace" (in 800) was marred by Danish incursions culminating in the Danelaw becoming an independent region. The "Peace of Guthrum" (886), altered its boundaries in favour of Alfred the Great.

© Arthur Banks 1972

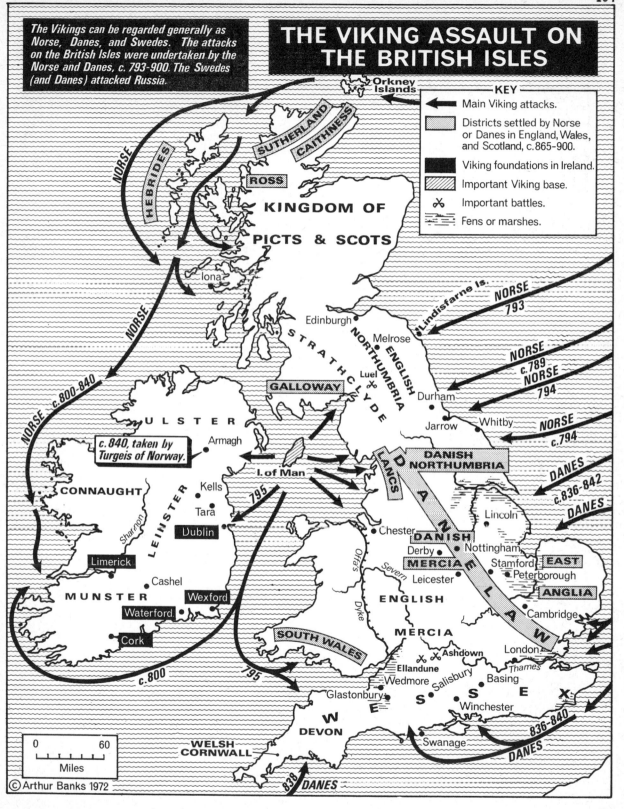

The Vikings can be regarded generally as Norse, Danes, and Swedes. The attacks on the British Isles were undertaken by the Norse and Danes, c. 793-900. The Swedes (and Danes) attacked Russia.

THE VIKING ASSAULT ON THE BRITISH ISLES

KEY

- Main Viking attacks.
- Districts settled by Norse or Danes in England, Wales, and Scotland, c.865-900.
- Viking foundations in Ireland.
- Important Viking base.
- Important battles.
- Fens or marshes.

Orkney Islands

SUTHERLAND
CAITHNESS
ROSS
HEBRIDES
NORSE

KINGDOM OF PICTS & SCOTS

Iona

NORSE

Edinburgh
Melrose
Lindisfarne Is.
NORSE 793
NORSE c.789
NORSE 794

STRATHCLYDE
NORTHUMBRIA
ENGLISH
Luel
Durham
Jarrow
Whitby
NORSE c.794

GALLOWAY

DANES c.836-842
DANES

NORSE c.800-840

ULSTER
Armagh
c. 840, taken by Turgeis of Norway.
I. of Man

DANISH NORTHUMBRIA
LANCS
Lincoln

NORSE c.800-840

CONNAUGHT
Shannon
Kells
Tara
795
Dublin
LEINSTER
Chester
Derby
Nottingham
DANISH MERCIA
Leicester
Stamford
Peterborough
EAST ANGLIA

Limerick
Cashel
MUNSTER
Wexford
Waterford
Cork

Offa's Dyke
Severn
ENGLISH MERCIA
Cambridge
London
Thames

c.800

SOUTH WALES

795
Ashdown
Ellandune
Wedmore
Salisbury
Basing
Glastonbury
ESSEX
Winchester
DANES 836-840

W DEVON

WELSH CORNWALL

Swanage

838 DANES

0 60
Miles

© Arthur Banks 1972

ALFRED THE GREAT 849–899

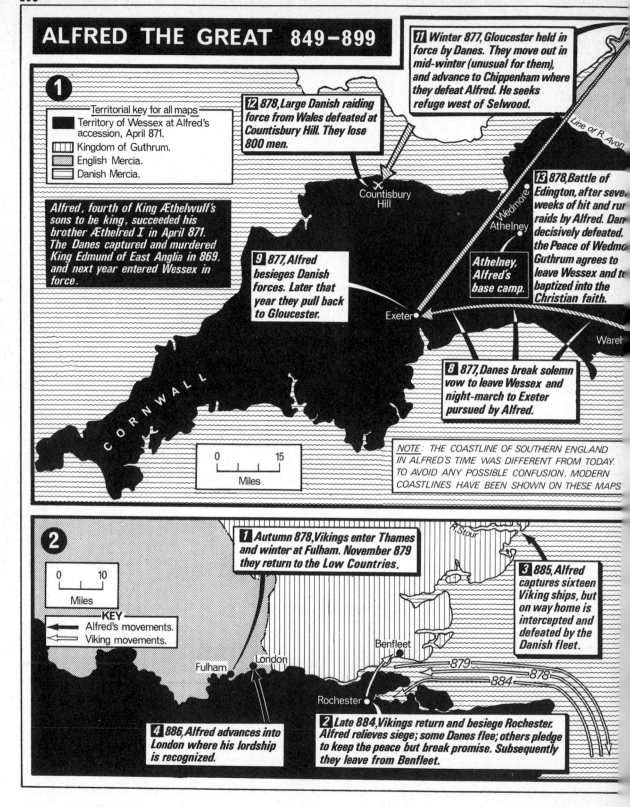

1

Territorial key for all maps
- ■ Territory of Wessex at Alfred's accession, April 871.
- ⊞ Kingdom of Guthrum.
- ▨ English Mercia.
- ▤ Danish Mercia.

Alfred, fourth of King Æthelwulf's sons to be king, succeeded his brother Æthelred I in April 871. The Danes captured and murdered King Edmund of East Anglia in 869, and next year entered Wessex in force.

11 Winter 877, Gloucester held in force by Danes. They move out in mid-winter (unusual for them), and advance to Chippenham where they defeat Alfred. He seeks refuge west of Selwood.

12 878, Large Danish raiding force from Wales defeated at Countisbury Hill. They lose 800 men.

13 878, Battle of Edington, after seve... weeks of hit and run raids by Alfred. Dan... decisively defeated. the Peace of Wedmo... Guthrum agrees to leave Wessex and t... baptized into the Christian faith.

9 877, Alfred besieges Danish forces. Later that year they pull back to Gloucester.

Athelney, Alfred's base camp.

Countisbury Hill

Exeter

Wareh...

8 877, Danes break solemn vow to leave Wessex and night-march to Exeter pursued by Alfred.

CORNWALL

Line of R. Avon

Wedmore

Athelney

0 — 15
Miles

NOTE: THE COASTLINE OF SOUTHERN ENGLAND IN ALFRED'S TIME WAS DIFFERENT FROM TODAY. TO AVOID ANY POSSIBLE CONFUSION, MODERN COASTLINES HAVE BEEN SHOWN ON THESE MAPS

2

0 — 10
Miles

KEY
→ Alfred's movements.
⇨ Viking movements.

1 Autumn 878, Vikings enter Thames and winter at Fulham. November 879 they return to the Low Countries.

R. Stour

3 885, Alfred captures sixteen Viking ships, but on way home is intercepted and defeated by the Danish fleet.

Benfleet

Fulham   London

Rochester

879
884
878

4 886, Alfred advances into London where his lordship is recognized.

2 Late 884, Vikings return and besiege Rochester. Alfred relieves siege; some Danes flee; others pledge to keep the peace but break promise. Subsequently they leave from Benfleet.

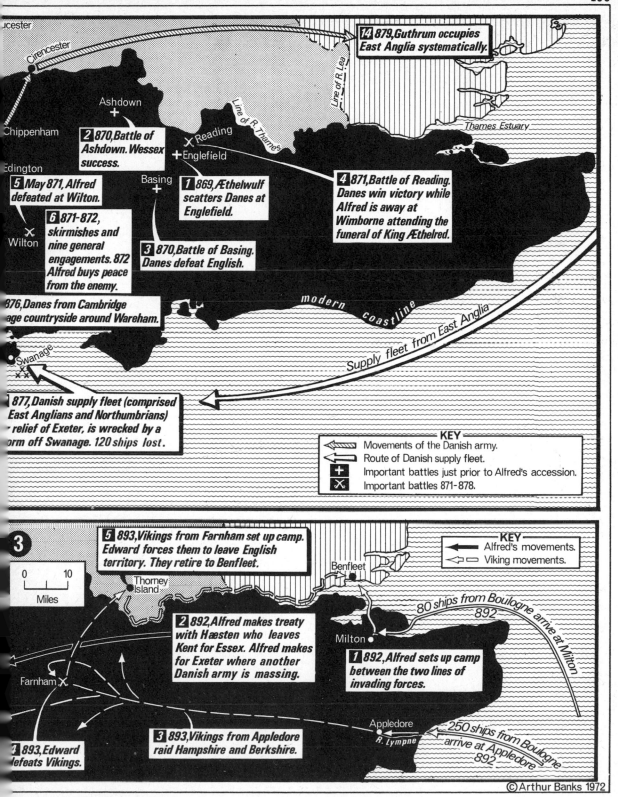

Gloucester
Cirencester
Ashdown +
Chippenham

2 *870, Battle of Ashdown. Wessex success.*

Edington

5 *May 871, Alfred defeated at Wilton.*

6 *871-872, skirmishes and nine general engagements. 872 Alfred buys peace from the enemy.*

× Wilton

Basing +

× Reading
+ Englefield

1 *869, Æthelwulf scatters Danes at Englefield.*

4 *871, Battle of Reading. Danes win victory while Alfred is away at Wimborne attending the funeral of King Æthelred.*

3 *870, Battle of Basing. Danes defeat English.*

Line of R. Thames
Line of R. Lea

14 *879, Guthrum occupies East Anglia systematically.*

Thames Estuary

876, Danes from Cambridge ravage countryside around Wareham.

modern coastline

Supply fleet from East Anglia

○ Swanage
× ×

877, Danish supply fleet (comprised East Anglians and Northumbrians) for relief of Exeter, is wrecked by a storm off Swanage. 120 ships lost.

KEY
Movements of the Danish army.
Route of Danish supply fleet.
+ Important battles just prior to Alfred's accession.
× Important battles 871-878.

3

0   10
Miles

5 *893, Vikings from Farnham set up camp. Edward forces them to leave English territory. They retire to Benfleet.*

Thorney Island
Benfleet

KEY
Alfred's movements.
Viking movements.

80 ships from Boulogne arrive at Milton 892

2 *892, Alfred makes treaty with Hæsten who leaves Kent for Essex. Alfred makes for Exeter where another Danish army is massing.*

Milton

1 *892, Alfred sets up camp between the two lines of invading forces.*

Farnham ×

3 *893, Vikings from Appledore raid Hampshire and Berkshire.*

Appledore
R. Lympne

250 ships from Boulogne arrive at Appledore 892

4 *893, Edward defeats Vikings.*

© Arthur Banks 1972

107

ALFRED THE GREAT – continued

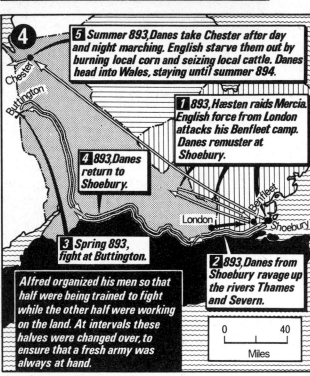

5 Summer 893, Danes take Chester after day and night marching. English starve them out by burning local corn and seizing local cattle. Danes head into Wales, staying until summer 894.

1 893, Hæsten raids Mercia. English force from London attacks his Benfleet camp. Danes remuster at Shoebury.

4 893, Danes return to Shoebury.

3 Spring 893, fight at Buttington.

Alfred organized his men so that half were being trained to fight while the other half were working on the land. At intervals these halves were changed over, to ensure that a fresh army was always at hand.

2 893, Danes from Shoebury ravage up the rivers Thames and Severn.

0 — 40 Miles

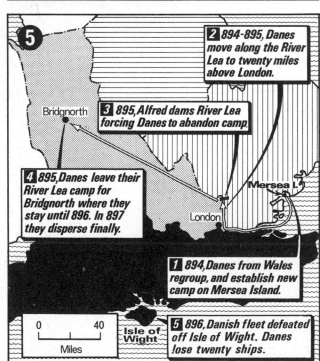

2 894-895, Danes move along the River Lea to twenty miles above London.

3 895, Alfred dams River Lea forcing Danes to abandon camp.

4 895, Danes leave their River Lea camp for Bridgnorth where they stay until 896. In 897 they disperse finally.

1 894, Danes from Wales regroup, and establish new camp on Mersea Island.

5 896, Danish fleet defeated off Isle of Wight. Danes lose twenty ships.

0 — 40 Miles

ALFRED'S SYSTEM OF FORTIFIED TOWNS

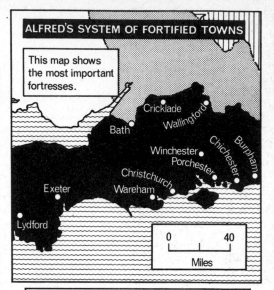

This map shows the most important fortresses.

0 — 40 Miles

The story of Alfred "burning the cakes", is based on an interpolation from the annals of St. Neot in Asser's "Life of Alfred".

THE ANGLO-SAXON CHRONICLE

The Anglo-Saxon Chronicle consists collectively of 7 annalistic compilations written in Old English. (There are, too, at least 3 Latin versions.) Each begins with an outline of history from Julius Caesar until the ⑤. Until the entry for 891 the compilations are remarkably similar and until 915 much common material is used. Then the details recorded in each manuscript diverge considerably. The latest entry of all the manuscripts is for 1154 in that written at Peterborough Abbey.

The story of Alfred wandering in the Danish camp dressed as a minstrel is based on an account told in William of Malmesbury's "De Gestis Regum".

Alfred, born 849 at Wantage. Before the age of 7 he had undertaken two journeys to Rome. He was taught Latin later in life by Asser, and between 892 and 899 when he died, he produced five Latin works. (Translations of Gregory's Cura Pastoralis, Orosius's history of the ancient world, Bede's Historia Ecclesiastica, Boethius's De Consolatione Philosophiae, and St. Augustine's Soliloquies).

108

EUROPE c. 800

The principal historical event in Europe at this period was the creation of the Holy Roman Empire as the main power in Western Europe. As established by Charlemagne it comprised Gallo-Latin Neustria, Lombard Italy, and Teutonic Austrasia. In Spain, the Ummayad emirate was established by Abd-er-Rahman. Islam was in control of Africa and western Asia (but not Asia Minor). Finally, Bulgarian and Serbian kingdoms were coming into being.

781, Alcuin of York appointed by Charlemagne to lead revival of learning.

Charlemagne's capital.

778, Charlemagne's rearguard ambushed by Wascones.

798, allied with Charlemagne.

773-4, Charlemagne helps Pope against Lombard invasion.

Charlemagne subdues Saxons (772-804), Bavarians (788), and Avars (791-796).

800, Charlemagne crowned Holy Roman Emperor.

810, Charlemagne makes peace with Emir of Cordova.

KEY
Charlemagne's Empire.
Lands tributary to Charlemagne.
The Eastern Roman Empire.
The Caliphate of the Abbasids.

KHAZARS, MAGYARS (HUNGARIANS), POLES, LETTS, SLAVS, WENDS, BOHEMIA, AVARS, SERBS, CROATIA, BULGARIANS, BAVARIA, AUSTRASIA, NEUSTRIA, BURGUNDY, AQUITAINE, BRETONS, ITALY, BENEVENTO, NORSEMEN, DANES, FRISIANS, SAXONS, PICTS, SCOTS, BRITONS, ANGLO-SAXON KINGDOMS, KINGDOM OF ASTURIAS, UMMAYAD EMIRATE OF CORDOVA, TUNIS, ASIA MINOR, CYPRUS, Crete, Sicily, Sardinia, Corsica

Cities: Edessa, Damascus, Jerusalem, Angora, Constantinople, Athens, Durazzo, Venice, Rome, Naples, Palermo, Tripoli, Turin, Pavia, Genoa, Marseilles, Barcelona, Toulouse, Tours, Poitiers, Paris, London, Roncesvalles, Saragossa, Cordova, Seville, Tangiers, Jebel Tarik (Gibraltar), Strasbourg, Aachen, Paderborn

Seas/Rivers: Black Sea, Mediterranean Sea, Baltic Sea, Dnieper, Vistula, Elbe, Danube, Rhine, Rhône, Seine, Ebro, Douro, Tagus

0 200 Miles

© Arthur Banks 1972

THE SHORT-LIVED KITAN ASCENDANCY IN CHINA

① Later Liang 907 - 923

KITAN (reindeer-using people)

UIGURS
Kan
Liang
TU-FAN
SHA-T'O
c.923
CH'I
LATER
TERRITORY OF SHENG-SHIH
CHU
FORMER SHU
Ch'eng-tu
TSIN
T'ai yuan
W.Capital
E.Capital
CHING-NAN
Ching
Yang
LIANG
WU
Hang
WU-YUEH
YEN
Yu
MIN
Fu
Kuang

Struggles for power dominated the period 907 - 960 (the main moves are shown by arrows on maps). The Kitan were granted land in northern China for aid extended to the Later Tsin in their fight for supremacy. Thus, the Kitan gained a strategic foothold for their invasion.

0   300
Miles

② Later T'ang 923 - 936

KITAN 936

UIGURS
Kan
SHA-T'O
Ling
LATER T'ANG
W.Capital
E.Capital
TU-FAN
LATER SHU
S.P'ING
Ching
T'an
C'HU
TA-TIEN-HSING
TA-I-NING
Ta-li
ANNAM
Ta-lo
S. HAN
Kuang
Yu
N. Residency
Chiang-tu
Hang
WU-YUEH
Hung
WU
MIN
Ch'ang-lo

0   300
Miles

**③ Later Tsin 936 - 946 and
Later Han 947 - 950**

KITAN

UIGURS
Kan
SHA-T'O
947
Ling
LATER TSIN (KITAN)
N. Residency
W.Capital
E.Capital
LATER HAN
S.P'ING
T'U FAN
LATER SHU
Ching
T'an
LO-TIEN
CH'U
TA-LI
Ta-li
ANNAM
Ta-lo
S. HAN
Kuang
Yun
S. Residency
Chiang-tu
Hang
WU YUEH
YIN
Fu
T'ANG
MIN

0   300
Miles

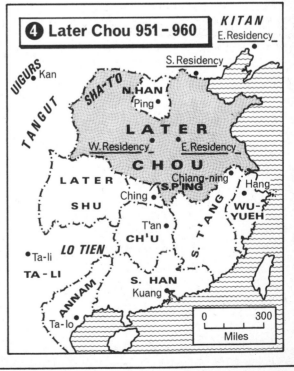

④ Later Chou 951 - 960

KITAN E.Residency

UIGURS
Kan
TANGUT
SHA-TO
N.HAN
Ping
LATER CHOU
W.Residency
E.Residency
LATER SHU
Ching
S.P'ING
Chiang-ning
Hang
T'an
CH'U
LO TIEN
TA-LI
Ta-li
ANNAM
Ta-lo
S. HAN
Kuang
S. Residency
WU-YUEH
T'ANG

0   300
Miles

© Arthur Banks 1972

110

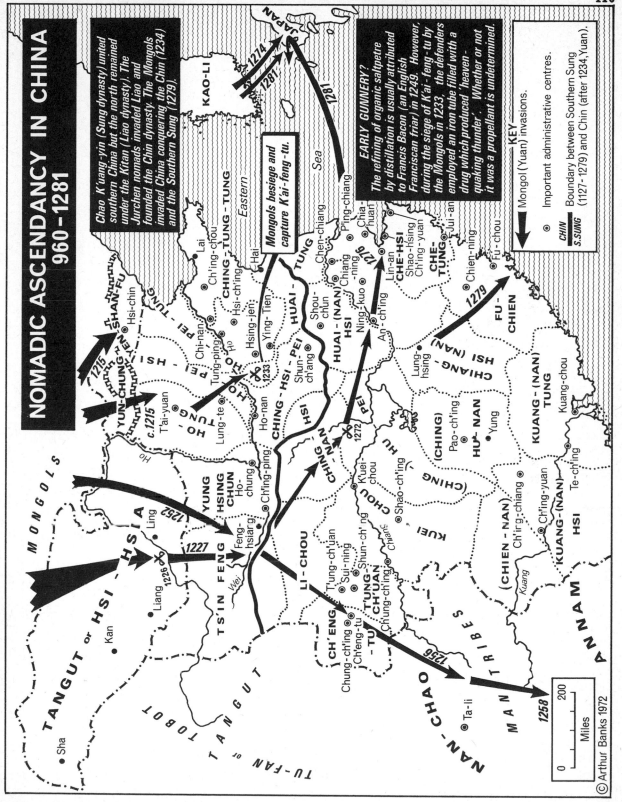

NOMADIC ASCENDANCY IN CHINA 960-1281

Chao K'uang-yin (Sung dynasty) united southern China but the north remained under the Kitan (Liao dynasty). The Jurchen nomads invaded Liao and founded the Chin dynasty. The Mongols invaded China conquering the Chin (1234) and the Southern Sung (1279).

Mongols besiege and capture K'ai-feng-fu.

EARLY GUNNERY?
The refining of organic saltpetre by distillation is usually attributed to Francis Bacon (an English Franciscan friar) in 1249. However, during the siege of K'ai-feng-tu by the Mongols in 1233, the defenders employed an iron tube filled with a drug which produced 'heaven-quaking thunder'. Whether or not it was a propellant is undetermined.

KEY
Mongol (Yuan) invasions.
Important administrative centres.
Boundary between Southern Sung (1127-1279) and Chin (after 1234, Yuan).
CHIN
S.SUNG

© Arthur Banks 1972

0   200
Miles

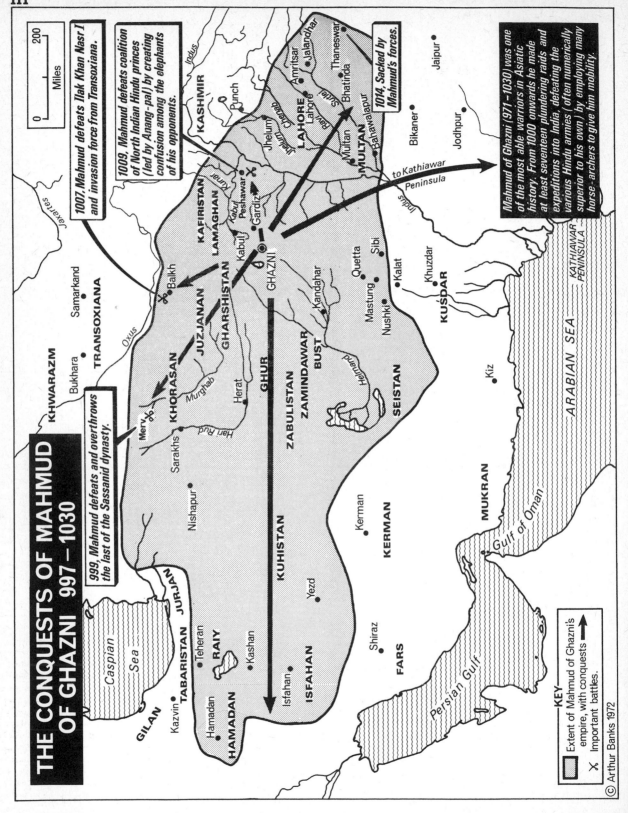

THE CONQUESTS OF MAHMUD OF GHAZNI 997–1030

1007. Mahmud defeats Ilak Khan Nasr I and invasion force from Transoxiana.

1009. Mahmud defeats coalition of North Indian Hindu princes (led by Anang-pal) by creating confusion among the elephants of his opponents.

1014. Sacked by Mahmud's forces.

Mahmud of Ghazni (971–1030) was one of the most able warriors in Asiatic history. From 1000 onwards he made at least seventeen plundering raids and expeditions into India, defeating the various Hindu armies (often numerically superior to his own) by employing many horse-archers to give him mobility.

999. Mahmud defeats and overthrows the last of the Sassanid dynasty.

KHWARAZM

Bukhara •

Samarkand •

TRANSOXIANA

KASHMIR

Punch •

Amritsar • Jalandhar •
Thaneswar •
Lahore • Bhatinda •
LAHORE
Multan •
MULTAN
Bahawalpur •

Jaipur •

Bikaner •

Jodhpur •

to Kathiawar Peninsula

Balkh •

KAFIRISTAN
LAMAGHAN
Kabul •
Peshawar •
Gardiz •
GHAZNI

JUZJANAN
GHARSHISTAN
Quetta •
Sibi •
Mastung •
Nushki •
• Kalat
Khuzdar •

KUSDAR

KHORASAN
Merv •
Sarakhs •
Herat •
GHUR
ZABULISTAN
ZAMINDAWAR
Kandahar •
BUST
SEISTAN

MUKRAN

ARABIAN SEA

KATHIAWAR PENINSULA

Nishapur •

KUHISTAN

Kerman •

KERMAN

Kiz •

Gulf of Oman

Yezd •

Isfahan •
ISFAHAN

Shiraz •

FARS

Persian Gulf

GILAN
Kazvin •
Hamadan •
HAMADAN
TABARISTAN
Teheran •
RAIY
• Kashan
JURJAN
Caspian Sea

KEY

Extent of Mahmud of Ghazni's empire, with conquests

X Important battles.

© Arthur Banks 1972

0 — 200 Miles

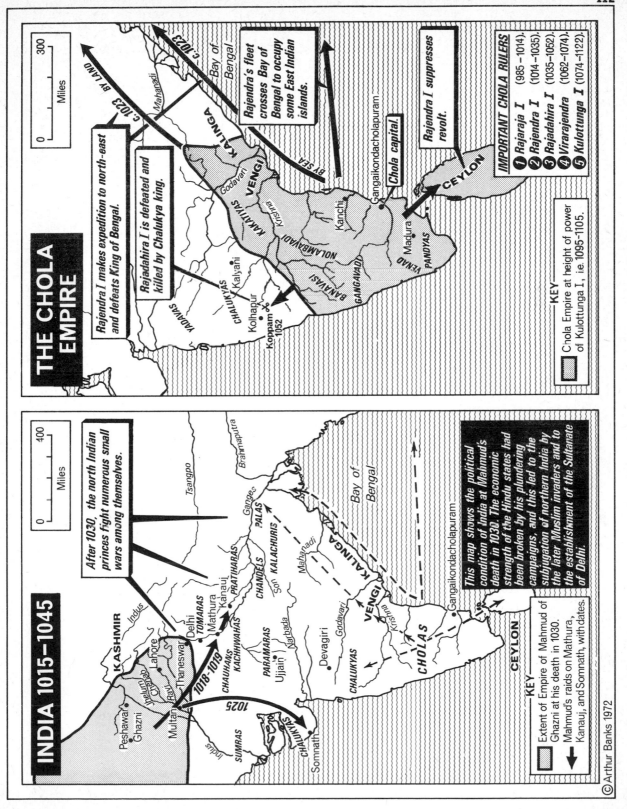

THE NORMAN INVASION OF ENGLAND 1066

0   50
Miles

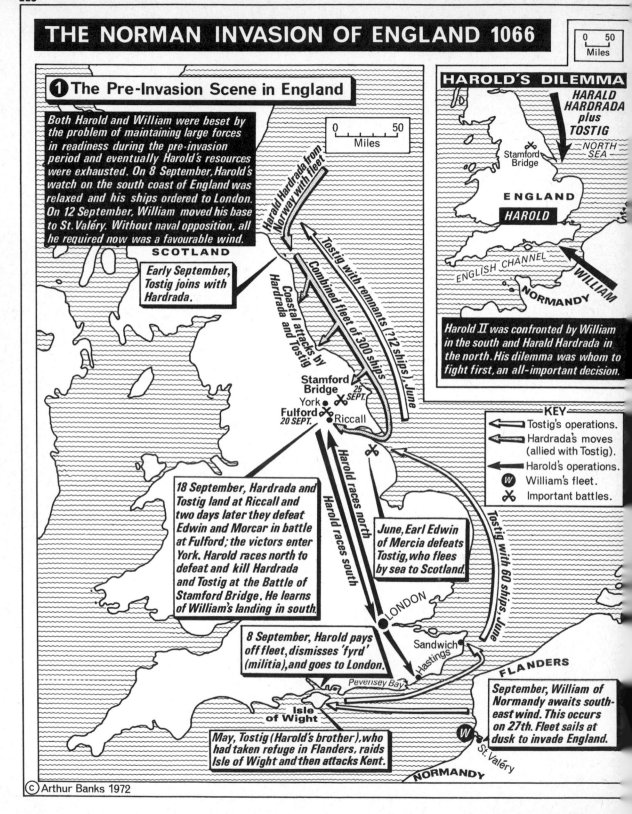

① The Pre-Invasion Scene in England

Both Harold and William were beset by the problem of maintaining large forces in readiness during the pre-invasion period and eventually Harold's resources were exhausted. On 8 September, Harold's watch on the south coast of England was relaxed and his ships ordered to London. On 12 September, William moved his base to St. Valéry. Without naval opposition, all he required now was a favourable wind.

0   50
Miles

SCOTLAND

Early September, Tostig joins with Hardrada.

Harald Hardrada from Norway with fleet

Tostig with remnants (112 ships) June

Combined fleet of 300 ships

Coastal attacks by Hardrada and Tostig

Stamford Bridge 25 SEPT.

York

Fulford 20 SEPT.

Riccall

Harold races north

Harold races south

18 September, Hardrada and Tostig land at Riccall and two days later they defeat Edwin and Morcar in battle at Fulford; the victors enter York. Harold races north to defeat and kill Hardrada and Tostig at the Battle of Stamford Bridge. He learns of William's landing in south.

June, Earl Edwin of Mercia defeats Tostig, who flees by sea to Scotland.

Tostig with 60 ships, June

LONDON

Sandwich

Hastings

8 September, Harold pays off fleet, dismisses 'fyrd' (militia), and goes to London.

Pevensey Bay

FLANDERS

Isle of Wight

W

St. Valéry

September, William of Normandy awaits south-east wind. This occurs on 27th. Fleet sails at dusk to invade England.

May, Tostig (Harold's brother), who had taken refuge in Flanders, raids Isle of Wight and then attacks Kent.

NORMANDY

© Arthur Banks 1972

HAROLD'S DILEMMA

HARALD HARDRADA plus TOSTIG

NORTH SEA

Stamford Bridge

ENGLAND

HAROLD

ENGLISH CHANNEL

WILLIAM

NORMANDY

Harold II was confronted by William in the south and Harald Hardrada in the north. His dilemma was whom to fight first, an all-important decision.

KEY

⟵ Tostig's operations.

⟵ Hardrada's moves (allied with Tostig).

⟵ Harold's operations.

Ⓦ William's fleet.

✕ Important battles.

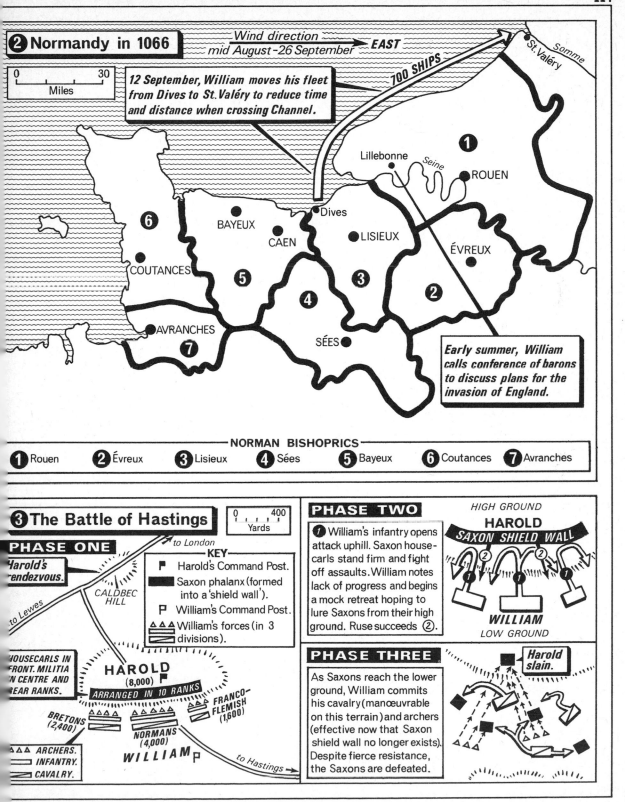

❷ Normandy in 1066

Wind direction
mid August - 26 September ➡ **EAST**

700 SHIPS

Somme
• St. Valéry

0 ─────── 30
Miles

12 September, William moves his fleet from Dives to St. Valéry to reduce time and distance when crossing Channel.

❶
Lillebonne
Seine
• ROUEN

❻
BAYEUX •
CAEN •
• Dives
• LISIEUX

❸

ÉVREUX
•

❷

COUTANCES •

❺

❹

SÉES •

AVRANCHES •

❼

Early summer, William calls conference of barons to discuss plans for the invasion of England.

─── **NORMAN BISHOPRICS** ───

❶ Rouen ❷ Évreux ❸ Lisieux ❹ Sées ❺ Bayeux ❻ Coutances ❼ Avranches

❸ The Battle of Hastings

0 ──┴──┴──┴── 400
Yards

PHASE ONE

Harold's rendezvous.

to London

─── **KEY** ───

▐🏴 Harold's Command Post.

▬ Saxon phalanx (formed into a 'shield wall').

🏴▌ William's Command Post.

▲▲▲ William's forces (in 3 divisions).

to Lewes

CALDBEC HILL

HOUSECARLS IN FRONT. MILITIA IN CENTRE AND REAR RANKS.

HAROLD
(8,000) 🏴
ARRANGED IN 10 RANKS

FRANCO-FLEMISH (1,600)

BRETONS (2,400)

NORMANS (4,000)

WILLIAM 🏴

to Hastings ➡

▲▲▲ ARCHERS.
▭ INFANTRY.
▱ CAVALRY.

PHASE TWO

HIGH GROUND

HAROLD
SAXON SHIELD WALL

❶ William's infantry opens attack uphill. Saxon house-carls stand firm and fight off assaults. William notes lack of progress and begins a mock retreat hoping to lure Saxons from their high ground. Ruse succeeds ❷.

WILLIAM
LOW GROUND

PHASE THREE

Harold slain.

As Saxons reach the lower ground, William commits his cavalry (manœuvrable on this terrain) and archers (effective now that Saxon shield wall no longer exists). Despite fierce resistance, the Saxons are defeated.

THE IMPORTANCE OF THE ENGLISH CHANNEL IN WAR

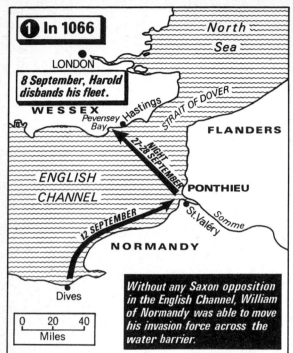

1 In 1066

8 September, Harold disbands his fleet.

LONDON

WESSEX

Pevensey Bay — Hastings

NIGHT 27-28 SEPTEMBER

STRAIT OF DOVER

FLANDERS

North Sea

ENGLISH CHANNEL

PONTHIEU

12 SEPTEMBER

St. Valéry

Somme

NORMANDY

Dives

Without any Saxon opposition in the English Channel, William of Normandy was able to move his invasion force across the water barrier.

0 20 40
Miles

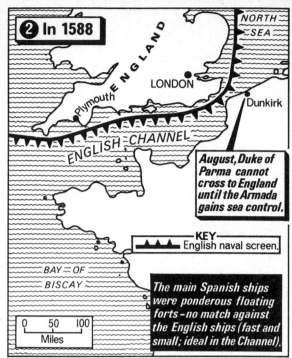

2 In 1588

NORTH SEA

ENGLAND

Plymouth

LONDON

Dunkirk

ENGLISH CHANNEL

August, Duke of Parma cannot cross to England until the Armada gains sea control.

BAY OF BISCAY

KEY
English naval screen.

The main Spanish ships were ponderous floating forts – no match against the English ships (fast and small; ideal in the Channel).

0 50 100
Miles

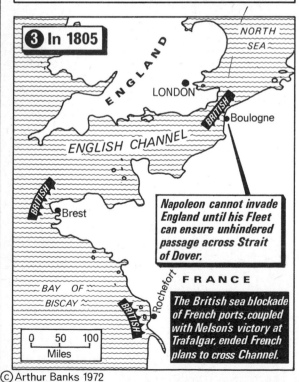

3 In 1805

NORTH SEA

ENGLAND

LONDON

BRITISH

Boulogne

ENGLISH CHANNEL

BRITISH

Brest

Napoleon cannot invade England until his Fleet can ensure unhindered passage across Strait of Dover.

BAY OF BISCAY

Rochefort

BRITISH

FRANCE

The British sea blockade of French ports, coupled with Nelson's victory at Trafalgar, ended French plans to cross Channel.

0 50 100
Miles

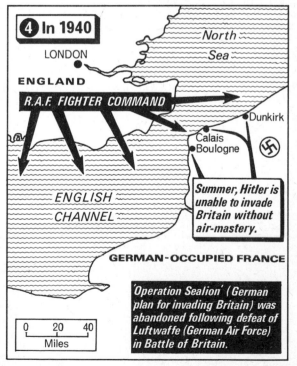

4 In 1940

North Sea

LONDON

ENGLAND

R.A.F. FIGHTER COMMAND

Dunkirk

Calais
Boulogne

ENGLISH CHANNEL

Summer, Hitler is unable to invade Britain without air-mastery.

GERMAN-OCCUPIED FRANCE

'Operation Sealion' (German plan for invading Britain) was abandoned following defeat of Luftwaffe (German Air Force) in Battle of Britain.

0 20 40
Miles

© Arthur Banks 1972

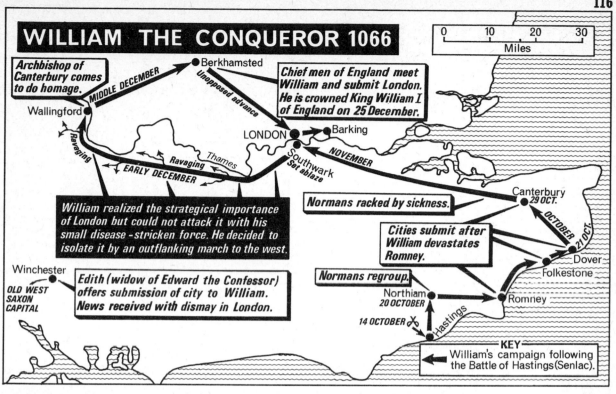

WILLIAM THE CONQUEROR 1066

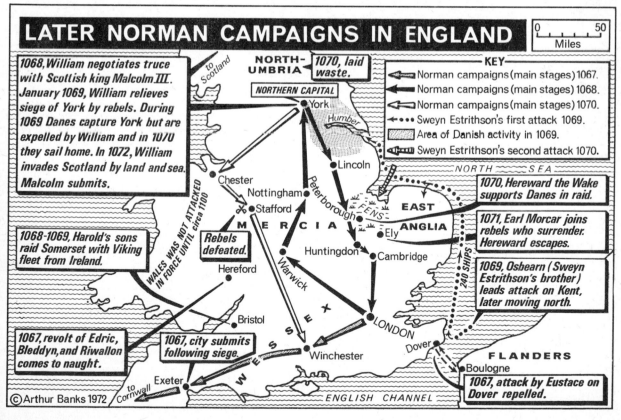

LATER NORMAN CAMPAIGNS IN ENGLAND

© Arthur Banks 1972

116

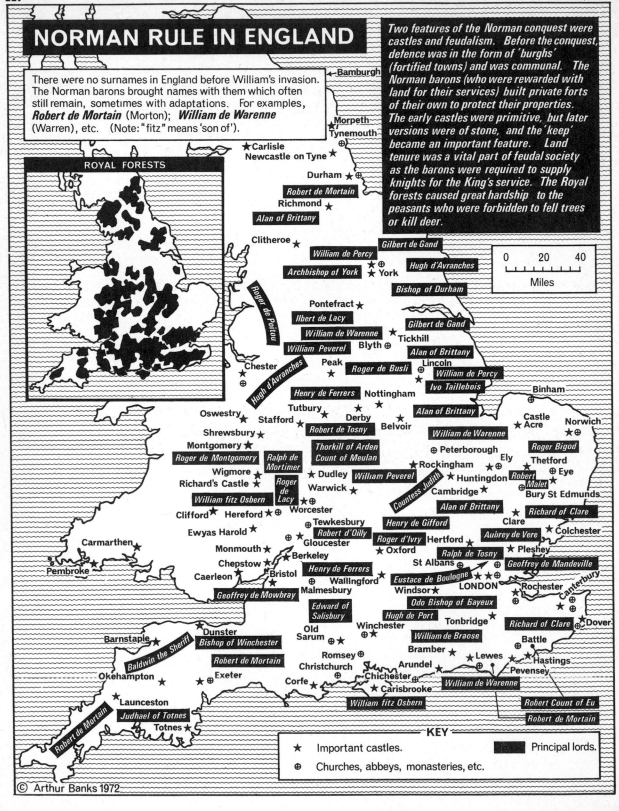

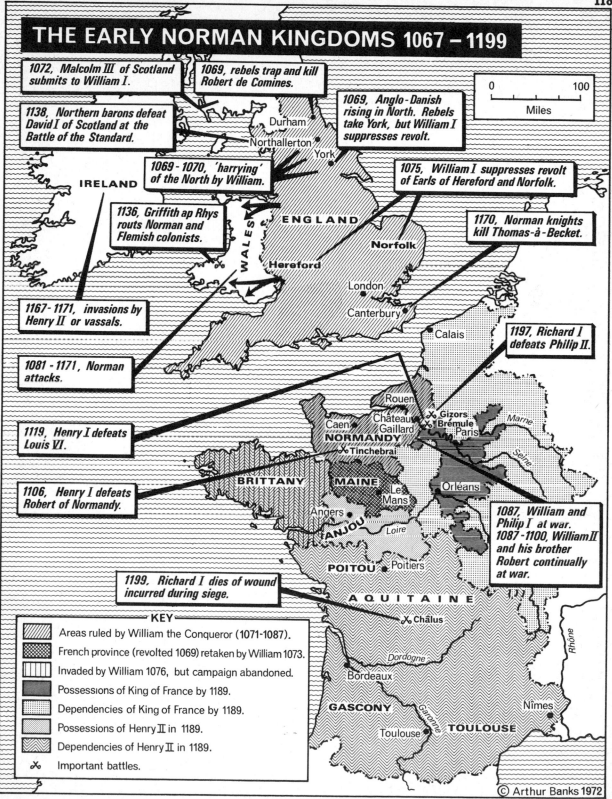

THE EARLY NORMAN KINGDOMS 1067–1199

1072, Malcolm III of Scotland submits to William I.

1069, rebels trap and kill Robert de Comines.

1069, Anglo-Danish rising in North. Rebels take York, but William I suppresses revolt.

1138, Northern barons defeat David I of Scotland at the Battle of the Standard.

1069–1070, 'harrying' of the North by William.

1075, William I suppresses revolt of Earls of Hereford and Norfolk.

1136, Griffith ap Rhys routs Norman and Flemish colonists.

1170, Norman knights kill Thomas-à-Becket.

1167–1171, invasions by Henry II or vassals.

1197, Richard I defeats Philip II.

1081–1171, Norman attacks.

1119, Henry I defeats Louis VI.

1106, Henry I defeats Robert of Normandy.

1087, William and Philip I at war. 1087–1100, William II and his brother Robert continually at war.

1199, Richard I dies of wound incurred during siege.

0 ——— 100
Miles

IRELAND

Durham
Northallerton
York
ENGLAND
Norfolk
London
Canterbury
WALES
Hereford
Calais
Rouen
Château Gaillard
Caen
Gizors
Brémule
Paris
Marne
Seine
NORMANDY
Tinchebrai
BRITTANY
MAINE
Le Mans
Orléans
Angers
ANJOU
Loire
POITOU
Poitiers
AQUITAINE
Châlus
Dordogne
Rhône
Bordeaux
GASCONY
Garonne
Nîmes
Toulouse
TOULOUSE

KEY

- Areas ruled by William the Conqueror (1071-1087).
- French province (revolted 1069) retaken by William 1073.
- Invaded by William 1076, but campaign abandoned.
- Possessions of King of France by 1189.
- Dependencies of King of France by 1189.
- Possessions of Henry II in 1189.
- Dependencies of Henry II in 1189.
- ✕ Important battles.

© Arthur Banks 1972

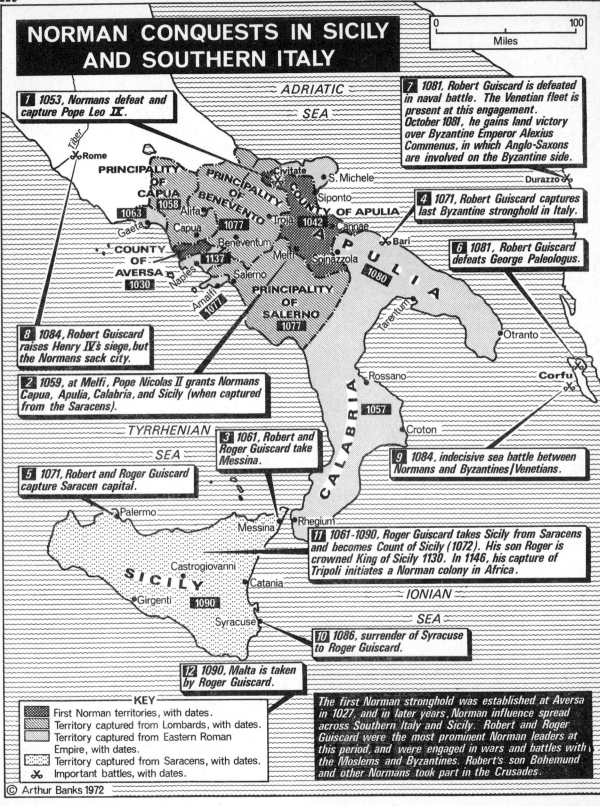

NORMAN CONQUESTS IN SICILY AND SOUTHERN ITALY

0   100
Miles

1 1053, Normans defeat and capture Pope Leo IX.

7 1081, Robert Guiscard is defeated in naval battle. The Venetian fleet is present at this engagement. October 1081, he gains land victory over Byzantine Emperor Alexius Commenus, in which Anglo-Saxons are involved on the Byzantine side.

4 1071, Robert Guiscard captures last Byzantine stronghold in Italy.

6 1081, Robert Guiscard defeats George Paleologus.

8 1084, Robert Guiscard raises Henry IV's siege, but the Normans sack city.

2 1059, at Melfi, Pope Nicolas II grants Normans Capua, Apulia, Calabria, and Sicily (when captured from the Saracens).

3 1061, Robert and Roger Guiscard take Messina.

5 1071, Robert and Roger Guiscard capture Saracen capital.

9 1084, indecisive sea battle between Normans and Byzantines/Venetians.

11 1061-1090, Roger Guiscard takes Sicily from Saracens and becomes Count of Sicily (1072). His son Roger is crowned King of Sicily 1130. In 1146, his capture of Tripoli initiates a Norman colony in Africa.

10 1086, surrender of Syracuse to Roger Guiscard.

12 1090, Malta is taken by Roger Guiscard.

ADRIATIC SEA

Tiber

Rome

PRINCIPALITY OF CAPUA

PRINCIPALITY OF BENEVENTO

Civitate

S. Michele

Siponto

COUNTY OF APULIA

1058

1063

Alifa

Capua

1077

Troia

1042

Cannae

Durazzo

Gaeta

Beneventum

Melfi

Bari

COUNTY OF AVERSA

1137

Spinazzola

1030

Naples

Salerno

PRINCIPALITY OF SALERNO

1077

1080

A P U L I A

Amalfi

1077

1077

TYRRHENIAN SEA

Tarentum

Otranto

Corfu

Rossano

C A L A B R I A

1057

Croton

Rhegium

Palermo

Messina

S I C I L Y

Castrogiovanni

IONIAN SEA

Girgenti

1090

Catania

Syracuse

KEY

First Norman territories, with dates.
Territory captured from Lombards, with dates.
Territory captured from Eastern Roman Empire, with dates.
Territory captured from Saracens, with dates.
Important battles, with dates.

© Arthur Banks 1972

The first Norman stronghold was established at Aversa in 1027, and in later years, Norman influence spread across Southern Italy and Sicily. Robert and Roger Guiscard were the most prominent Norman leaders at this period, and were engaged in wars and battles with the Moslems and Byzantines. Robert's son Bohemund and other Normans took part in the Crusades.

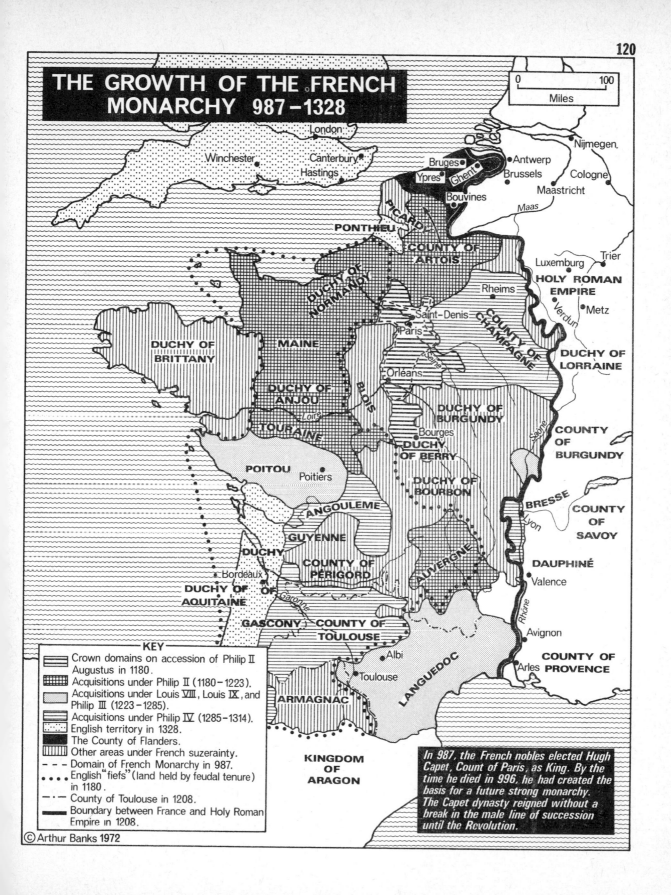

THE GROWTH OF THE FRENCH MONARCHY 987–1328

0   100
Miles

London
Winchester   Canterbury
Hastings

Nijmegen
Bruges   Antwerp
Ypres   Ghent   Brussels   Cologne
Bouvines   Maastricht
Maas

PICARDY
PONTHIEU
COUNTY OF ARTOIS
Luxemburg   Trier

HOLY ROMAN EMPIRE
Rheims
Verdun   Metz

DUCHY OF NORMANDY
Saint-Denis
Paris
COUNTY OF CHAMPAGNE
DUCHY OF LORRAINE

DUCHY OF BRITTANY
MAINE
Orléans
BLOIS

DUCHY OF ANJOU
Loire
TOURAINE
DUCHY OF BURGUNDY
Bourges
DUCHY OF BERRY
COUNTY OF BURGUNDY

POITOU
Poitiers
DUCHY OF BOURBON
BRESSE
COUNTY OF SAVOY

ANGOULEME
GUYENNE
AUVERGNE
Lyon
DAUPHINÉ
Valence

DUCHY OF AQUITAINE
Bordeaux
COUNTY OF PERIGORD
Rhone

GASCONY   COUNTY OF TOULOUSE
Avignon
COUNTY OF PROVENCE
Arles

ARMAGNAC
Albi
Toulouse
LANGUEDOC

KINGDOM OF ARAGON

KEY

Crown domains on accession of Philip II Augustus in 1180.

Acquisitions under Philip II (1180–1223).

Acquisitions under Louis VIII, Louis IX, and Philip III (1223–1285).

Acquisitions under Philip IV (1285–1314).

English territory in 1328.

The County of Flanders.

Other areas under French suzerainty.

– – – Domain of French Monarchy in 987.

• • • • English "fiefs" (land held by feudal tenure) in 1180.

– • – County of Toulouse in 1208.

Boundary between France and Holy Roman Empire in 1208.

© Arthur Banks 1972

In 987, the French nobles elected Hugh Capet, Count of Paris, as King. By the time he died in 996, he had created the basis for a future strong monarchy. The Capet dynasty reigned without a break in the male line of succession until the Revolution.

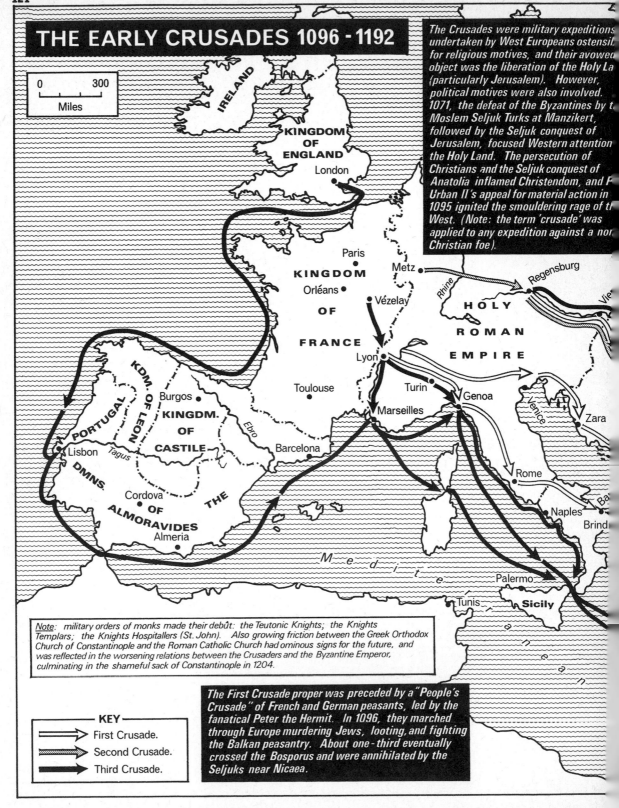

THE EARLY CRUSADES 1096 - 1192

0 ——— 300
Miles

The Crusades were military expeditions
undertaken by West Europeans ostensibl[y]
for religious motives, and their avowed
object was the liberation of the Holy La[nd]
(particularly Jerusalem). However,
political motives were also involved.
1071, the defeat of the Byzantines by t[he]
Moslem Seljuk Turks at Manzikert,
followed by the Seljuk conquest of
Jerusalem, focused Western attention [on]
the Holy Land. The persecution of
Christians and the Seljuk conquest of
Anatolia inflamed Christendom, and P[ope]
Urban II's appeal for material action in
1095 ignited the smouldering rage of t[he]
West. (Note: the term 'crusade' was
applied to any expedition against a no[n]
Christian foe).

IRELAND

KINGDOM
OF
ENGLAND
London

Paris
Metz
Rhine
Regensburg
Vie[nna]

KINGDOM
Orléans
Vézelay
HOLY

OF
Lyon
ROMAN

FRANCE
Turin
Genoa
EMPIRE

Toulouse
Marseilles
Venice
Zara

KDM.
OF LEON
Burgos
KINGDM.
Ebro
Barcelona
Rome

PORTUGAL
OF
Naples
Ba[ri]

Lisbon
Tagus
CASTILE
Brind[isi]

DMNS.
THE

Cordova
OF

ALMORAVIDES
Palermo

Almeria
M e d i t e
Tunis
Sicily

Note: military orders of monks made their debût: the Teutonic Knights; the Knights
Templars; the Knights Hospitallers (St. John). Also growing friction between the Greek Orthodox
Church of Constantinople and the Roman Catholic Church had ominous signs for the future, and
was reflected in the worsening relations between the Crusaders and the Byzantine Emperor,
culminating in the shameful sack of Constantinople in 1204.

The First Crusade proper was preceded by a "People's
Crusade" of French and German peasants, led by the
fanatical Peter the Hermit. In 1096, they marched
through Europe murdering Jews, looting, and fighting
the Balkan peasantry. About one-third eventually
crossed the Bosporus and were annihilated by the
Seljuks near Nicaea.

KEY

⇒ First Crusade.

⇒ Second Crusade.

→ Third Crusade.

FIRST CRUSADE 1096-1099

ADERS
...hemar de Monteil (Papal Legate).
...hemund of Taranto.
...cred (Bohemund's nephew).
...ymond of Toulouse.
...ffrey de Bouillon of Lorraine.
...dwin (Godfrey's brother).
...gh of Vermandois.(Louis VI's brother)
...bert of Normandy.(William I's son).
...phen of Blois.(William I's son-in-law).
...bert of Flanders.

...te: Leaders of later Crusades are
...wn on map entitled:
...he Later Crusades 1202 - 1270"

SECOND CRUSADE 1147-1149

LEADERS
Conrad III of Germany.
Louis VII of France.
Baldwin III of Jerusalem.

THIRD CRUSADE 1189-1192

LEADERS
Frederick I (Barbarossa) of Germany.
Philip II (Augustus) of France.
Richard I (Cœur de Lion) of England.
Leopold of Austria.

MILITARY LESSONS OF THE CRUSADES

TACTICS
The value of manœuvrability; the use of light cavalry
for reconnaissance; the significance of horse-archery;
the importance of combining cavalry and infantry.

FORTIFICATIONS
Castle and city defence systems were completely
revised in the West. The turreted walls (with double
or triple concentric defence lines) of Byzantine
strongpoints were noted in particular.

LOGISTICS
The importance of sea-power; the need for supply
bases; the improvement of organization techniques.

1109, Norman, Lombard, and German Crusaders under Raymond and Stephen of Blois, severely defeated in attempt to rescue Bohemund.

1100 - 1103, Bohemund imprisoned here.

Caspian Sea

KINGDOM
st
OF
...UNGARY

Belgrade

Danube

KDM. OF BULGARIA

...RBIA

Adrianople

Thessalonica

Athens

Black Sea

Constantinople

Sinope

Trebizond

Kastamuni

Mersivan
SELJUK KINGDOM
OF
ICONIUM

Sivas

Nicaea 1101

Dorylaeum

Angora

Iconium
(Konya)

Edessa

COUNTY
OF EDESSA

Tigris

Smyrna

Aleppo
Antioch
PRIN. OF
ANTIOCH

Euphrates

Cyprus

Tripoli

KINGDOM

Crete

Tyre
Acre

OF

JERUSALEM

Sea

Jaffa

Jerusalem

Damietta

Ascalon

Cairo

© Arthur Banks 1972

123

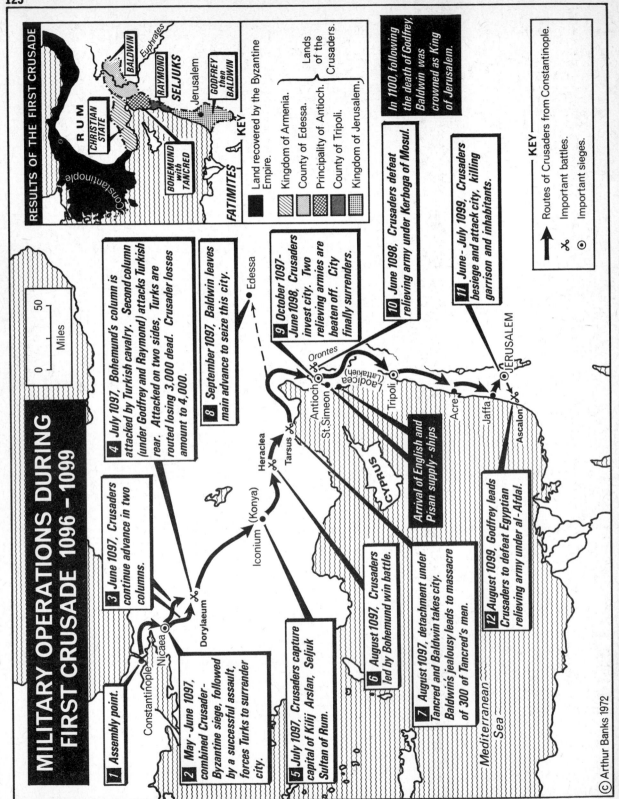

MILITARY OPERATIONS DURING FIRST CRUSADE 1096–1099

1 Assembly point.

2 May–June 1097, combined Crusader-Byzantine siege, followed by a successful assault, forces Turks to surrender city.

3 June 1097, Crusaders continue advance in two columns.

4 July 1097, Bohemund's column is attacked by Turkish cavalry. Second column (under Godfrey and Raymond) attacks Turkish rear. Attacked on two sides, Turks are routed losing 3,000 dead. Crusader losses amount to 4,000.

5 July 1097, Crusaders capture capital of Kilij Arslan, Seljuk Sultan of Rum.

6 August 1097, Crusaders led by Bohemund win battle.

7 August 1097, detachment under Tancred and Baldwin takes city. Baldwin's jealousy leads to massacre of 300 of Tancred's men.

8 September 1097, Baldwin leaves main advance to seize this city.

9 October 1097–June 1098, Crusaders invest city. Two relieving armies are beaten off. City finally surrenders.

10 June 1098, Crusaders defeat relieving army under Kerboga of Mosul.

11 June–July 1099, Crusaders besiege and attack city, killing garrison and inhabitants.

12 August 1099, Godfrey leads Crusaders to defeat Egyptian relieving army under al-Afdal.

Arrival of English and Pisan supply-ships

In 1100, following the death of Godfrey, Baldwin was crowned as King of Jerusalem.

Constantinople

Nicaea

Dorylaeum

Iconium (Konya)

Heraclea

Tarsus

St.Simeon

Antioch

Laodicea (Latakien)

Orontes

Tripoli

Acre

Jaffa

Ascalon

JERUSALEM

Edessa

CYPRUS

Mediterranean Sea

50 0 Miles

© Arthur Banks 1972

RESULTS OF THE FIRST CRUSADE

R U M CHRISTIAN STATE

BALDWIN

Euphrates

RAYMOND

SELJUKS

BOHEMUND with TANCRED

GODFREY then BALDWIN

Jerusalem

FATIMITES

Constantinople

KEY

Land recovered by the Byzantine Empire.

Lands of the Crusaders.

Kingdom of Armenia.
County of Edessa.
Principality of Antioch.
County of Tripoli.
Kingdom of Jerusalem.

KEY

→ Routes of Crusaders from Constantinople.

✗ Important battles.

⊙ Important sieges.

THE CRUSADERS IN THE MIDDLE EAST 1100 - 1146

This map depicts the Middle East in turmoil after most of the First Crusaders had returned home. The four leaders remaining in the area were Godfrey (who died in 1100), Baldwin, Bohemund, and Raymond. Godfrey was succeeded by his brother Baldwin, who became King of Jerusalem. The Crusaders' objective was to consolidate their positions, and reinforcements were sent from Europe to assist them. Their main asset was not their strength, but disunity among their enemies.

17 1144, city falls to Imad-al-Din Zengi. Papal call for a Second Crusade.

9 1104, Bohemund, released from imprisonment, is defeated.

1 1100, Bohemund is captured by Turks and is imprisoned for three years at Sivas. Tancred rules in Antioch.

16 1125, Baldwin II wins major victory over Moslems.

4 1101, Baldwin defeats Egyptian Saad-el-Dawleh.

6 1102, Baldwin is defeated by Egyptian army, but he escapes and regroups. Stephen of Blois is killed.

11 1105, in third battle of Ramleh, Baldwin defeats Egyptians.

2 August 1101. William of Nevers' expedition smashed by Turks.

15 1119, Roger of Antioch is defeated and killed by Ilghazi of Aleppo.

12 1109, surrenders to Baldwin.

14 1111 - 1112, Crusaders unsuccessful in attempt to capture this city. It falls to Venetians and Crusaders in 1124.

Fortress built by Baldwin.

3 September 1101, armies of Bavaria and Aquitaine annihilated by Turks. Hugh of Vermandois dies of wounds.

8 1103, besieged and taken by Tancred from Byzantines.

5 1102, Raymond destroys Moslem army.

13 1110, captured by Baldwin, assisted by Sigurd I of Norway.

10 1104, taken by Baldwin.

7 27 May 1102, Baldwin defeats Egyptians.

KEY

- Baldwin's expedition 1116 - 1117.
- Baldwin's unsuccessful expedition to Egypt 1118.
- Crusaders' successful raid 1146.

Tigris

Euphrates

Melitene

Edessa

Harran

Azaz

Antioch

Lattakieh (Laodicea)

Tripoli

Sidon

Acre

Tyre

Jaffa

Ramleh

Jerusalem

Ascalon

Bosra

Jordan

Le Krak de Montreal

Eilat

SINAI

Nile

EGYPT

Heraclea

Mediterranean Sea

0   100   Miles

125

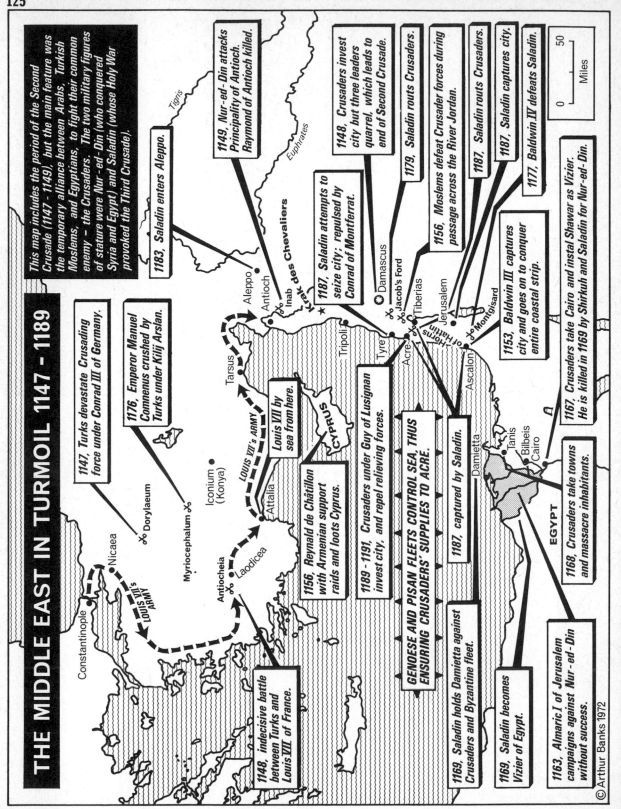

THE MIDDLE EAST IN TURMOIL 1147 - 1189

This map includes the period of the Second Crusade (1147 - 1149), but the main feature was the temporary alliance between Arabs, Turkish Moslems, and Egyptians, to fight their common enemy — the Crusaders. The two military figures of stature were Nur-ed-Din (who conquered Syria and Egypt) and Saladin (whose Holy War provoked the Third Crusade).

1183, Saladin enters Aleppo.

1149, Nur-ed-Din attacks Principality of Antioch. Raymond of Antioch killed.

1148, Crusaders invest city but three leaders quarrel, which leads to end of Second Crusade.

1179, Saladin routs Crusaders.

1187, Saladin routs Crusaders.

1187, Saladin captures city.

1177, Baldwin IV defeats Saladin.

1156, Moslems defeat Crusader forces during passage across the River Jordan.

1187, Saladin attempts to seize city; repulsed by Conrad of Montferrat.

1153, Baldwin III captures city and goes on to conquer entire coastal strip.

1167, Crusaders take Cairo and instal Shawar as Vizier. He is killed in 1169 by Shirkuh and Saladin for Nur-ed-Din.

1147, Turks devastate Crusading force under Conrad III of Germany.

1176, Emperor Manuel Comnenus crushed by Turks under Kilij Arslan.

Louis VII by sea from here.

1156, Reynald de Châtillon with Armenian support raids and loots Cyprus.

1189 - 1191, Crusaders under Guy of Lusignan invest city, and repel relieving forces.

GENOESE AND PISAN FLEETS CONTROL SEA, THUS ENSURING CRUSADERS' SUPPLIES TO ACRE.

1187, captured by Saladin.

1168, Crusaders take towns and massacre inhabitants.

1148, indecisive battle between Turks and Louis VII of France.

1169, Saladin holds Damietta against Crusaders and Byzantine fleet.

1169, Saladin becomes Vizier of Egypt.

1163, Almaric I of Jerusalem campaigns against Nur-ed-Din without success.

Constantinople

Nicaea

Dorylaeum

Myriocephalum

Iconium (Konya)

LOUIS VII's ARMY

Antiocheia

Laodicea

Attalia

CYPRUS

Tarsus

LOUIS VII's ARMY

Aleppo

Antioch

Inab

Krak des Chevaliers

Tigris

Euphrates

Tripoli

Tyre

Acre

Ascalon

Damietta

Tanis

Bilbeis

Cairo

EGYPT

Jerusalem

Horns of Hattin

Tiberias

Jacob's Ford

Damascus

Montgisard

0   50
Miles

© Arthur Banks 1972

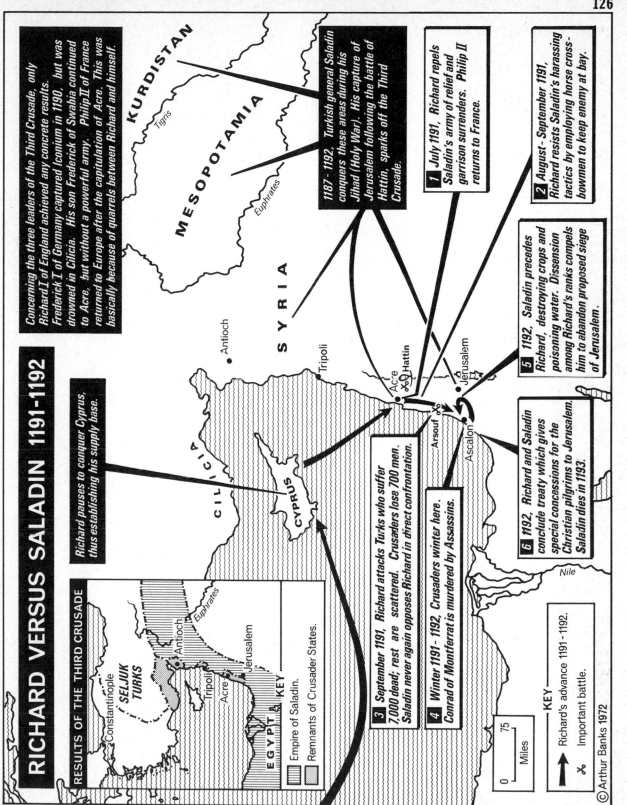

RICHARD VERSUS SALADIN 1191-1192

Concerning the three leaders of the Third Crusade, only Richard I of England achieved any concrete results. Frederick I of Germany captured Iconium in 1190, but was drowned in Cilicia. His son Frederick of Swabia continued to Acre, but without a powerful army. Philip II of France returned to Europe after the capitulation of Acre. This was basically because of quarrels between Richard and himself.

RESULTS OF THE THIRD CRUSADE

1187 - 1192, Turkish general Saladin conquers these areas during his Jihad (Holy War). His capture of Jerusalem following the battle of Hattin, sparks off the Third Crusade.

1 July 1191, Richard repels Saladin's army of relief and garrison surrenders. Philip II returns to France.

2 August - September 1191, Richard resists Saladin's harassing tactics by employing horse cross-bowmen to keep enemy at bay.

5 1192, Saladin precedes Richard, destroying crops and poisoning water. Dissension among Richard's ranks compels him to abandon proposed siege of Jerusalem.

6 1192, Richard and Saladin conclude treaty which gives special concessions for the Christian pilgrims to Jerusalem. Saladin dies in 1193.

Richard pauses to conquer Cyprus, thus establishing his supply base.

3 September 1191, Richard attacks Turks who suffer 7,000 dead; rest are scattered. Crusaders lose 700 men. Saladin never again opposes Richard in direct confrontation.

4 Winter 1191 - 1192, Crusaders winter here. Conrad of Montferrat is murdered by Assassins.

KEY
Empire of Saladin.
Remnants of Crusader States.

KEY
Richard's advance 1191 - 1192.
Important battle.

0 75
Miles

© Arthur Banks 1972

KURDISTAN, MESOPOTAMIA, SYRIA, CILICIA, CYPRUS, EGYPT, Tigris, Euphrates, Nile, Antioch, Tripoli, Acre, Hattin, Jerusalem, Arsouf, Ascalon, Constantinople, SELJUK TURKS

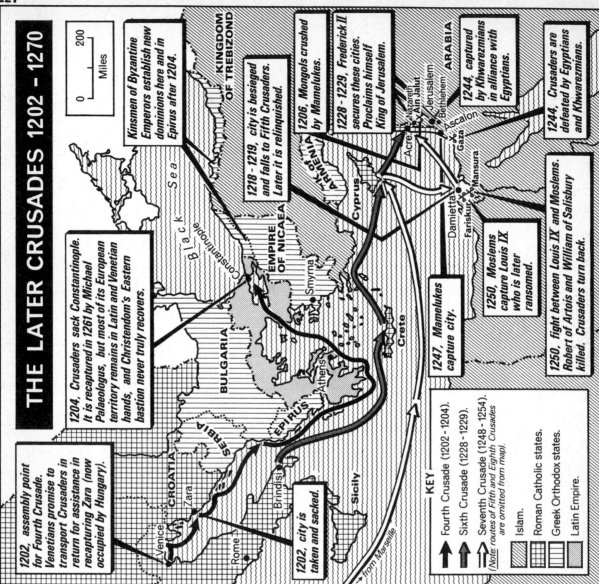

THE LATER CRUSADES 1202 – 1270

200 Miles
0

KINGDOM OF TREBIZOND

Kinsmen of Byzantine Emperors establish new dominions here and in Epirus after 1204.

1218 – 1219, city is besieged and falls to Fifth Crusaders. Later it is relinquished.

1206, Mongols crushed by Mamelukes.

1228 – 1229, Frederick II secures these cities. Proclaims himself King of Jerusalem.

ARABIA

1244, captured by Khwarezmians in alliance with Egyptians.

1244, Crusaders are defeated by Egyptians and Khwarezmians.

Nazareth
Ain Jalut
Jerusalem
Bethlehem
Ascalon
Gaza
Acre

1204, Crusaders sack Constantinople. It is recaptured in 1261 by Michael Palaeologus, but most of its European territory remains in Latin and Venetian hands, and Christendom's Eastern bastion never truly recovers.

ARMENIA

Damietta
Fariskur
Mansura

Cyprus

EMPIRE OF NICAEA

Constantinople

1250, Moslems capture Louis IX who is later ransomed.

Black Sea

Smyrna

1247, Mamelukes capture city.

1250, fight between Louis IX and Moslems. Robert of Artois and William of Salisbury killed. Crusaders turn back.

1202, assembly point for Fourth Crusade. Venetians promise to transport Crusaders in return for assistance in recapturing Zara (now occupied by Hungary).

BULGARIA

SERBIA

CROATIA

Athens
Crete

EPIRUS

Sicily

Brindisi

Venice
Zara
Rome

from Marseille

1202, city is taken and sacked.

KEY

Fourth Crusade (1202 – 1204).
Sixth Crusade (1228 – 1229).
Seventh Crusade (1248 – 1254).
(Note: routes of Fifth and Eighth Crusades are omitted from map).

Islam.
Roman Catholic states.
Greek Orthodox states.
Latin Empire.

FOURTH CRUSADE 1202–1204

LEADERS
Boniface of Montferrat.
Louis of Blois.
Baldwin of Flanders.
Henry (brother of Baldwin).
Henry Dandolo, Doge of Venice.
Simon de Montfort.

FIFTH CRUSADE 1218–1221

LEADERS
Frederick II of Germany. *(who never participated)*
John of Brienne, King of Jerusalem.
Hugh of Cyprus.
Cardinal Pelagius.
Hermann von Salza.
Louis of Bavaria.
Andrew of Hungary.
Leopold of Austria.

CHILDREN'S CRUSADES 1212

There were two crusades by children. The first was led by a French shepherd boy named Stephen; the second by a German boy named Nicholas. Both crusades were marked by intense suffering.

SIXTH CRUSADE 1228 – 1229

LEADERS
Frederick II of Germany.
Hermann von Salza.

SEVENTH CRUSADE 1248 – 1254

LEADERS
Louis IX of France.
Robert of Artois } brothers of Louis IX
Charles of Anjou
William, *Earl of Salisbury.*

EIGHTH CRUSADE 1270

LEADERS
Louis IX of France, (died at Tunis).
Charles of Anjou.

Note: Prince Edward of England arrived in the Holy Land (1271) to find that the Crusade had ended. After a year in Acre he made a truce and returned to England.

© Arthur Banks 1972

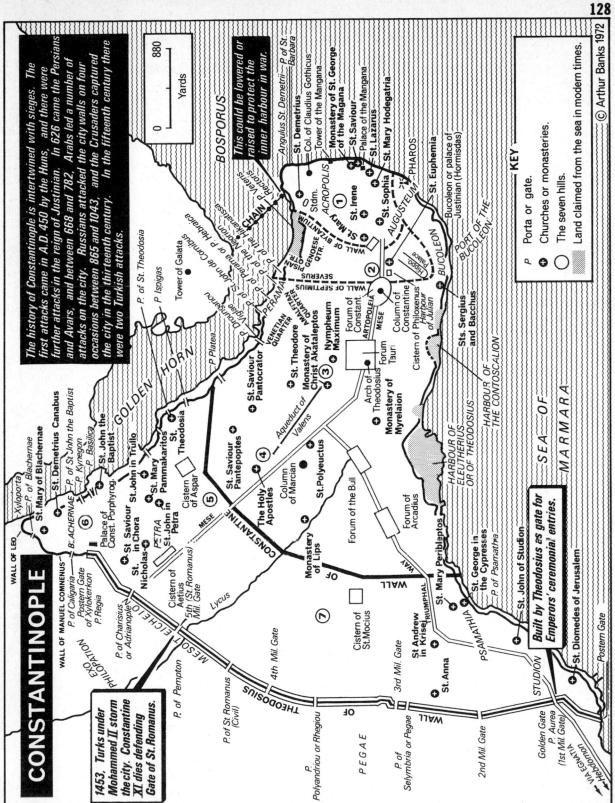

CONSTANTINOPLE

128

© Arthur Banks 1972

The history of Constantinople is intertwined with sieges. The first attacks came in A.D. 450 by the Huns, and there were further attacks in the reign of Justinian. In 626 came the Persians and Avars, and between 668 and 782, Arabs led a number of attacks on the city. Russians attacked the city walls on four occasions between 865 and 1043, and the Crusaders captured the city in the thirteenth century. In the fifteenth century there were two Turkish attacks.

1453, Turks under Mohammed II storm the city. Constantine XI dies defending Gate of St. Romanus.

This could be lowered or raised to protect the inner harbour in war.

Built by Theodosius as gate for Emperors' ceremonial entries.

KEY.

P   Porta or gate.
✠   Churches or monasteries.
◯   The seven hills.
    Land claimed from the sea in modern times.

BOSPORUS

GOLDEN HORN

SEA OF MARMARA

Tower of Galata

CHAIN

ACROPOLIS

St. Irene

St. Mary

St. Sophia

AUGUSTEUM

PHAROS

St. Euphemia

BUCOLEON

Bucoleon or palace of Justinian (Hormisdas)

PORT OF THE BUCOLEON

Angulus St. Demetrii

St. Demetrius

Col. of Claudius Gothicus

Tower of the Mangana

Monastery of St. George of the Mangana

St. Saviour

Palace of the Magana

St. Lazarus

St. Mary Hodegatria

P. of St. Barbara

WALL OF BYZANTIUM

GENOESE QTR.

PISAN QTR.

WALL OF SEVERUS

WALL OF SEPTIMIUS SEVERUS

Hippo.

ARTOPOLEIA

Column of Constantine

Forum of Constant.

MESE

Sts. Sergius and Bacchus

Cistern of Philoxenus

Column of Philoxenus

Forum Tauri

Arch of Theodosius

Monastery of Myrelaion

HARBOUR OF THE CONTOSCALION

HARBOUR OF ELEUTHERIUS OR OF THEODOSIUS

Nympheum Maximum

Monastery of Christ Akataleptos

St. Theodore

VENETIAN QUARTER

AMALFITAN QUARTER

PERAMA

P. of the Neorion

P. of St. John de Cornibus

P. of Perama or p. Hebraica

Droungarios

P. Vigla or p. of the Tzikanisterion

St. Mary of the Veneti

P. Veteris

P. of the Rectors

St. Saviour Pantocrator

Aqueduct of Valens

P. of St. Theodosia

P. Ispigas

P. Platea

P. of Cornibus

St. John the Baptist

P. of Kynegon

P. Basilica

St. Demetrius Canabus

P. of St John the Baptist

St. Mary of Blachernae

P. of Blachernae

Xyloporta

WALL OF LEO

WALL OF MANUEL COMNENUS

P. of Caligaria

Postern Gate of Xylokerkon

P. Regia

BLACHERNAE

Palace of Const. Porphyrog.

St. Saviour in Chora

St. Nicholas

St. John in Trullo

St. Mary Pammakaritos

St. Theodosia

PETRA

St. John in Petra

Cistern of Aspar

Cistern of Aetius

5th (St. Romanus) Mil. Gate

Lycus

P. of Charisius or Adrianople

EXOPATION

P. of Pempton

PHILOPATION

MESOTEICHEION

P. of St Romanus (Civil)

4th Mil. Gate

WALL OF THEODOSIUS

P. Polyandriou or Rhegiou

P. of Selymbria or Pegae

3rd Mil. Gate

Cistern of St.Mocius

St Andrew in Krise

TRIUMPHAL WAY

St. Anna

St. George in the Cypresses

P. of Psamathia

St. Mary Peribleptos

St. John of Studion

STUDION

PSAMATHIA

PEGAE

2nd Mil. Gate

Golden Gate P. Aurea (1st Mil Gate)

VIA EGNATIA

Hebdomon

Postern Gate

St. Diomedes of Jerusalem

St. Saviour Pantepoptes

Column of Marcian

St. Polyeuctus

The Holy Apostles

Monastery of Lips

Forum of the Bull

Forum of Arcadius

St. John the Baptist

① St. Irene
② Hippodrome area
③ Monastery of Christ Akataleptos
④ St. Saviour Pantepoptes
⑤ Cistern of Aspar
⑥ Blachernae
⑦ Cistern of St. Mocius

0   880
Yards

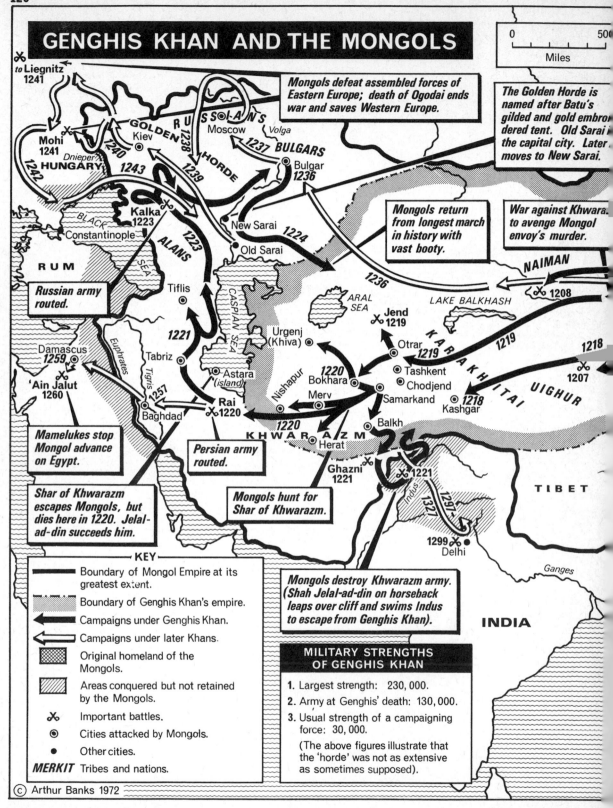

GENGHIS KHAN AND THE MONGOLS

0   500
Miles

to Liegnitz 1241

Mohi 1241

HUNGARY

1242

1243

Mongols defeat assembled forces of Eastern Europe; death of Ogodai ends war and saves Western Europe.

The Golden Horde is named after Batu's gilded and gold embroidered tent. Old Sarai the capital city. Later moves to New Sarai.

GOLDEN

Kiev

1238

1240

1239

HORDE

Moscow

1237

BULGARS

Bulgar 1236

Volga

RUSSIANS

Dnieper

BLACK

Kalka 1223

Constantinople

1223

ALANS

1223

New Sarai

1224

Old Sarai

1236

Mongols return from longest march in history with vast booty.

War against Khwara. to avenge Mongol envoy's murder.

NAIMAN

1208

SEA

RUM

Russian army routed.

Tiflis

CASPIAN SEA

ARAL SEA

Jend 1219

LAKE BALKHASH

1219

Urgenj (Khiva)

1221

Damascus 1259

'Ain Jalut 1260

Euphrates

Tabriz

Tigris

1257

Astara (island)

Rai 1220

Baghdad

Nishapur

Otrar 1219

1218

1219

1207

Tashkent

Bokhara

Chodjend

1220

Merv

Samarkand

Kashgar

1218

KARAKHITAI

UIGHUR

Mamelukes stop Mongol advance on Egypt.

Persian army routed.

KHWARAZM

Herat

Balkh

Mongols hunt for Shar of Khwarazm.

Ghazni 1221

1221

TIBET

Shar of Khwarazm escapes Mongols, but dies here in 1220. Jelal-ad-din succeeds him.

1327

1291

1299

Delhi

Indus

Ganges

Mongols destroy Khwarazm army. (Shah Jelal-ad-din on horseback leaps over cliff and swims Indus to escape from Genghis Khan).

INDIA

KEY

— Boundary of Mongol Empire at its greatest extent.

▒ Boundary of Genghis Khan's empire.

◄ Campaigns under Genghis Khan.

◁ Campaigns under later Khans.

▦ Original homeland of the Mongols.

▨ Areas conquered but not retained by the Mongols.

✕ Important battles.

◉ Cities attacked by Mongols.

• Other cities.

MERKIT Tribes and nations.

MILITARY STRENGTHS OF GENGHIS KHAN

1. Largest strength: 230,000.
2. Army at Genghis' death: 130,000.
3. Usual strength of a campaigning force: 30,000.

(The above figures illustrate that the 'horde' was not as extensive as sometimes supposed).

© Arthur Banks 1972

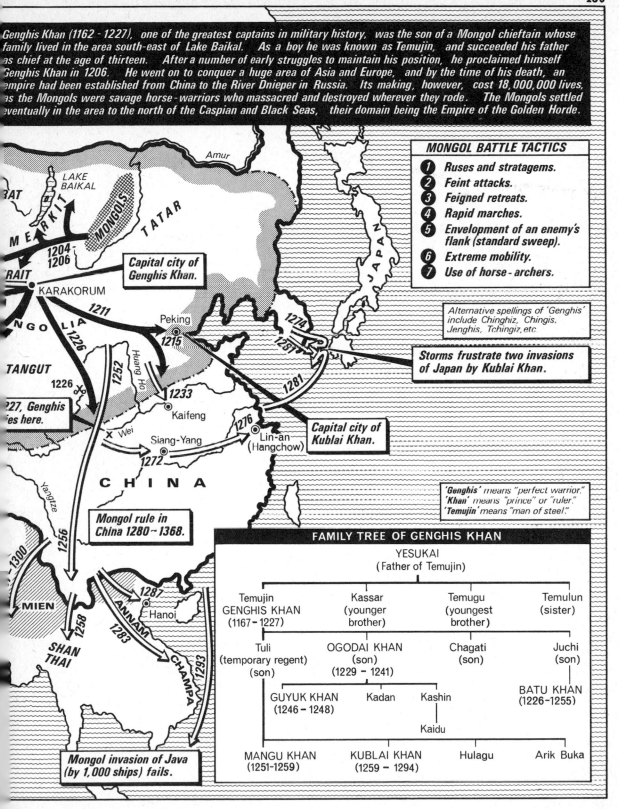

Genghis Khan (1162 - 1227), one of the greatest captains in military history, was the son of a Mongol chieftain whose family lived in the area south-east of Lake Baikal. As a boy he was known as Temujin, and succeeded his father as chief at the age of thirteen. After a number of early struggles to maintain his position, he proclaimed himself Genghis Khan in 1206. He went on to conquer a huge area of Asia and Europe, and by the time of his death, an Empire had been established from China to the River Dnieper in Russia. Its making, however, cost 18,000,000 lives, as the Mongols were savage horse-warriors who massacred and destroyed wherever they rode. The Mongols settled eventually in the area to the north of the Caspian and Black Seas, their domain being the Empire of the Golden Horde.

MONGOL BATTLE TACTICS

1. Ruses and stratagems.
2. Feint attacks.
3. Feigned retreats.
4. Rapid marches.
5. Envelopment of an enemy's flank (standard sweep).
6. Extreme mobility.
7. Use of horse-archers.

Alternative spellings of 'Genghis' include Chinghiz, Chingis, Jenghis, Tchingiz, etc.

Capital city of Genghis Khan.

Storms frustrate two invasions of Japan by Kublai Khan.

Capital city of Kublai Khan.

'Genghis' means "perfect warrior." 'Khan' means "prince" or "ruler." 'Temujin' means "man of steel."

1227, Genghis dies here.

Mongol rule in China 1280~1368.

Mongol invasion of Java (by 1,000 ships) fails.

FAMILY TREE OF GENGHIS KHAN

YESUKAI
(Father of Temujin)

Temujin GENGHIS KHAN (1167 - 1227) — Kassar (younger brother) — Temugu (youngest brother) — Temulun (sister)

Tuli (temporary regent) (son) — OGODAI KHAN (son) (1229 - 1241) — Chagati (son) — Juchi (son)

GUYUK KHAN (1246 - 1248) — Kadan — Kashin — BATU KHAN (1226-1255)

Kaidu

MANGU KHAN (1251-1259) — KUBLAI KHAN (1259 - 1294) — Hulagu — Arik Buka

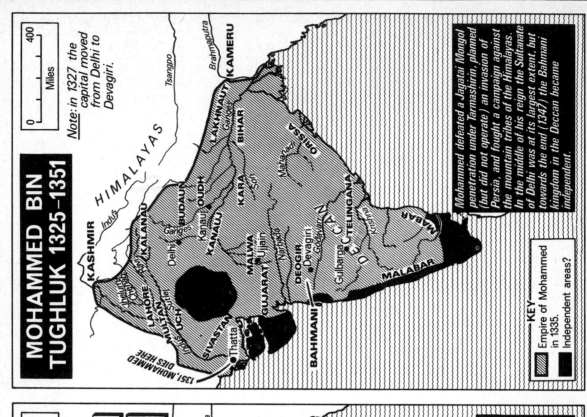

MOHAMMED BIN TUGHLUK 1325–1351

400 | Miles | 0

Note: in 1327 the capital moved from Delhi to Devagiri.

1351, MOHAMMED DIES HERE

KAMERU

HIMALAYAS

KASHMIR

Indus

Jhelum
Chenab
Ravi
Sutlej

LAHORE
MULTAN
UCH
SIVASTAN
Thatta

Ganges
BUDAUN
KALANAUR
OUDH
Kanauj
Delhi
MALWA
Ujjain
GUJARAT
DEOGIR
Devagiri
Gulbarga
BAHMANI

LAKHNAUTI
BIHAR
Gogra
Son
KARA
Narbada
DECCAN
TELINGANA
Godavari
Krishna

Brahmaputra
Tsangpo
ORISSA
Mahanadi
MALABAR

Mohammed defeated a Jagatai Mongol penetration under Tarmashirin, planned (but did not operate) an invasion of Persia, and fought a campaign against the mountain tribes of the Himalayas. In the middle of his reign the Sultanate of Delhi was at its largest extent, but towards the end (1347) the Bahmani kingdom in the Deccan became independent.

KEY
▧ Empire of Mohammed in 1335.
■ Independent areas?

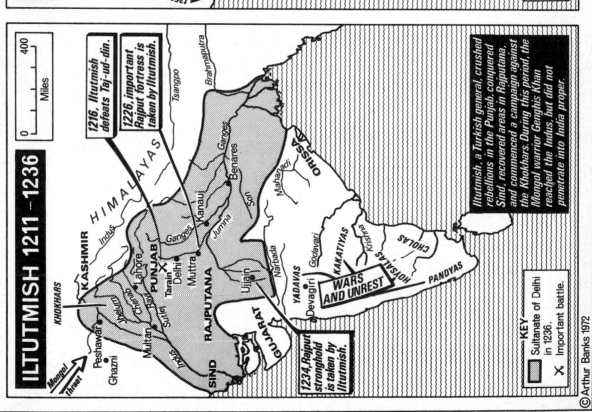

ILTUTMISH 1211–1236

400 | Miles | 0

1216, Iltutmish defeats Taj-ud-din.

1226, important Rajput fortress is taken by Iltutmish.

1234, Rajput stronghold is taken by Iltutmish.

Mongol threat

HIMALAYAS

KASHMIR
KHOKHARS
Peshawar
Ghazni
Multan
SIND
Indus
Jhelum
Chenab
Ravi
Sutlej
Lahore
PUNJAB
Tarain
Delhi
Muttra
RAJPUTANA
GUJARAT
Ujjain

Ganges
Kanauj
Jumna
Benares
Son
Narbada
YADAVAS
Devagiri

Brahmaputra
Tsangpo
Ganges
Mahanadi
ORISSA
Godavari
KAKATIYAS
Krishna
HOYSALAS
CHOLAS
PANDYAS

WARS AND UNREST

Iltutmish, a Turkish general, crushed rebellions in the Punjab, conquered Sind, recovered areas in Rajputana, and commenced a campaign against the Khokhars. During this period, the Mongol warrior Genghis Khan reached the Indus, but did not penetrate into India proper.

KEY
▨ Sultanate of Delhi in 1236.
✗ Important battle.

© Arthur Banks 1972

THE IMPORTANCE OF GEOGRAPHY IN THE MILITARY HISTORY OF NORTHERN INDIA

NOTE: *modern coastlines and river courses shown on this map.*

CONTOURS (in feet)

■	Over 18,000'
■	12,000'–18,000'
■	4,500'–12,000'
▦	1,200'–4,500'
▨	600'–1,200'
□	0'–600'

TIBETAN PLATEAUX

H I M A L A Y A S

Nanda Devi 25,645'

29,028' ▲ Mt. Everest

Tsangpo

Brahmaputra

PLAIN OF THE GANGES

Ganges

Ganges

Yamuna

Sutlej

Ravi

Chenab

Jhelum

INDUS

Indus

PLAIN OF THE

THAR OR INDIAN DESERT

KHYBER PASS

GOMAL PASS

KHOJAK PASS

BOLAN PASS

MALWA FLAT

Narbeda

DECCAN PLATEAU

Godavari

Kistna

Mahanadi

THE RANN OF CUTCH

Arabian Sea

KEY

■	Over – 12,000'
▦	1,200' – 12,000'
□	0' – 1,200'

➤ General direction of attacks on northern India.

INVASIONS

Ganges

Indus

0 ___ 300 Miles

0 ___ 100 ___ 200 Miles

Before the development of sea-power by the European nations, the invaders of India invariably attacked from the north–west direction. The Himalayas and Tibetan Plateaux proved to be an "impenetrable" barrier in the north-east, whereas the mountain passes in the north-west were fully exploited by generals such as Alexander, Timur, and Babur.

© Arthur Banks 1972

THE CAMPAIGNS OF TIMUR (TAMERLANE)
1369 – 1405

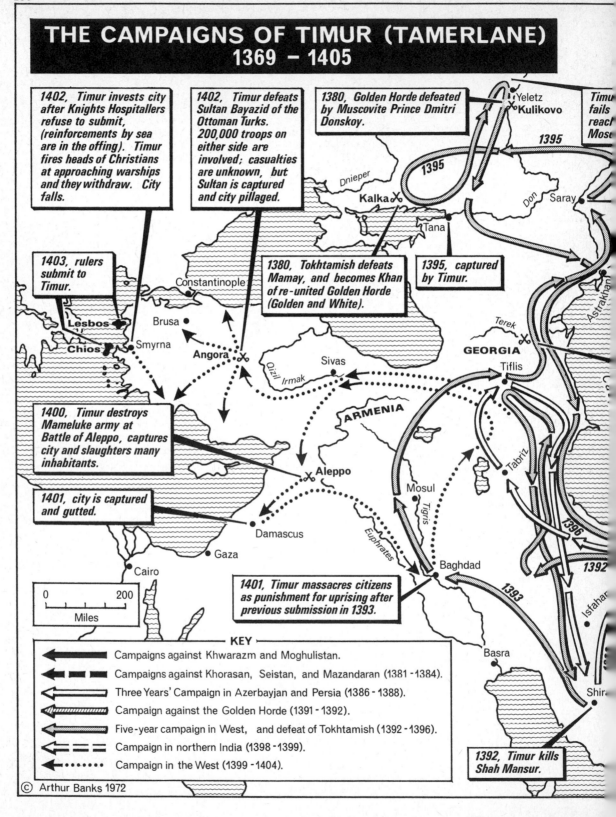

1402, Timur invests city after Knights Hospitallers refuse to submit, (reinforcements by sea are in the offing). Timur fires heads of Christians at approaching warships and they withdraw. City falls.

1402, Timur defeats Sultan Bayazid of the Ottoman Turks. 200,000 troops on either side are involved; casualties are unknown, but Sultan is captured and city pillaged.

1380, Golden Horde defeated by Muscovite Prince Dmitri Donskoy.

Timu fails reach Mos

1403, rulers submit to Timur.

1380, Tokhtamish defeats Mamay, and becomes Khan of re-united Golden Horde (Golden and White).

1395, captured by Timur.

1400, Timur destroys Mameluke army at Battle of Aleppo, captures city and slaughters many inhabitants.

1401, city is captured and gutted.

1401, Timur massacres citizens as punishment for uprising after previous submission in 1393.

1392, Timur kills Shah Mansur.

Yeletz
Kulikovo
Dnieper
Kalka
Tana
Saray
Don
1395
1395
Astrakhan
Constantinople
Brusa
Lesbos
Chios
Smyrna
Angora
Qizil Irmak
Sivas
GEORGIA
Tiflis
Terek
Tabriz
ARMENIA
Mosul
Tigris
Aleppo
Euphrates
Baghdad
1396
1393
1392
Damascus
Gaza
Cairo
Isfahan
Basra
Shir

```
0        200
   Miles
```

KEY
- Campaigns against Khwarazm and Moghulistan.
- Campaigns against Khorasan, Seistan, and Mazandaran (1381-1384).
- Three Years' Campaign in Azerbaijan and Persia (1386-1388).
- Campaign against the Golden Horde (1391-1392).
- Five-year campaign in West, and defeat of Tokhtamish (1392-1396).
- Campaign in northern India (1398-1399).
- Campaign in the West (1399-1404).

© Arthur Banks 1972

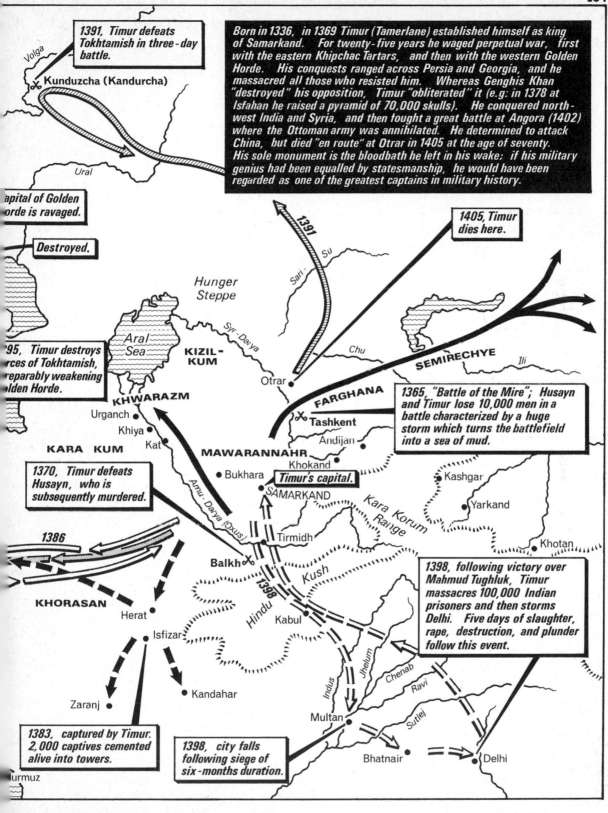

1391, Timur defeats Tokhtamish in three-day battle.

Volga

✕ Kunduzcha (Kandurcha)

Ural

Born in 1336, in 1369 Timur (Tamerlane) established himself as king of Samarkand. For twenty-five years he waged perpetual war, first with the eastern Khipchac Tartars, and then with the western Golden Horde. His conquests ranged across Persia and Georgia, and he massacred all those who resisted him. Whereas Genghis Khan "destroyed" his opposition, Timur "obliterated" it (e.g: in 1378 at Isfahan he raised a pyramid of 70,000 skulls). He conquered north-west India and Syria, and then fought a great battle at Angora (1402) where the Ottoman army was annihilated. He determined to attack China, but died "en route" at Otrar in 1405 at the age of seventy. His sole monument is the bloodbath he left in his wake; if his military genius had been equalled by statesmanship, he would have been regarded as one of the greatest captains in military history.

...apital of Golden ...orde is ravaged.

Destroyed.

...95, Timur destroys ...ces of Tokhtamish, ...reparably weakening ...olden Horde.

1405, Timur dies here.

Hunger Steppe

1391

Sarl - Su

Chu

Ili

SEMIRECHYE

Aral Sea

KIZIL-KUM

Syr - Da·ya

Otrar

FARGHANA

KHWARAZM

Urganch

Khiya

Kat

Amu - Darya (Oxus)

KARA KUM

Tashkent ✕

Andijan

1365, "Battle of the Mire"; Husayn and Timur lose 10,000 men in a battle characterized by a huge storm which turns the battlefield into a sea of mud.

MAWARANNAHR

Bukhara

Khokand

Timur's capital.

Kashgar

Yarkand

1370, Timur defeats Husayn, who is subsequently murdered.

SAMARKAND

Kara Korum Range

Tirmidh

Khotan

1386

Balkh ✕

1398

Kush

Hindu

KHORASAN

Herat

Isfizar

Kabul

1398, following victory over Mahmud Tughluk, Timur massacres 100,000 Indian prisoners and then storms Delhi. Five days of slaughter, rape, destruction, and plunder follow this event.

Indus

Jhelum

Chenab

Ravi

Kandahar

Zaranj

Multan

Sutlej

1383, captured by Timur. 2,000 captives cemented alive into towers.

1398, city falls following siege of six-months duration.

Bhatnair

Delhi

...urmuz

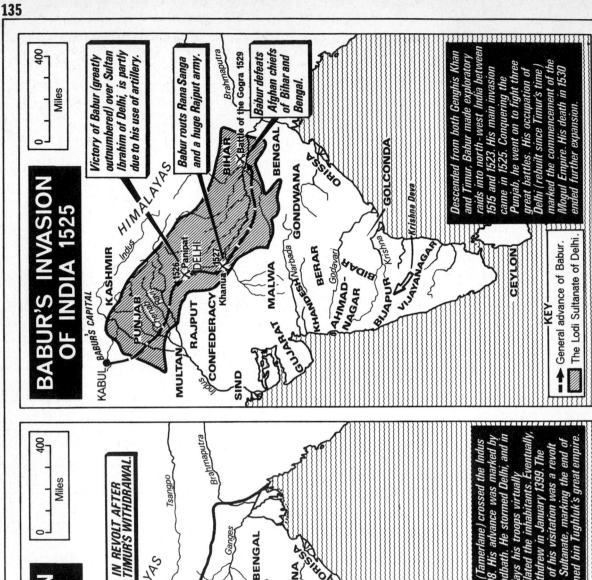

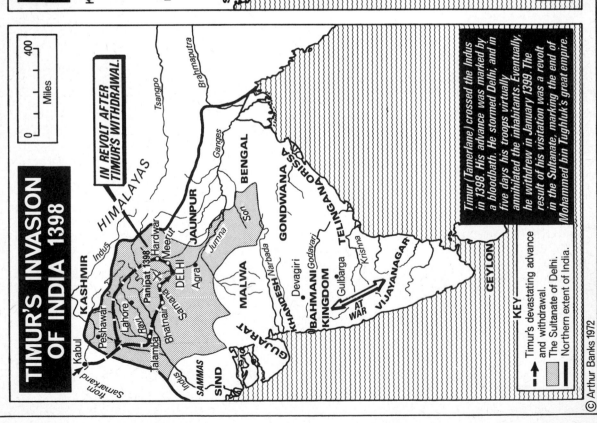

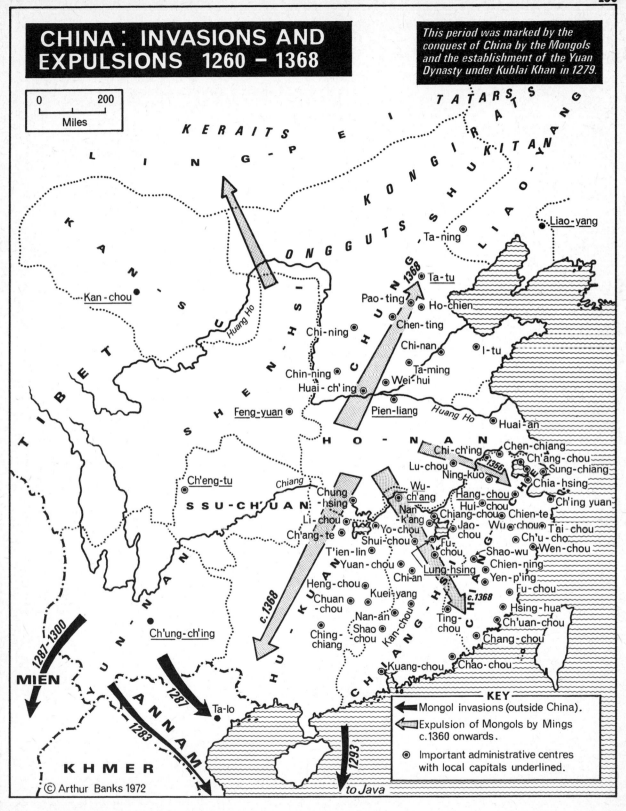

CHINA: INVASIONS AND EXPULSIONS 1260 – 1368

This period was marked by the conquest of China by the Mongols and the establishment of the Yuan Dynasty under Kublai Khan in 1279.

0 — 200
Miles

KERAITS

TATARS

LING-PEI

KAN'SU

Kan-chou

TIBET

Huang Ho

SHEN-HSI

Ch'eng-tu

Chiang

SSU-CH'UAN

Ch'ung-ch'ing

Feng-yuan

KONGIRATS

ONGGUTS SHUKITAN

LIAO-YANG

Liao-yang

Ta-ning

CHUNG 1368

Ta-tu

Pao-ting

Ho-chien

Chi-ning

Chen-ting

Chi-nan

I-tu

Chin-ning

Ta-ming

Wei-hui

Huai-ch'ing

Pien-liang

Huang Ho

Huai-an

HO-NAN

Chi-ch'ing

Chen-chiang

Ch'ang-chou

Lu-chou

1356

Sung-chiang

Ning-kuo

CHE

Chia-hsing

Wu-ch'ang

Hang-chou

Ch'ing yuan

Chung-hsing

Nan-k'ang

Hui-chou

Chien-te

Li-chou

Chiang-chou

Jao-chou

Wu-chou

T'ai-chou

Ch'ang-te

Yo-chou

Fu-chou

Shao-wu

Ch'u-cho

Wen-chou

Shui-chou

HU-KUANG

Lung-hsing

Chien-ning

T'ien-lin

Yen-p'ing

Yuan-chou

Chi-an

Fu-chou

Heng-chou

Kuei-yang

c.1368

Hsing-hua

Chuan-chou

Nan-an

Shao-chou

Kan-chou

Ting-chou

CHIANG-HSI

Ch'uan-chou

YUN-NAN

Ching-chiang

1287-1300

MIEN

Ta-lo

1287

ANNAM

1283

KHMER

© Arthur Banks 1972

CHIANG-HSI c.1368

Chang-chou

Kuang-chou

Chao-chou

1293

to Java

KEY
— Mongol invasions (outside China).

← Expulsion of Mongols by Mings c.1360 onwards.

⊙ Important administrative centres with local capitals underlined.

TWO IMPORTANT SIEGES OF CONSTANTINOPLE

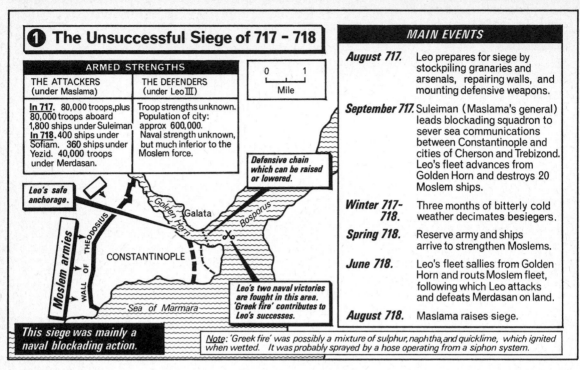

❶ The Unsuccessful Siege of 717 - 718

ARMED STRENGTHS

THE ATTACKERS (under Maslama)	THE DEFENDERS (under Leo III)
In 717. 80,000 troops, plus 80,000 troops aboard 1,800 ships under Suleiman. **In 718.** 400 ships under Sofiam. 360 ships under Yezid. 40,000 troops under Merdasan.	Troop strengths unknown. Population of city: approx 600,000. Naval strength unknown, but much inferior to the Moslem force.

0   1
Mile

Defensive chain which can be raised or lowered.

Leo's safe anchorage.

Golden Horn

Galata

Bosporus

Moslem armies

WALL OF THEODOSIUS

CONSTANTINOPLE

Leo's two naval victories are fought in this area. 'Greek fire' contributes to Leo's successes.

Sea of Marmara

This siege was mainly a naval blockading action.

MAIN EVENTS

August 717. Leo prepares for siege by stockpiling granaries and arsenals, repairing walls, and mounting defensive weapons.

September 717. Suleiman (Maslama's general) leads blockading squadron to sever sea communications between Constantinople and cities of Cherson and Trebizond. Leo's fleet advances from Golden Horn and destroys 20 Moslem ships.

Winter 717-718. Three months of bitterly cold weather decimates besiegers.

Spring 718. Reserve army and ships arrive to strengthen Moslems.

June 718. Leo's fleet sallies from Golden Horn and routs Moslem fleet, following which Leo attacks and defeats Merdasan on land.

August 718. Maslama raises siege.

<u>Note</u>: 'Greek fire' was possibly a mixture of sulphur, naphtha, and quicklime, which ignited when wetted. It was probably sprayed by a hose operating from a siphon system.

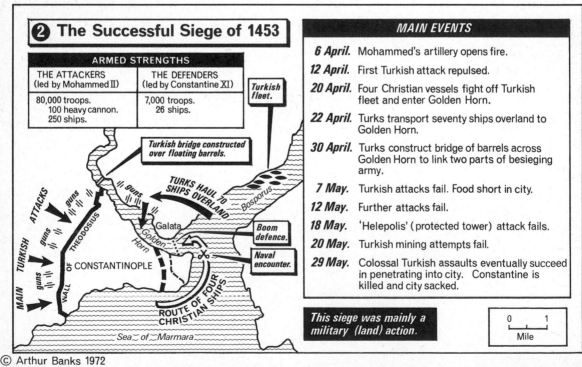

❷ The Successful Siege of 1453

ARMED STRENGTHS

THE ATTACKERS (led by Mohammed II)	THE DEFENDERS (led by Constantine XI)
80,000 troops. 100 heavy cannon. 250 ships.	7,000 troops. 26 ships.

Turkish fleet.

Turkish bridge constructed over floating barrels.

TURKS HAUL 70 SHIPS OVERLAND

TURKISH ATTACKS

guns

guns

MAIN TURKISH ATTACKS

guns

guns

WALL OF THEODOSIUS

CONSTANTINOPLE

Galata

Golden Horn

Bosporus

Boom defence.

Naval encounter.

ROUTE OF FOUR CHRISTIAN SHIPS

Sea of Marmara

This siege was mainly a military (land) action.

0   1
Mile

MAIN EVENTS

6 April. Mohammed's artillery opens fire.

12 April. First Turkish attack repulsed.

20 April. Four Christian vessels fight off Turkish fleet and enter Golden Horn.

22 April. Turks transport seventy ships overland to Golden Horn.

30 April. Turks construct bridge of barrels across Golden Horn to link two parts of besieging army.

7 May. Turkish attacks fail. Food short in city.

12 May. Further attacks fail.

18 May. 'Helepolis' (protected tower) attack fails.

20 May. Turkish mining attempts fail.

29 May. Colossal Turkish assaults eventually succeed in penetrating into city. Constantine is killed and city sacked.

138

TWO IMPORTANT SIEGES OF RHODES

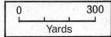

0 — 300
Yards

❶ The Unsuccessful Siege of 1480

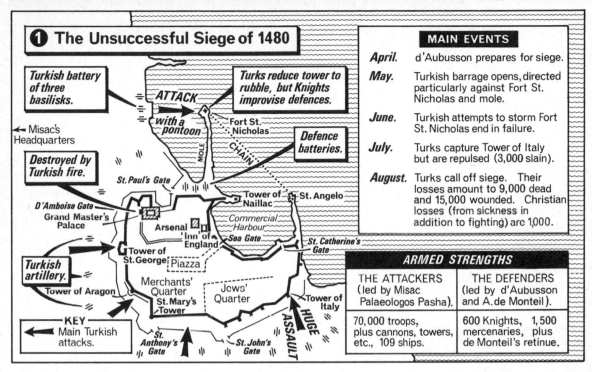

MAIN EVENTS

April. d'Aubusson prepares for siege.

May. Turkish barrage opens, directed particularly against Fort St. Nicholas and mole.

June. Turkish attempts to storm Fort St. Nicholas end in failure.

July. Turks capture Tower of Italy but are repulsed (3,000 slain).

August. Turks call off siege. Their losses amount to 9,000 dead and 15,000 wounded. Christian losses (from sickness in addition to fighting) are 1,000.

ARMED STRENGTHS

THE ATTACKERS (led by Misac Palaeologos Pasha).	THE DEFENDERS (led by d'Aubusson and A. de Monteil).
70,000 troops, plus cannons, towers, etc., 109 ships.	600 Knights, 1,500 mercenaries, plus de Monteil's retinue.

❷ The Successful Siege of 1522

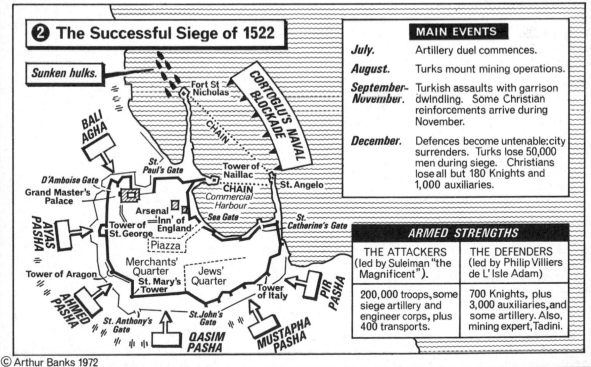

MAIN EVENTS

July. Artillery duel commences.

August. Turks mount mining operations.

September– November. Turkish assaults with garrison dwindling. Some Christian reinforcements arrive during November.

December. Defences become untenable: city surrenders. Turks lose 50,000 men during siege. Christians lose all but 180 Knights and 1,000 auxiliaries.

ARMED STRENGTHS

THE ATTACKERS (led by Suleiman "the Magnificent").	THE DEFENDERS (led by Philip Villiers de L'Isle Adam)
200,000 troops, some siege artillery and engineer corps, plus 400 transports.	700 Knights, plus 3,000 auxiliaries, and some artillery. Also, mining expert, Tadini.

© Arthur Banks 1972

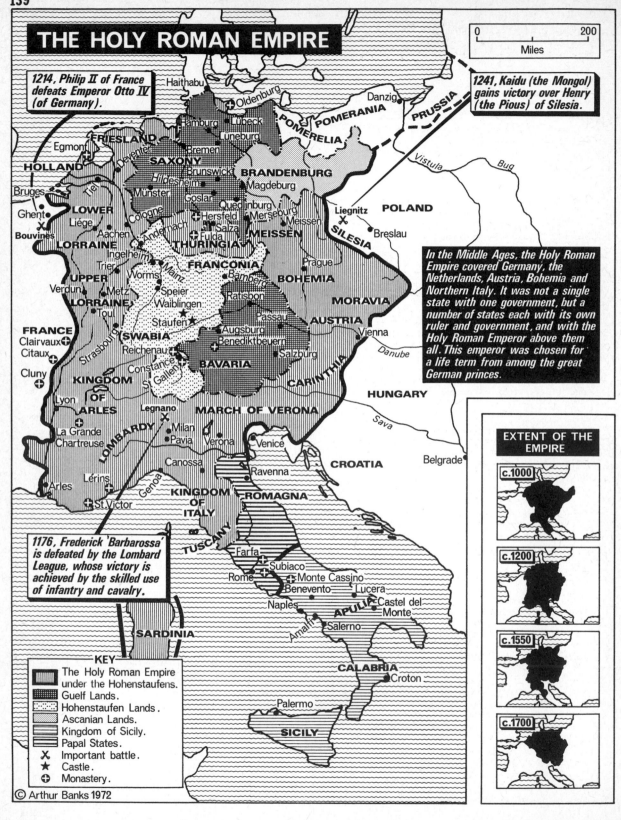

THE HOLY ROMAN EMPIRE

0   200
Miles

1214, Philip II of France defeats Emperor Otto IV (of Germany).

1241, Kaidu (the Mongol) gains victory over Henry (the Pious) of Silesia.

Haithabu
Danzig
PRUSSIA
Oldenburg
POMERANIA
Hamburg   Lübeck
POMERELIA
Egmont
FRIESLAND
Bremen
Lüneburg
HOLLAND
Deventer
SAXONY
Brunswick
Vistula
Bug
Bruges
Trier
Hildesheim
BRANDENBURG
Ghent
Münster
Magdeburg
LOWER
Goslar
Bouvines
Cologne
Quedlinburg
Merseburg
Liegnitz
POLAND
Liège
Andernach
Hersfeld   Salza
Meissen
Breslau
Aachen
Fulda
SILESIA
LORRAINE
THURINGIA
MEISSEN
Ingelheim
FRANCONIA
Prague
UPPER
Trier   Mainz
Worms
Bamberg
BOHEMIA
Verdun
Speier
Metz
Waiblingen
Ratisbon
MORAVIA
LORRAINE
Toul
Staufen
Passau
AUSTRIA
FRANCE
SWABIA
Augsburg
Vienna
Clairvaux
Reichenau
Benedictbeuern
Citaux
Constance
Salzburg
Danube
Cluny
St. Gallen
BAVARIA
CARINTHIA
Lyon
KINGDOM
OF
ARLES
Legnano
MARCH OF VERONA
HUNGARY
Sava
La Grande
Milan
Chartreuse
Pavia
Verona
Venice
Arles
Lérins
LOMBARDY
Canossa
Belgrade
CROATIA
Genoa
Ravenna
St.Victor
KINGDOM
OF
ITALY
ROMAGNA
TUSCANY
Farfa
Rome
Subiaco
Monte Cassino
Benevento
Lucera
SARDINIA
Naples
Castel del
Monte
Amalfi
APULIA
Salerno
CALABRIA
Croton
Palermo
SICILY

1176, Frederick 'Barbarossa' is defeated by the Lombard League, whose victory is achieved by the skilled use of infantry and cavalry.

In the Middle Ages, the Holy Roman Empire covered Germany, the Netherlands, Austria, Bohemia and Northern Italy. It was not a single state with one government, but a number of states each with its own ruler and government, and with the Holy Roman Emperor above them all. This emperor was chosen for a life term from among the great German princes.

EXTENT OF THE EMPIRE

c.1000

c.1200

c.1550

c.1700

KEY
|||
The Holy Roman Empire under the Hohenstaufens.
Guelf Lands.
Hohenstaufen Lands.
Ascanian Lands.
Kingdom of Sicily.
Papal States.
X Important battle.
★ Castle.
✚ Monastery.

© Arthur Banks 1972

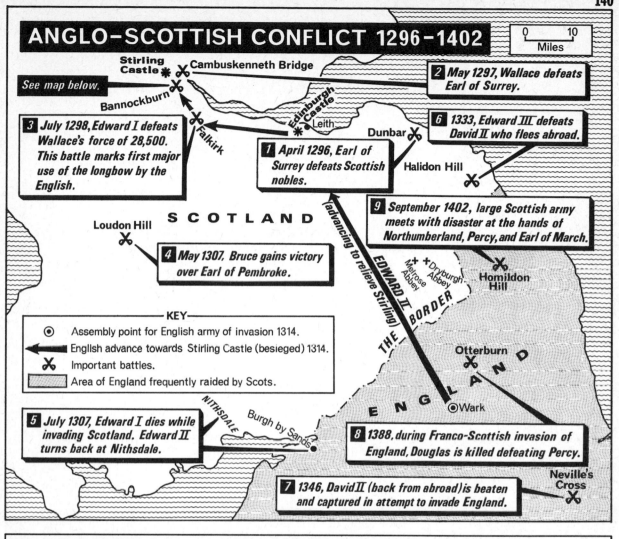

ANGLO-SCOTTISH CONFLICT 1296-1402

0 — 10 Miles

2 May 1297, Wallace defeats Earl of Surrey.

6 1333, Edward III defeats David II who flees abroad.

See map below.

Stirling Castle — Cambuskenneth Bridge

Bannockburn

3 July 1298, Edward I defeats Wallace's force of 28,500. This battle marks first major use of the longbow by the English.

Falkirk

Edinburgh Castle — Leith

Dunbar

Halidon Hill

1 April 1296, Earl of Surrey defeats Scottish nobles.

9 September 1402, large Scottish army meets with disaster at the hands of Northumberland, Percy, and Earl of March.

S C O T L A N D

(advancing to relieve Stirling)

EDWARD II

Loudon Hill

4 May 1307, Bruce gains victory over Earl of Pembroke.

Melrose Abbey — Dryburgh Abbey

THE BORDER

Homildon Hill

— **KEY** —

⊙ Assembly point for English army of invasion 1314.

← English advance towards Stirling Castle (besieged) 1314.

✂ Important battles.

▨ Area of England frequently raided by Scots.

Otterburn

E N G L A N D

⊙ Wark

5 July 1307, Edward I dies while invading Scotland. Edward II turns back at Nithsdale.

NITHSDALE

Burgh by Sands

8 1388, during Franco-Scottish invasion of England, Douglas is killed defeating Percy.

Neville's Cross

7 1346, David II (back from abroad) is beaten and captured in attempt to invade England.

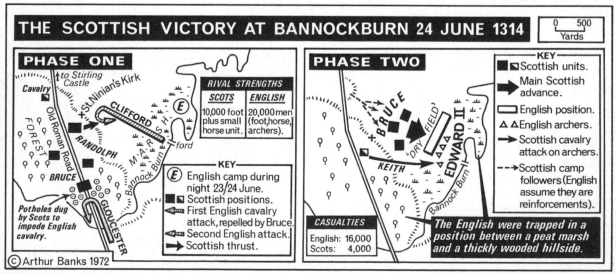

THE SCOTTISH VICTORY AT BANNOCKBURN 24 JUNE 1314

0 — 500 Yards

PHASE ONE

to Stirling Castle
Cavalry
St Ninian's Kirk
Old Roman Road
CLIFFORD
FOREST
RANDOLPH
M A R S H
ford
E
BRUCE
Bannock Burn
GLOUCESTER

Potholes dug by Scots to impede English cavalry.

RIVAL STRENGTHS

SCOTS	ENGLISH
10,000 foot plus small horse unit.	20,000 men (foot, horse, archers).

— **KEY** —

E English camp during night 23/24 June.
▨ Scottish positions.
⟨ First English cavalry attack, repelled by Bruce.
⟨ Second English attack.
➤ Scottish thrust.

PHASE TWO

BRUCE
'DRY FIELD'
KEITH
EDWARD II
Bannock Burn

— **KEY** —

■▨ Scottish units.
➤ Main Scottish advance.
▭ English position.
△△ English archers.
→ Scottish cavalry attack on archers.
--→ Scottish camp followers (English assume they are reinforcements).

CASUALTIES

English: 16,000
Scots: 4,000

The English were trapped in a position between a peat marsh and a thickly wooded hillside.

© Arthur Banks 1972

THE HUNDRED YEARS' WAR 1337–1453

Note: the war actually spanned 120 years as French raids across the English Channel went on until 1457.

❶ The Sluys-Crécy Period 1337-1347

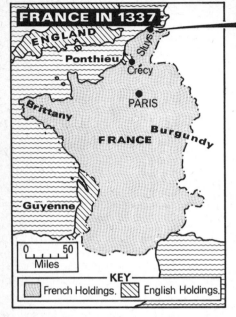

FRANCE IN 1337

ENGLAND
Ponthieu
Sluys
Crécy
PARIS
Brittany
Burgundy
FRANCE
Guyenne

0   50
Miles

KEY
French Holdings.   English Holdings.

THE ENGLISH NAVAL VICTORY AT SLUYS 24 JUNE 1340

A French fleet of 190 ships, anchored in the Zwin river, is attacked by an English fleet of 150 ships. The English steer straight in to the French, and their archers lay down a hail of arrows. Blinded by the onslaught, the French are also cramped for movement because of their moorings. The English men-at-arms complete the carnage. 166 French ships are sunk or captured, and this victory gives England command of the English Channel.

MAIN CAUSES OF THE HUNDRED YEARS' WAR

1. English rage over French support for the Scots in their wars with England.
2. French suspicions concerning English commercial interests in Flanders.
3. The feudal relationship between French and English kings in France.

TEN BASIC STAGES OF THE HUNDRED YEARS' WAR

❶ 1337–1347, Sluys/Crecy period.
❷ 1347–1354, Period of truce.
❸ 1355–1360, Poitiers period.
❹ 1360–1367, Period of uneasy peace.
❺ 1368–1396, Du Guesclin and after.
❻ 1396–1413, Period of uneasy truce.
❼ 1413–1428, Period of Henry V.
❽ 1429–1444, Joan of Arc's influence.
❾ 1444–1449, Truce of Tours.
❿ 1449–1453, The French resurgence.

EDWARD III's CAMPAIGN IN NORTHERN FRANCE 1346-1347

ENGLAND
Portsmouth
St. Helens
Calais

ENGLISH SEA MASTERY

4 September 1346, Edward besieges port. It surrenders on 4 August 1347. A truce is signed on 28 September 1347.

11 July 1346, Edward's invasion force sets sail for France. It includes some 3,600 archers, 3,500 Welsh spearmen and archers, 2,740 hobelers, and 1,140 men-at-arms.

ENGLISH SEA MASTERY

ENGLISH FLEET

1-4 Sept.
Montreuil 28 August
Crécy
Abbeville
24 August
Somme
Amiens

26 August 1346, Edward defeats Philip VI.

St. Vaast 12 July

St. Lô 22 July

Caen
2 August

Lisieux
Elboeuf 7 August
RAVAGING
Seine
Rouen

LOCATION OF FRENCH ARMY ON 2 AUGUST 1346

15-23 August

Poissy
PARIS
13 August

Note: the capture of the port of Calais, although it was England's only land gain, meant that England was immune from invasion

26 July 1346, English storm and sack city. Fleet lends support.

0   50
Miles

KEY
➤ Route of Edward's advance to Calais.

© Arthur Banks 1972

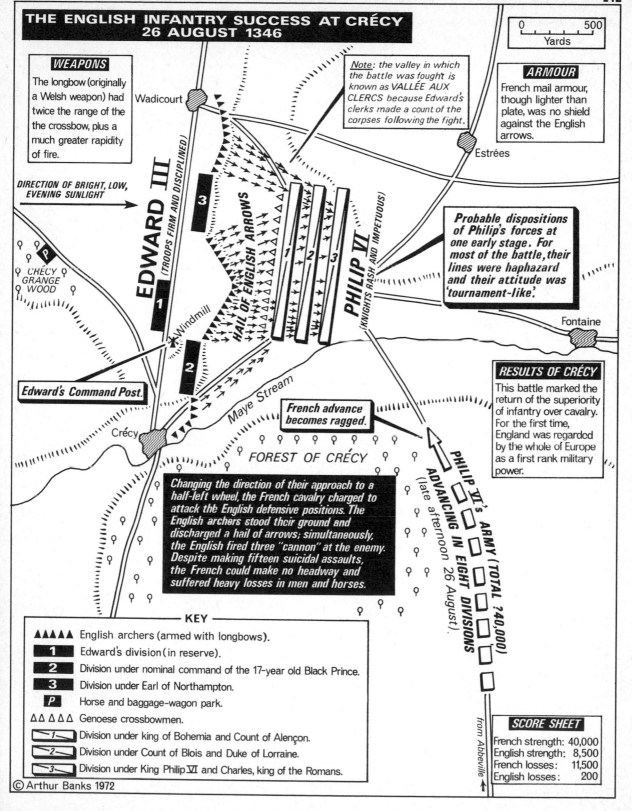

THE ENGLISH INFANTRY SUCCESS AT CRÉCY 26 AUGUST 1346

WEAPONS

The longbow (originally a Welsh weapon) had twice the range of the the crossbow, plus a much greater rapidity of fire.

Note: the valley in which the battle was fought is known as VALLÉE AUX CLERCS because Edward's clerks made a count of the corpses following the fight.

ARMOUR

French mail armour, though lighter than plate, was no shield against the English arrows.

0   500
Yards

Wadicourt

Estrées

DIRECTION OF BRIGHT, LOW, EVENING SUNLIGHT

EDWARD III (TROOPS FIRM AND DISCIPLINED)

3

HAIL OF ENGLISH ARROWS

PHILIP VI (KNIGHTS RASH AND IMPETUOUS)

Probable dispositions of Philip's forces at one early stage. For most of the battle, their lines were haphazard and their attitude was 'tournament-like'.

P

CRÉCY GRANGE WOOD

1

Windmill

2

Edward's Command Post.

Crécy

Maye Stream

French advance becomes ragged.

Fontaine

RESULTS OF CRÉCY

This battle marked the return of the superiority of infantry over cavalry. For the first time, England was regarded by the whole of Europe as a first rank military power.

FOREST OF CRÉCY

PHILIP VI's ARMY (TOTAL ?40,000) ADVANCING IN EIGHT DIVISIONS (late afternoon 26 August).

Changing the direction of their approach to a half-left wheel, the French cavalry charged to attack the English defensive positions. The English archers stood their ground and discharged a hail of arrows; simultaneously, the English fired three "cannon" at the enemy. Despite making fifteen suicidal assaults, the French could make no headway and suffered heavy losses in men and horses.

from Abbeville

— **KEY** —

▲▲▲▲▲ English archers (armed with longbows).

1 Edward's division (in reserve).

2 Division under nominal command of the 17-year old Black Prince.

3 Division under Earl of Northampton.

P Horse and baggage-wagon park.

△△ △ △△ Genoese crossbowmen.

_1_ Division under king of Bohemia and Count of Alençon.

_2_ Division under Count of Blois and Duke of Lorraine.

_3_ Division under King Philip VI and Charles, king of the Romans.

© Arthur Banks 1972

SCORE SHEET

French strength: 40,000
English strength: 8,500
French losses: 11,500
English losses: 200

THE HUNDRED YEARS' WAR – continued

❷ Spread of the Black Death to Europe

The Black Death, a form of bubonic plague, apparently commenced in China and was carried west by traders. In 1348 it devastated France and England alike, and one third of the population of each country died. During this period, the two states were in a state of truce, but no major campaigns could be undertaken while the pestilence raged. There were later visitations of the disease, but the first one was the most deadly in terms of numbers.

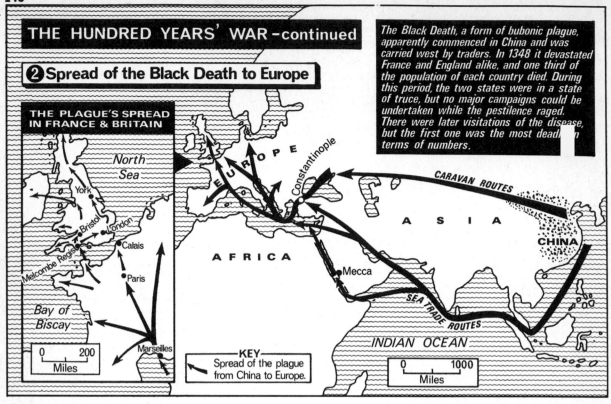

THE PLAGUE'S SPREAD IN FRANCE & BRITAIN

North Sea

York
Bristol
London
Calais
Melcombe Regis
Paris
Bay of Biscay
Marseilles

0 200 Miles

EUROPE
Constantinople
CARAVAN ROUTES
ASIA
CHINA
AFRICA
Mecca
SEA TRADE ROUTES
INDIAN OCEAN

0 1000 Miles

KEY
→ Spread of the plague from China to Europe.

❸ The Black Prince's Campaigns

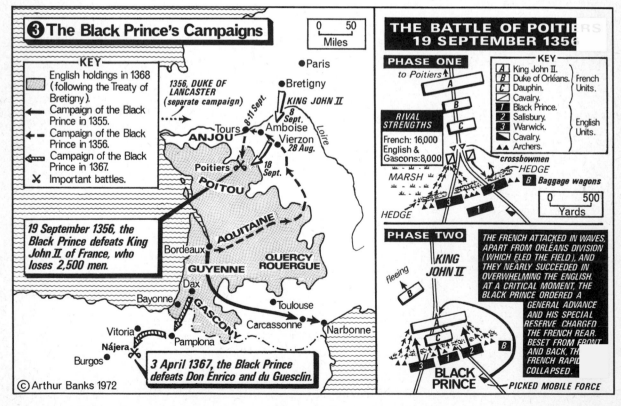

0 50 Miles

KEY
▨ English holdings in 1368 (following the Treaty of Bretigny).
← Campaign of the Black Prince in 1355.
⟵- Campaign of the Black Prince in 1356.
⇜ Campaign of the Black Prince in 1367.
✕ Important battles.

19 September 1356, the Black Prince defeats King John II of France, who loses 2,500 men.

3 April 1367, the Black Prince defeats Don Enrico and du Guesclin.

© Arthur Banks 1972

Paris
Bretigny
1356, DUKE OF LANCASTER (separate campaign)
KING JOHN II
8-11 Sept.
8 Sept.
Amboise
Vierzon
28 Aug.
Loire
Tours
ANJOU
18 Sept.
Poitiers
POITOU
AQUITAINE
Bordeaux
QUERCY ROUERGUE
GUYENNE
Dax
Bayonne
GASCONY
Toulouse
Carcassonne
Narbonne
Vitoria
Nájera
Pamplona
Burgos

THE BATTLE OF POITIERS 19 SEPTEMBER 1356

PHASE ONE
to Poitiers ↑

KEY
A King John II.
B Duke of Orléans. — French Units.
C Dauphin.
▱ Cavalry.
1 Black Prince.
2 Salisbury. — English Units.
3 Warwick.
▰ Cavalry.
▲▲ Archers.

RIVAL STRENGTHS
French: 16,000
English & Gascons: 8,000

crossbowmen
HEDGE
MARSH
B Baggage wagons
HEDGE

0 500 Yards

PHASE TWO
KING JOHN II
fleeing
BLACK PRINCE
PICKED MOBILE FORCE

THE FRENCH ATTACKED IN WAVES, APART FROM ORLEANS DIVISION (WHICH FLED THE FIELD), AND THEY NEARLY SUCCEEDED IN OVERWHELMING THE ENGLISH. AT A CRITICAL MOMENT, THE BLACK PRINCE ORDERED A GENERAL ADVANCE AND HIS SPECIAL RESERVE CHARGED THE FRENCH REAR. BESET FROM FRONT AND BACK, THE FRENCH RAPIDLY COLLAPSED.

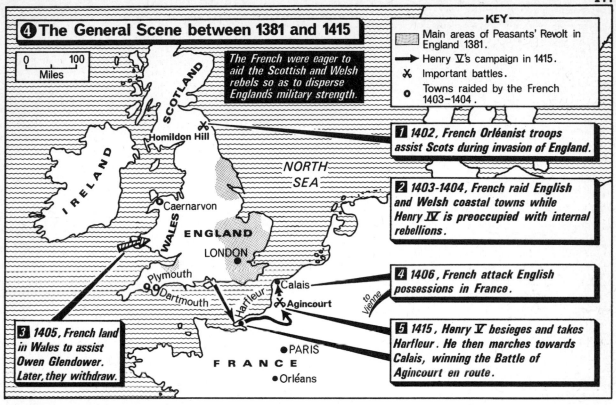

❹ The General Scene between 1381 and 1415

KEY

- ▨ Main areas of Peasants' Revolt in England 1381.
- ➤ Henry Ⅴ's campaign in 1415.
- ✕ Important battles.
- ○ Towns raided by the French 1403–1404.

The French were eager to aid the Scottish and Welsh rebels so as to disperse England's military strength.

1 *1402, French Orléanist troops assist Scots during invasion of England.*

2 *1403-1404, French raid English and Welsh coastal towns while Henry Ⅳ is preoccupied with internal rebellions.*

4 *1406, French attack English possessions in France.*

3 *1405, French land in Wales to assist Owen Glendower. Later, they withdraw.*

5 *1415, Henry Ⅴ besieges and takes Harfleur. He then marches towards Calais, winning the Battle of Agincourt en route.*

SCOTLAND
Homildon Hill
IRELAND
WALES
Caernarvon
ENGLAND
LONDON
NORTH SEA
Plymouth
Dartmouth
Harfleur
Calais
Agincourt
to Vienne
FRANCE
PARIS
Orléans

0 100 Miles

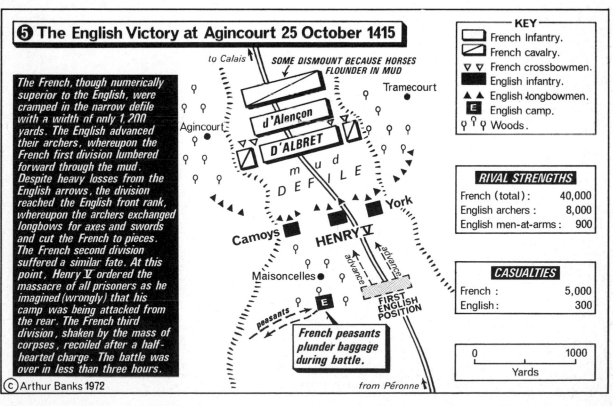

❺ The English Victory at Agincourt 25 October 1415

KEY

- ▢ French Infantry.
- ▧ French cavalry.
- ▽ ▽ French crossbowmen.
- ▬ English infantry.
- ▲ ▲ English longbowmen.
- **E** English camp.
- ♀ ♀ ♀ Woods.

The French, though numerically superior to the English, were cramped in the narrow defile with a width of only 1,200 yards. The English advanced their archers, whereupon the French first division lumbered forward through the mud. Despite heavy losses from the English arrows, the division reached the English front rank, whereupon the archers exchanged longbows for axes and swords and cut the French to pieces. The French second division suffered a similar fate. At this point, Henry Ⅴ ordered the massacre of all prisoners as he imagined (wrongly) that his camp was being attacked from the rear. The French third division, shaken by the mass of corpses, recoiled after a half-hearted charge. The battle was over in less than three hours.

to Calais
SOME DISMOUNT BECAUSE HORSES FLOUNDER IN MUD
Tramecourt
Agincourt
d'Alençon
D'ALBRET
m u d
DEFILE
York
Camoys
HENRY Ⅴ
advance
advance
Maisoncelles
E
peasants
FIRST ENGLISH POSITION
French peasants plunder baggage during battle.
from Péronne

RIVAL STRENGTHS

French (total):	40,000
English archers:	8,000
English men-at-arms:	900

CASUALTIES

French:	5,000
English:	300

0 1000 Yards

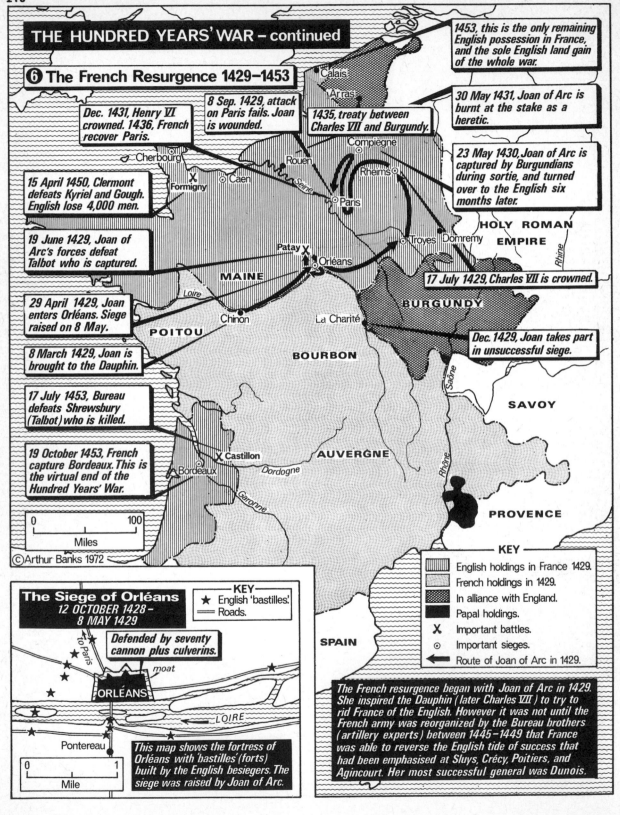

THE HUNDRED YEARS' WAR – continued

❻ The French Resurgence 1429–1453

1453, this is the only remaining English possession in France, and the sole English land gain of the whole war.

Dec. 1431, Henry VI crowned. 1436, French recover Paris.

8 Sep. 1429, attack on Paris fails. Joan is wounded.

1435, treaty between Charles VII and Burgundy.

30 May 1431, Joan of Arc is burnt at the stake as a heretic.

23 May 1430, Joan of Arc is captured by Burgundians during sortie, and turned over to the English six months later.

15 April 1450, Clermont defeats Kyriel and Gough. English lose 4,000 men.

19 June 1429, Joan of Arc's forces defeat Talbot who is captured.

29 April 1429, Joan enters Orléans. Siege raised on 8 May.

8 March 1429, Joan is brought to the Dauphin.

17 July 1453, Bureau defeats Shrewsbury (Talbot) who is killed.

19 October 1453, French capture Bordeaux. This is the virtual end of the Hundred Years' War.

17 July 1429, Charles VII is crowned.

Dec. 1429, Joan takes part in unsuccessful siege.

Calais
Arras
Cherbourg
Formigny
Caen
Rouen
Compiègne
Rheims
Seine
Paris
Patay
Orléans
MAINE
Loire
Chinon
La Charité
Troyes
Domremy
POITOU
BOURBON
BURGUNDY
Rhine
HOLY ROMAN EMPIRE
Saône
SAVOY
AUVERGNE
Dordogne
Castillon
Bordeaux
Garonne
Rhône
PROVENCE
SPAIN

0   100
Miles

© Arthur Banks 1972

KEY

- ▥ English holdings in France 1429.
- ▦ French holdings in 1429.
- ▨ In alliance with England.
- ■ Papal holdings.
- X Important battles.
- ⊙ Important sieges.
- ← Route of Joan of Arc in 1429.

The Siege of Orléans
12 OCTOBER 1428 – 8 MAY 1429

KEY
- ★ English 'bastilles'.
- ═ Roads.

Defended by seventy cannon plus culverins.

to Paris
moat
ORLÉANS
LOIRE
Pontereau

0   1
Mile

This map shows the fortress of Orléans with 'bastilles' (forts) built by the English besiegers. The siege was raised by Joan of Arc.

The French resurgence began with Joan of Arc in 1429. She inspired the Dauphin (later Charles VII) to try to rid France of the English. However it was not until the French army was reorganized by the Bureau brothers (artillery experts) between 1445–1449 that France was able to reverse the English tide of success that had been emphasised at Sluys, Crécy, Poitiers, and Agincourt. Her most successful general was Dunois.

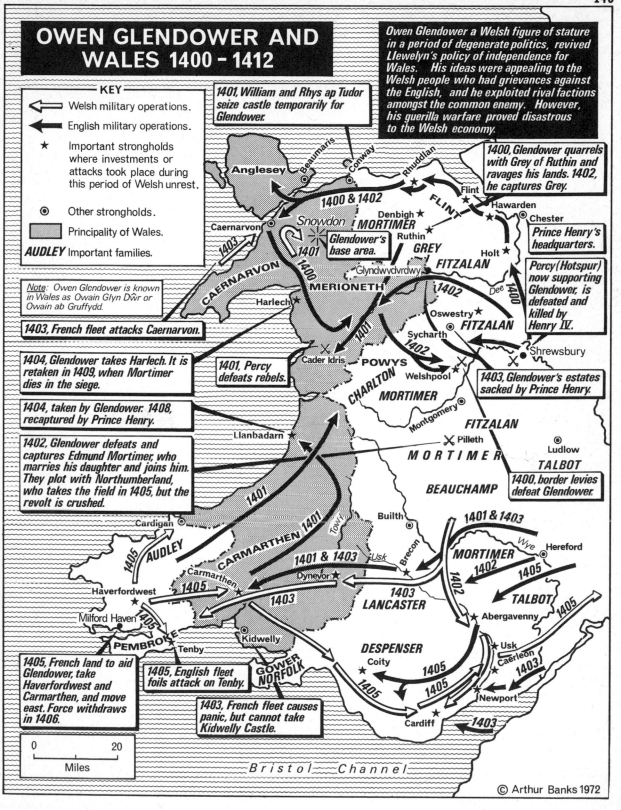

OWEN GLENDOWER AND WALES 1400 - 1412

Owen Glendower a Welsh figure of stature in a period of degenerate politics, revived Llewelyn's policy of independence for Wales. His ideas were appealing to the Welsh people who had grievances against the English, and he exploited rival factions amongst the common enemy. However, his guerilla warfare proved disastrous to the Welsh economy.

KEY

⇐ Welsh military operations.

← English military operations.

★ Important strongholds where investments or attacks took place during this period of Welsh unrest.

◉ Other strongholds.

▨ Principality of Wales.

AUDLEY Important families.

Note: Owen Glendower is known in Wales as Owain Glyn Dŵr or Owain ab Gruffydd.

1401, William and Rhys ap Tudor seize castle temporarily for Glendower.

1400, Glendower quarrels with Grey of Ruthin and ravages his lands. 1402, he captures Grey.

Prince Henry's headquarters.

Percy (Hotspur) now supporting Glendower, is defeated and killed by Henry IV.

1403, French fleet attacks Caernarvon.

1404, Glendower takes Harlech. It is retaken in 1409, when Mortimer dies in the siege.

1401, Percy defeats rebels.

1403, Glendower's estates sacked by Prince Henry.

1404, taken by Glendower. 1408, recaptured by Prince Henry.

1402, Glendower defeats and captures Edmund Mortimer, who marries his daughter and joins him. They plot with Northumberland, who takes the field in 1405, but the revolt is crushed.

1400, border levies defeat Glendower.

1405, French land to aid Glendower, take Haverfordwest and Carmarthen, and move east. Force withdraws in 1406.

1405, English fleet foils attack on Tenby.

1403, French fleet causes panic, but cannot take Kidwelly Castle.

Glendower's base area.

Snowdon

Anglesey — Beaumaris — Conway — Rhuddlan — Flint — Hawarden — Chester

1400 & 1402

Caernarvon — CAERNARVON — 1403 — 1400 — 1401

Denbigh — MORTIMER — Ruthin — GREY — Holt — FITZALAN

Glyndwvdvdwy — MERIONETH — Oswestry — FITZALAN — Shrewsbury

Harlech — Cader Idris — POWYS — Sycharth — Welshpool — CHARLTON — MORTIMER — Montgomery

FITZALAN

Llanbadarn — Pilleth — M O R T I M E R — Ludlow — TALBOT

BEAUCHAMP

Cardigan — AUDLEY — CARMARTHEN — Towy — Builth — Brecon — MORTIMER — Hereford — Wye — TALBOT

1401 & 1403

Dynevor — 1401 & 1403 — Usk — 1403 — LANCASTER — Abergavenny

Haverfordwest — Milford Haven — PEMBROKE — Tenby — Kidwelly — GOWER NORFOLK — DESPENSER — Coity — Usk — Caerleon — Newport

Cardiff

0 ——— 20

Miles

Bristol Channel

© Arthur Banks 1972

THE WARS OF THE ROSES 1455 – 1485

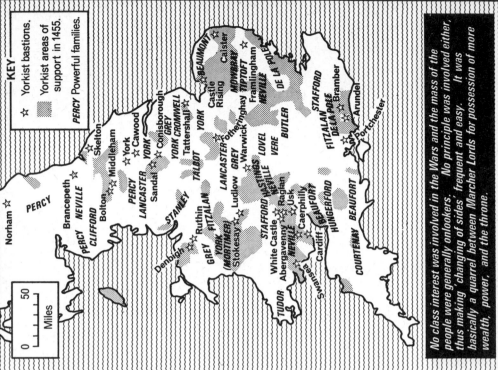

② Yorkist Strongholds and Areas of Support 1455

KEY
- ☆ Yorkist bastions.
- ▓ Yorkist areas of support in 1455.
- *PERCY* Powerful families.

0 — 50 Miles

No class interest was involved in the Wars and the mass of the people were generally onlookers. No principle was involved either, thus making 'changing of sides' frequent and easy. It was basically a quarrel between Marcher Lords for possession of more wealth, power, and the throne.

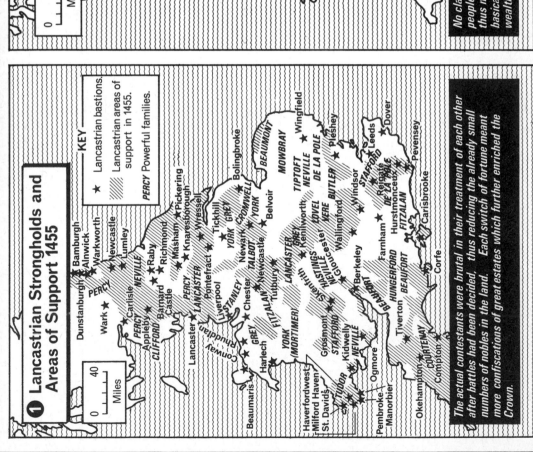

① Lancastrian Strongholds and Areas of Support 1455

KEY
- ★ Lancastrian bastions.
- ▨ Lancastrian areas of support in 1455.
- *PERCY* Powerful families.

0 — 40 Miles

The actual contestants were brutal in their treatment of each other after battles had been decided, thus reducing the already small numbers of nobles in the land. Each switch of fortune meant more confiscations of great estates which further enriched the Crown.

© Arthur Banks 1972

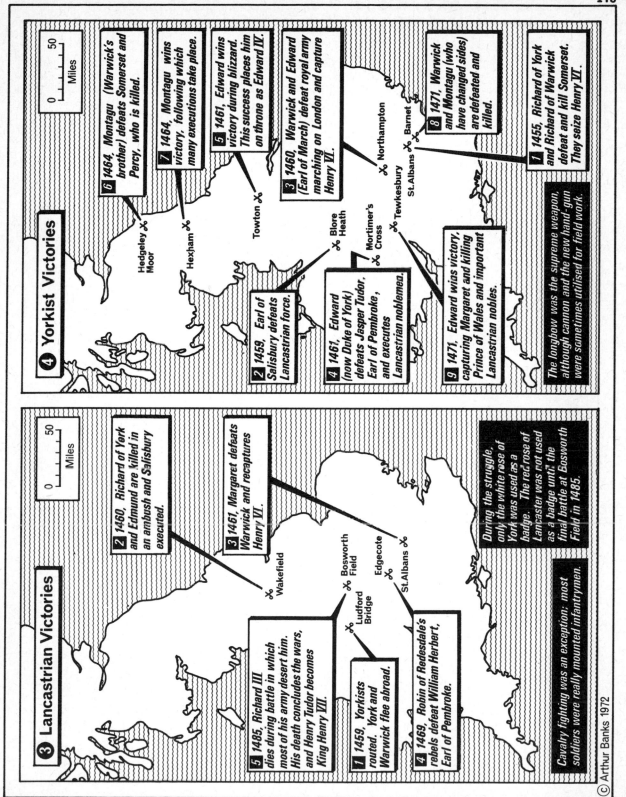

④ Yorkist Victories

50 Miles

6 1464, Montagu (Warwick's brother) defeats Somerset and Percy, who is killed.

7 1464, Montagu wins victory, following which many executions take place.

5 1461, Edward wins victory during blizzard. This success places him on throne as Edward IV.

3 1460, Warwick and Edward (Earl of March) defeat royal army marching on London and capture Henry VI.

8 1471, Warwick and Montagu (who have changed sides) are defeated and killed.

1 1455, Richard of York and Richard of Warwick defeat and kill Somerset. They seize Henry VI.

Hedgeley Moor · Hexham · Towton · Blore Heath · Mortimer's Cross · Tewkesbury · Northampton · St.Albans · Barnet

2 1459, Earl of Salisbury defeats Lancastrian force.

4 1461, Edward (now Duke of York) defeats Jasper Tudor, Earl of Pembroke, and executes Lancastrian noblemen.

9 1471, Edward wins victory, capturing Margaret and killing Prince of Wales and important Lancastrian nobles.

The longbow was the supreme weapon, although cannon and the new hand-gun were sometimes utilised for field work.

③ Lancastrian Victories

50 Miles

2 1460, Richard of York and Edmund are killed in an ambush and Salisbury executed.

3 1461, Margaret defeats Warwick and recaptures Henry VI.

Wakefield · Bosworth Field · Edgecote · St.Albans · Ludford Bridge

5 1485, Richard III dies during battle in which most of his army desert him. His death concludes the wars, and Henry Tudor becomes King Henry VII.

1 1459, Yorkists routed. York and Warwick flee abroad.

4 1469, Robin of Redesdale's rebels defeat William Herbert, Earl of Pembroke.

During the struggle, only the white rose of York was used as a badge. The red rose of Lancaster was not used as a badge until the final battle at Bosworth Field in 1485.

Cavalry fighting was an exception: most soldiers were really mounted infantrymen.

© Arthur Banks 1972

THE RISE OF SWITZERLAND AS A MILITARY POWER

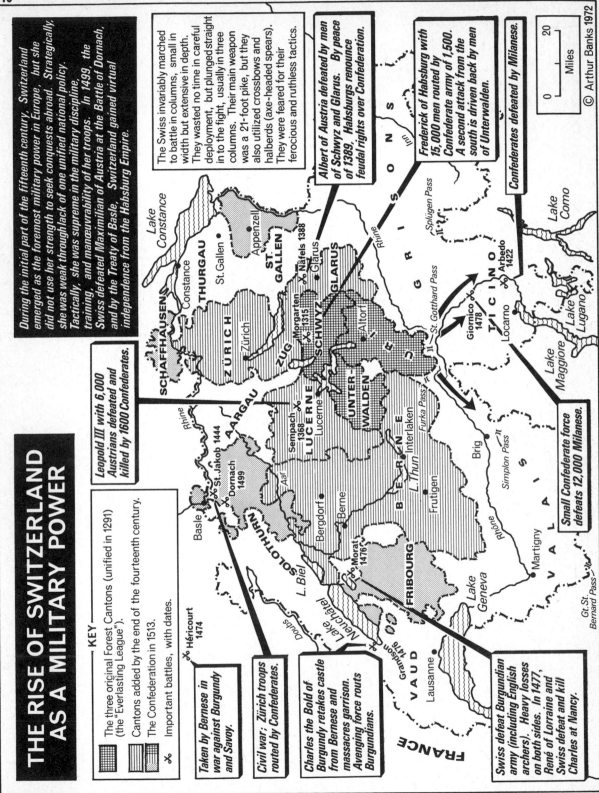

During the initial part of the fifteenth century, Switzerland emerged as the foremost military power in Europe, but she did not use her strength to seek conquests abroad. Strategically, she was weak throughout lack of one unified national policy. Tactically, she was supreme in the military discipline, training, and manoeuvrability of her troops. In 1499, the Swiss defeated Maximilian of Austria at the Battle of Dornach, and by the Treaty of Basle, Switzerland gained virtual independence from the Habsburg Empire.

The Swiss invariably marched to battle in columns, small in width but extensive in depth. They wasted no time in careful deployment, but plunged straight in to the fight, usually in three columns. Their main weapon was a 21-foot pike, but they also utilized crossbows and halberds (axe-headed spears). They were feared for their ferocious and ruthless tactics.

KEY
- The three original Forest Cantons (unified in 1291) (the "Everlasting League").
- Cantons added by the end of the fourteenth century.
- The Confederation in 1513.
- Important battles, with dates.

Albert of Austria defeated by men of Schwyz and Glarus. By peace of 1389, Habsburgs renounce feudal rights over Confederation.

Frederick of Habsburg with 15,000 men routed by Confederate army of 1,500. A second attack from the south is driven back by men of Unterwalden.

Confederates defeated by Milanese.

Leopold III with 6,000 Austrians defeated and killed by 1600 Confederates.

Small Confederate force defeats 12,000 Milanese.

Taken by Bernese in war against Burgundy and Savoy.

Civil war; Zürich troops routed by Confederates.

Charles the Bold of Burgundy retakes castle from Bernese and massacres garrison. Avenging force routs Burgundians.

Swiss defeat Burgundian army (including English archers). Heavy losses on both sides. In 1477, René of Lorraine and Swiss defeat and kill Charles at Nancy.

© Arthur Banks 1972

0   20
Miles

Lake Constance
THURGAU
Appenzell
St. Gallen
Constance
ST. GALLEN
Näfels 1388
Glarus
GLARUS
SCHAFFHAUSEN
Zürich
ZÜRICH
Morgarten 1315
SCHWYZ
ZUG
Altorf
UNTERWALDEN
GRISONS
Rhine
Splügen Pass
St. Gotthard Pass
Giornico 1478
Arbedo 1422
TICINO
Locarno
Lake Como
Lake Lugano
Lake Maggiore
Rhine
Basle
St. Jakob 1444
Dornach 1499
AARGAU
Aaf
SOLOTHURN
Sempach 1368
Lucerne
LUCERNE
Interlaken
L. Thun
BERNE
Bergdorf
Berne
Furka Pass
Brig
Simplon Pass
VALAIS
Rhône
Héricourt 1474
Doubs
Morat 1476
FRIBOURG
Frutigen
Martigny
Gt. St. Bernard Pass
L. Biel
Lake Neuchâtel
Grandson 1476
VAUD
Lausanne
Lake Geneva
FRANCE

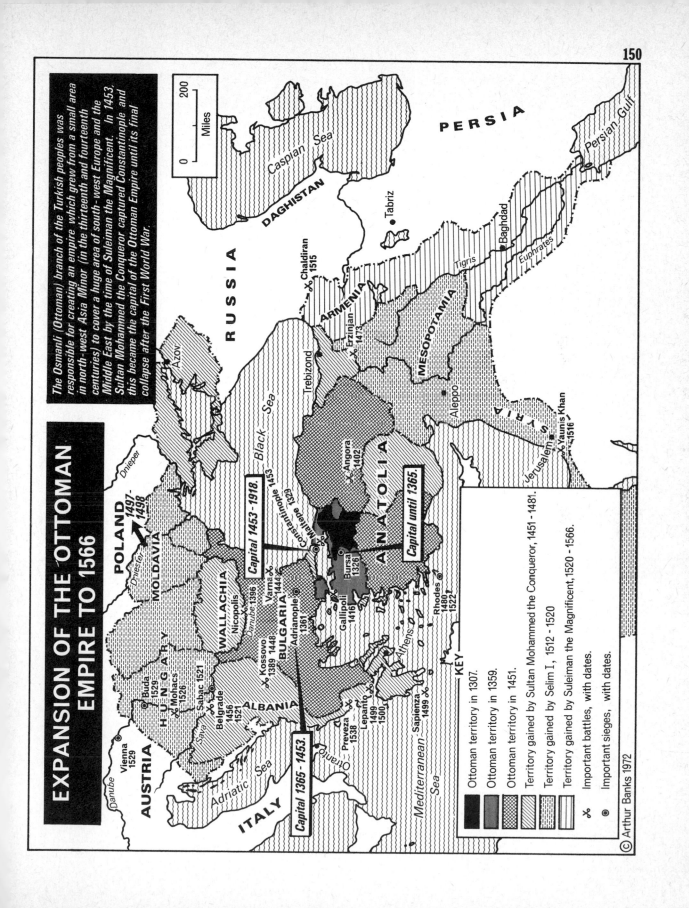

EXPANSION OF THE OTTOMAN EMPIRE TO 1566

The Osmanli (Ottoman) branch of the Turkish peoples was responsible for creating an empire which grew from a small area in north-west Asia Minor (in the thirteenth and fourteenth centuries) to cover a huge area of south-west Europe and the Middle East by the time of Suleiman the Magnificent. In 1453, Sultan Mohammed the Conqueror captured Constantinople and this became the capital of the Ottoman Empire until its final collapse after the First World War.

200

0

Miles

PERSIA

Persian Gulf

Caspian Sea

DAGHISTAN

RUSSIA

Tabriz

Baghdad

Chaldiran 1515

Tigris

Euphrates

ARMENIA

Erzinjan 1473

MESOPOTAMIA

Azov

Trebizond

Aleppo

SYRIA

Yaunis Khan 1516

Black Sea

Angora 1402

Jerusalem

Dnieper

POLAND 1497-1498

Capital 1453-1918.

Constantinople 1453

Chalcedon 1329

ANATOLIA

Capital until 1365.

MOLDAVIA

Dniester

WALLACHIA

Nicopolis

Danube 1396

Varna 1444

Adrianople 1361

BULGARIA

Gallipoli 1416

Bursa 1326

Rhodes 1480 1522

HUNGARY

Buda 1529

Mohacs 1526

Sabac 1521

Belgrade 1456 1521

ALBANIA

Kossovo 1389 1448

Sava

Danube

Athens

AUSTRIA

Vienna 1529

Capital 1365-1453.

Preveza 1538

Lepanto 1499 1500

Sapienza 1499

Mediterranean Sea

Adriatic Sea

Otranto

ITALY

KEY

	Ottoman territory in 1307.
	Ottoman territory in 1359.
	Ottoman territory in 1451.
	Territory gained by Sultan Mohammed the Conqueror, 1451 - 1481.
	Territory gained by Selim I, 1512 - 1520.
	Territory gained by Suleiman the Magnificent, 1520 - 1566.
✗	Important battles, with dates.
◉	Important sieges, with dates.

© Arthur Banks 1972

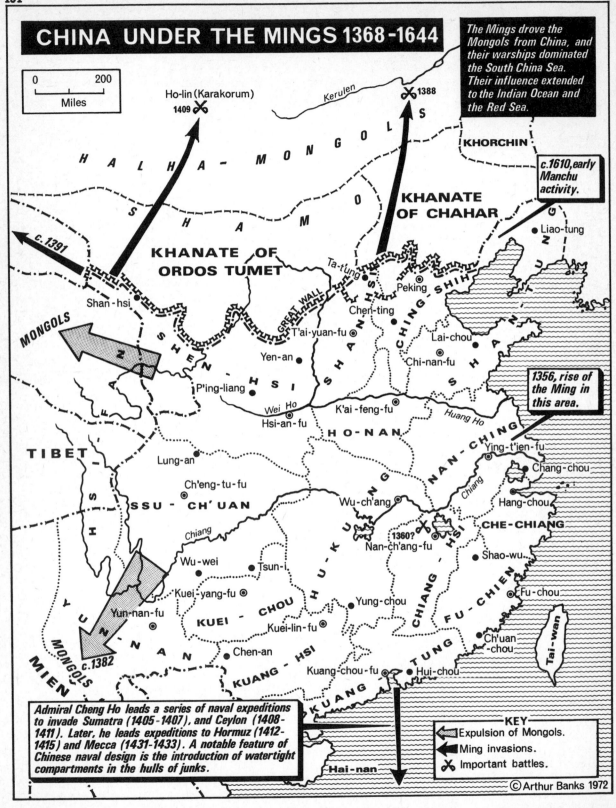

CHINA UNDER THE MINGS 1368-1644

The Mings drove the Mongols from China, and their warships dominated the South China Sea. Their influence extended to the Indian Ocean and the Red Sea.

0 200
Miles

Ho-lin (Karakorum)
1409 ✂

Kerulen

✂ 1388

KHORCHIN

c.1610, early Manchu activity.

H A L H A - M O N G O L S

KHANATE OF CHAHAR

Liao-tung

S H A M O

KHANATE OF ORDOS TUMET

c.1391

Ta-tung

Peking

CHING-SHIH

S H A N T U N G

MONGOLS

Shan-hsi

GREAT WALL

S H A N - H S I

Chen-ting

Lai-chou

1356, rise of the Ming in this area.

Yen-an

T'ai-yuan-fu

Chi-nan-fu

P'ing-liang

Wei Ho

Hsi-an-fu

K'ai-feng-fu

Huang Ho

H O - N A N

N A N - C H I N G

Ying-t'ien-fu

Chang-chou

TIBET

Lung-an

Hang-chou

H S I

Ch'eng-tu-fu

S S U - C H ' U A N

Chiang

Wu-ch'ang

H U - K U A N G

Chiang

CHE-CHIANG

Shao-wu

1360?

Nan-ch'ang-fu

C H I A N G - H S I

Wu-wei

Tsun-i

Kuei-yang-fu

K U E I - C H O U

Yung-chou

F U - C H I E N

Fu-chou

Y U - N A N

Kuei-lin-fu

Ch'uan-chou

MONGOLS

Yun-nan-fu

c.1382

Chen-an

K U A N G - H S I

Kuang-chou-fu

Hui-chou

K U A N G - T U N G

Tai-wan

M I E N

Hai-nan

Admiral Cheng Ho leads a series of naval expeditions to invade Sumatra (1405-1407), and Ceylon (1408-1411). Later, he leads expeditions to Hormuz (1412-1415) and Mecca (1431-1433). A notable feature of Chinese naval design is the introduction of watertight compartments in the hulls of junks.

KEY
▨ Expulsion of Mongols.
◀ Ming invasions.
✂ Important battles.

© Arthur Banks 1972

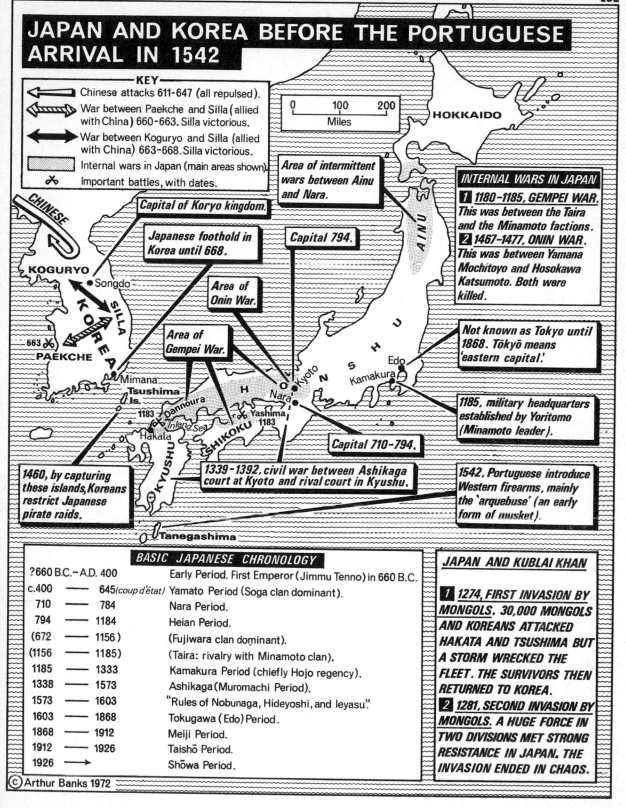

JAPAN AND KOREA BEFORE THE PORTUGUESE ARRIVAL IN 1542

KEY
- Chinese attacks 611-647 (all repulsed).
- War between Paekche and Silla (allied with China) 660-663. Silla victorious.
- War between Koguryo and Silla (allied with China) 663-668. Silla victorious.
- Internal wars in Japan (main areas shown).
- Important battles, with dates.

Area of intermittent wars between Ainu and Nara.

Capital of Koryo kingdom.

Japanese foothold in Korea until 668.

Capital 794.

Area of Onin War.

Area of Gempei War.

INTERNAL WARS IN JAPAN
1. 1180-1185, GEMPEI WAR. This was between the Taira and the Minamoto factions.
2. 1467-1477, ONIN WAR. This was between Yamana Mochitoyo and Hosokawa Katsumoto. Both were killed.

Not known as Tokyo until 1868. Tōkyō means 'eastern capital.'

1185, military headquarters established by Yoritomo (Minamoto leader).

Capital 710-794.

1339-1392, civil war between Ashikaga court at Kyoto and rival court in Kyushu.

1460, by capturing these islands, Koreans restrict Japanese pirate raids.

1542, Portuguese introduce Western firearms, mainly the 'arquebuse' (an early form of musket).

CHINESE, KOGURYO, Songdo, KOREA, SILLA, PAEKCHE, 663, Mimana, Tsushima Is., 1183, Dannoura, Inland Sea, Hakata, KYUSHU, SHIKOKU, Nara, Kyoto, Yashima 1183, Kamakura, Edo, HONSHU, HOKKAIDO, AINU, Tanegashima

0 100 200 Miles

BASIC JAPANESE CHRONOLOGY

?660 B.C.–A.D. 400		Early Period. First Emperor (Jimmu Tenno) in 660 B.C.
c.400 — 645(coup d'état)		Yamato Period (Soga clan dominant).
710 — 784		Nara Period.
794 — 1184		Heian Period.
(672 — 1156)		(Fujiwara clan dominant).
(1156 — 1185)		(Taira: rivalry with Minamoto clan).
1185 — 1333		Kamakura Period (chiefly Hojo regency).
1338 — 1573		Ashikaga (Muromachi Period).
1573 — 1603		"Rules of Nobunaga, Hideyoshi, and Ieyasu".
1603 — 1868		Tokugawa (Edo) Period.
1868 — 1912		Meiji Period.
1912 — 1926		Taishō Period.
1926 →		Shōwa Period.

© Arthur Banks 1972

JAPAN AND KUBLAI KHAN
1. 1274, FIRST INVASION BY MONGOLS. 30,000 MONGOLS AND KOREANS ATTACKED HAKATA AND TSUSHIMA BUT A STORM WRECKED THE FLEET. THE SURVIVORS THEN RETURNED TO KOREA.
2. 1281, SECOND INVASION BY MONGOLS. A HUGE FORCE IN TWO DIVISIONS MET STRONG RESISTANCE IN JAPAN. THE INVASION ENDED IN CHAOS.

FOUR LATER VIEWS OF THE WORLD

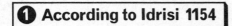

❶ According to Idrisi 1154

Mohammed al Idrisi, Arab geographer and scientist, was born at Ceuta in 1099. In 1154 he completed his "Kitāb Rūjār" (The Book of Roger) for the king of Sicily, Roger II. Prior to this he had travelled extensively.

Irland
England
EUROPE
Rum
Don
Turk
Khasar
ASIA
Sea of China
Africa
Aljir
Tibet
Sin
Said
Irak
Sind
Khorasan
Ind
Ghana
Hejaz
Serendip
Malay
Yemen
Sea of
Ind
AFRICA
Berbera Zenj Sofala
Wak Wak

❷ According to Fra Mauro 1450

Fra Mauro, a Venetian monk and cartographer, produced a world map from detail accumulated during the previous two centuries. His work was notable for details on Africa and Asia in particular.

Rossia
Permia
Svetia
Sibir
Mongul
Norvegia
Lituana
Alana
Samarkand
ASIA
EUROPE
Tartaria
Venice
Servia
Chatajo
Armenia
SERICA
Numidia
Siria
Cirenaica
Judaea
Babylonia
TEBET
EGYPT
Garamantia
Persia
INDIA
Arabia
AFRICA
Abasia
Ethiopia
Sophala

❸ According to Schöner 1523

Johannes Schöner (1477 - 1547) was a German mathematician and cosmographer at Nüremberg. He produced maps of the world in the form of wooden globes covered with paper "gores".

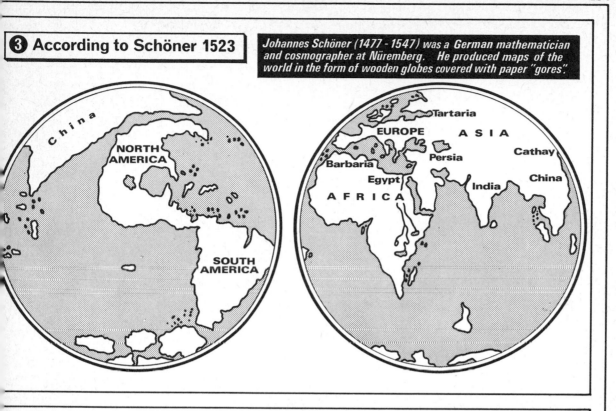

❹ According to Ortelius 1570

Abraham Ortelius, a Dutch cartographer (1527 - 1598), was a friend of Mercator. He produced an atlas of the world entitled "Theatrum Orbis Terrarum" containing seventy maps.

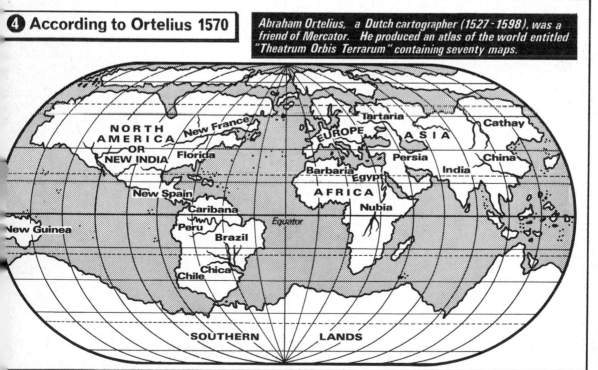

INDEX OF BATTLES,
SIEGES, WARS, CAMPAIGNS, ETC

In the case of battles, only the place name is given. Dates are given only when necessary to distinguish between battles at the same site.

INDEX OF INDIVIDUALS

INDEX OF RACES, TRIBES, AND ALL NAMED GROUPS OF PEOPLE

GEOGRAPHICAL INDEX